Playing for Real

Playing
for
Real

The World of a
Child Therapist

RICHARD BROMFIELD, Ph.D.

A DUTTON BOOK

DUTTON
Published by the Penguin Group
Penguin Books USA Inc., 375 Hudson Street,
New York, New York 10014, U.S.A.
Penguin Books Ltd, 27 Wrights Lane, London W8 5TZ, England
Penguin Books Australia Ltd, Ringwood, Victoria, Australia
Penguin Books Canada Ltd, 10 Alcorn Avenue,
Toronto, Ontario, Canada M4V 3B2
Penguin Books (N.Z.) Ltd, 182-190 Wairau Road,
Auckland 10, New Zealand

Penguin Books Ltd, Registered Offices:
Harmondsworth, Middlesex, England

First published by Dutton, an imprint of New American Library,
a division of Penguin Books USA Inc.
Distributed in Canada by McClelland & Stewart Inc.

First Printing, June, 1992
10 9 8 7 6 5 4 3 2 1

 REGISTERED TRADEMARK—MARCA REGISTRADA

LIBRARY OF CONGRESS CATALOGING IN PUBLICATION DATA:
Bromfield, Richard.
Playing for real: the world of a child therapist / Richard Bromfield.
    p.   cm.
ISBN 0-525-93461-8
1. Child psychotherapy.   2. Child psychotherapy—Case studies.
I. Title.
RJ504.B76   1992   91-36883
618.92'8914—dc20   CIP

Printed in the United States of America
Set in New Baskerville
Designed by Eve L. Kirch

With love,
for my wife, our children & my parents

"What is real?"
   —The Velveteen Rabbit to the Skinhorse

CONTENTS

ENDING

ACKNOWLEDGMENTS

Dean Inge suggested that originality is undetected plagiarism. I like to think there is something more in these pages, but his maxim speaks to the impossible task of giving all credit where it is due. Nearly every therapy hour I've conducted, every article I've read, and every conference I've attended has influenced my thinking. Having qualified the gross inadequacy of this acknowledgment, I wish to thank the following people: my agent, John Ware, especially for sensing potential in my initial rambling submission to him—a manuscript hardly resembling this one; Alexia Dorszynski, who needed no convincing that an earnest, as-it-is account of child therapy was of sufficient interest to publish, a belief thoroughly reflected in her thoughtful editorial suggestions; my many teachers and supervisors; Dr. Murray Cohen, who knows better than any (except, I hope, myself) where my words come from; the "patients [to quote Donald Winnicott] who have paid to teach me";* my best friend and wife, Debbie—staunchest and dearest supporter in this and every endeavor, doing more than her fair share so that I might write without sacrificing time with my family, and serving as first and last reader of every word—uncannily noting the awkward, vague, or tactless phrases that I overlooked; my children, who ever made perfectly clear that they much preferred my playing with them than my writing any old book; and of course, the children and families who generously consented to share their stories.

*In *Playing and Reality*. London: Penguin Press, 1971, p.v.

Prologue

He handed it to me without a word, then quickly took his regular seat in the overstuffed blue armchair to await my reaction. I stood holding a large folded sheet of hot orange construction paper. On its cover and in vivid purple, several misspelled and aborted attempts at writing my name were scratched over in heavier black marker. In the lower right corner he'd written the smaller, more legible message—"TO YOU"—in finer, dark green ink. The torrid, clashing colors foretold the turmoil behind Michael's gift and final hour with me.

"I know it's a mess. That's kinda weird, isn't it? I never knew I didn't know how to spell your name. Well, what are you waiting for? Open it!"

I sat down in a chair that was twin to and about seven feet opposite his own and carefully opened the card. A lone, primitively drawn human figure commanded my attention. His hair on end, gaping hole of a mouth, gauntly defined cheekbones, and large, hollow eye sockets conveyed true horror. Barely above the wavy blue ocean surface, the stick body clung desperately to a rope ladder suspended from a much better drawn and sturdy-looking helicopter. An angry and well-toothed shark swam dangerously close to the human bait.

"What do you think?" he asked.

"It's quite a drawing," I replied.

"Yeah," Michael responded proudly, having grown used to my not offering more candid or praising opinions of his words and works. In our first year together, he unquestionably would have read my neutral comment as critical and disapproving, but he had come to feel much better about himself. "I knew you'd really like it! And don't think it was easy to draw, either," he said, judging for himself. "Can you tell what's going on?"

"I sure can see that a lot is happening. Can you help me out?"

His spirits brightened as he told his story: "See, this guy's been exploring the world for a long time—two, maybe three years. At first he started going off to places he knew pretty well, like his backyard and his grandparents' house and the beach and places he went when he was a kid. It was easy then. Well, it wasn't that easy, because he wasn't used to leaving home and going places by himself. Hey, you remember the first time I came here?"

I smiled and nodded. I easily recalled the frightened little boy who had stared mutely while I introduced myself as the kind of doctor who plays and talks with children about their thoughts and feelings. Perhaps, his years of therapy coming to an end, those words now would make sense to him.

"I remember, too. I was sort of scared. After all, what did I know? I was just a little kid. Was I three when I first came here? Boy, that's dumb. Of course I wasn't. I couldn't be. I'm just ten now, so I was about seven, I guess. Are you just starting with any kids about seven years old? I don't envy them. They're just starting. I bet they'd be jealous 'cause I'm older and done here. I don't really care who comes here, anyway. It's not like it's my business. It's not like this is my house or anything." Suddenly aware of what he had said, he self-consciously straightened himself in the chair. "Where were we? Oh, yeah," he laughed joylessly, "I was talking about when this guy first learned to fly by himself. Yeah, he used to have a copilot that flew everywhere with him. And he liked that. Well, I gotta be honest just between us. Is that okay? I mean, we've known each other for—for how many years have I been coming here?"

"Almost three," I reminded him unnecessarily.

Michael held the back of his hand against his mouth and

spoke softly, as if to keep the person in his drawing from hearing. "He used to be afraid of his copilot."

"His copilot?"

"Yeah, his copilot. At first he didn't know if he could trust him. Don't laugh, but he worried he might get hurt or hijacked and never get to see his parents again. He'd be embarrassed," he whispered dramatically, "if he knew I was telling you this."

"I understand."

"Good. Hey, remember when you asked if it was all right if my father left the room and I said it wasn't, but you asked him to leave anyway?"

"You didn't like that."

"No. I bet you didn't even know that, did you? Did you even know I didn't like it?"

"I can remember what you did after he left."

"I don't know what you remember, 'cause I didn't do anything. I just crossed my arms and sat there. I didn't talk to you for a whole hour." Michael laughed, but this time with genuine pleasure.

"You're smiling," I observed aloud.

"I guess *I did let you know* how I felt." He pushed his sweater sleeve off his watch.

I glanced at the clock on the window ledge. "Three years has come down to this?" I wondered, sensing the irony that twenty-four minutes, negligible in a lifetime of minutes, now loomed so powerful and painful, and struck by the realization that I and the people whom I loved were all three years closer to the end, three years closer to *our* good-byes.

"You know all those mistakes I made on the front of the card? My father told me that's progress. He said that a couple of years ago I used to get so mad about mistakes I'd rip up papers and start fights."

"Your father's noticed changes?" I also remembered tantrums and wild sessions.

"About all kinds of things. I do, too, though I don't like, really think about myself as ..." Michael jumped up, raised his hands high above his head, and triumphantly proclaimed, "Ta-da! Introducing the new and improved—*me!*" The exaltation, however, faded fast. Deflated, as if by a slow leak, he sluggishly retook his seat. "I mean, if I'm that much improved, then I really must have been rotten. There's a restaurant near

my house that really stinks. It's the only restaurant I've ever
seen that smells like you wouldn't want to eat there. Restaurants are supposed to smell good, but this place, even dogs
don't hang around the back door where the kitchen is. Every
year new people buy this restaurant and paint it and buy new
tablecloths and rename it. They even use the same sign that
says it's new. But the food stinks worse every time. Come to
think of it," Michael said, perking up, "I'm nothing like that
restaurant. I'm the same person, and I'm not really under new
management 'cause I didn't get sold. It's like I'm changed.
Kinda like I got rid of the bad stuff about the old restaurant
and brought in some new, some better stuff. But that's not
quite right, either, 'cause I still have lots of the old stuff, but
it doesn't bother my parents or me as much anymore. It's like
I still make the cream of spinach soup, but it's not on the
menu. No, it's like it's still on the menu, but nobody orders
it." He frowned in concentration. "Mmmmm ... maybe it's
still on the menu, but I don't care if anyone buys it or likes
it. No, that's not it, either. This is getting to be a hole I can't
get out of. Can we forget this restaurant thing?" Michael
glanced at his watch. "Twenty—no, nineteen minutes left.
Where were we?" he asked again.

"Where were we, where?"

"In the picture, what was happening in the picture?"

"He was worried that his copilot might harm him or take
him from—"

"But," Michael interrupted, "he got over that and even
sometimes liked hanging out with his copilot. Ya know, the
copilot only saw him once a week, and so he had to do a lot
of exploring in between visits."

"By himself?" (Michael's pilot was quite right. Fifty minutes
weekly, the standard arrangement for outpatient therapy, was
not much time to examine his lifetime and be with someone
he loved.)

"He didn't like that. It's not like he was afraid or anything.
It was just more fun with someone else." He awkwardly leaned
forward. "Did I tell you I'm trying out for youth hockey next
month? I think I'm going to try out for goalie, though I'm a
pretty good skater, so maybe I should try another position.
But that's silly. Why am I telling you now? Tryouts are in a

few weeks. I can just wait and tell you what happens." He relaxed back in the chair, falsely reassured by his own words.

"In a few weeks?" I didn't remind him that today was our last day. He knew.

"Yeah, in a few weeks." A deep sigh betrayed the surety of his confirmation. "Do you ever go to see kids' games? I mean, I don't expect you to, like, cheer for me or act like you know me, 'cause you probably have to be careful about kids you see not seeing you with other kids. It's not like I'm worried or really care or anything. It's no big deal. Hey, let me see that picture. Hold it up," he requested, then laughed nervously. "Look at that nose." He pointed to the front end of the helicopter. "It looks like Sugar's." His smile flattened. "When I began here, she was still alive."

He consulted his watch. "Eleven minutes and counting to blast-off! Hey, where was I? No, don't tell me. I can find my own way. It's not easy drawing something so it looks like it's moving. See the propellers. Do you think they're moving? Do they look like they're really moving?"

"I can see curved lines drawn along the propellers."

Michael beamed. "That's what I did. If I didn't draw those lines, they wouldn't look like they're moving. That guy would really be in trouble if I didn't draw those lines. If I didn't, he'd be a goner. He's lucky he has someone looking out for him." He again checked the time. "Ten minutes. Whoa, I don't have much time to finish the picture." He sat up in his chair and shook his arms and legs. "Gotta hurry." Michael spoke quickly, "So—so—so there's, so there's this guy and he's, he's . . ." His speech could not keep pace with his pressured sense of time running out. He wiggled his legs open and shut, like a butterfly revving for flight. "So, there's this guy and he's climbing, he's—he's climbing down from his helicopter to see—to see, he's climbing down to see what's going on below and this mean shark's comin' along and—and he doesn't know if he's gonna get eaten or drown or get out alive. Do you think the shark looks mean? I made him look mean. I mean, I tried to make his teeth look sharp. See all the sharp little teeth? Do you think they could hurt someone? I bet they could." He checked his watch again. "Well, I did it—and with seven to go." Michael fell back, abandoning himself to the chair. "Well?"

"Well?"

"Don't just sit there. Say something. You're the expert."
The sarcasm feebly disguised his hurt.

"Michael, there's one thing about the picture you didn't
mention."

"What?" he fearfully asked, grimacing in uncomfortable apprehension.

"There's no copilot in the helicopter."

He looked away and toward the ceiling. His face visibly
tensed to hold back the tears and the sadness. But he was too
sad. A few discreet tears leaked before the dam broke. Michael buried his head in his lap and sobbed and sobbed.

I sat still and waited.

Gradually he unfolded, then grabbed a tissue to clear his
nose and dry his eyes.

"You know who the copilot is, don't you?" I inquired gently.
He nodded. "But I'll be okay."

"I know you will."

As Michael got up to leave, he noted that I'd seemed to
have gotten shorter since we'd begun three years ago.

Saying good-bye—to the people, places, things, ideas, and
past we love—hurts. Michael knew that. Everyone knows that.
So why do people willingly subject themselves or their children to that misery? Is there any good reason they should?

I am not trying to avoid these questions or imply that their
answers are obvious. Nor do I wish to leave you the opportunity to provide a work ethic or the masochistic rationale,
"It is good for you precisely because it hurts." This is not
necessarily true at all. Bad medicine can be bad medicine (and
bad therapy can be bad therapy) no matter how bad it tastes, or
at least, it can be worth neither its bitterness nor cost. And just
as certainly, things that do not hurt can be good and helpful.

I could now offer theoretical and technical arguments defending the pain of therapy, but they would leave you feeling
empty and unconvinced. I hope that by sharing some of my
world and reflections—as a child therapist—you will come to
experience and understand why its rewards merit the toil,
and why *children's playing in therapy,* being much more than
mere fun or pretend-to-be-taken-seriously, *is for real.*

NOTES TO THE READER

On my method

For the case studies constituting the core of *Playing for Real,* I began by asking my child patients and their parents whether they were willing to share their stories in a book about child therapy. Aware that such a request represented something important and could feel like both a prize and a burden, I encouraged them to think carefully before making a decision. The majority of families and children, sharing my view that this was not an endeavor to enter into lightly, took me up on my offer to meet and discuss what the experience could mean to them. To my pleasant surprise, every family agreed to consider the proposal.

Having received permission to proceed, I wrote each child's chapter—replicating events and language almost exactly as they occurred—and submitted it for review. Some children chose to read their chapters before their parents did (to make sure they approved of what I'd revealed); some preferred to read them along with their parents in my presence; and some younger children asked their parents to read and explain the chapters to them. Though invited to comment in any way— and explicitly informed of their unconditional veto power over anything which they found offensive, inaccurate, or simply bothersome—no one requested that a single word of substance be changed, and everyone consented to having the story in the book.

The children were given free rein to choose aliases (for themselves, family members, pets, parents' occupations and places lived), anonyms that they based on their favorite names, book heros, and secret clues known only to some best friends. The majority of children felt torn between the wish for confidentiality and a desire to see their real names in print, for readers to know their true identities. Some expressed worry that friends would not believe the book was about them. The older ones spontaneously expressed great pride that their stories might help and comfort other children, and were pleased that their parents, by reading the chapters, might better understand them.

For the book's other, and typically briefer, clinical snippets, I followed ethical guidelines, disguising potentially identifying information, while endeavoring to maintain the integrity of the dialogue, play events, and therapeutic themes. In order to protect all of the children and parents, I have not described anyone's physical appearance. To concoct such information—for example, making a skinny child fat—though certainly making for more vivid prose, would have compromised the truer case material presented, as who we are certainly has something critical to do with the bodies in which we live.

Be acutely aware, however, that every clinical recounting—by virtue of its reconstructed and second-hand nature—appears more coherent and neatly organized than was the original therapy. Translating hours and hours of often confusing play and talk into a book form that is readable, comprehensible, and correspondingly emotional requires deliberate writing and editing that inevitably transforms what previously occurred. If I had simply printed hundreds of pages of verbatim therapy notes, most readers would find them to be some combination of tedious, overwhelming, irrelevant, obscure—and not very revealing or informative.

On my language

I have attempted to describe children and their therapy in a realistically complex and sophisticated, yet clear and accessible manner. Though psychoanalytic principles are lived out in these pages, the reader will not encounter jargon-laden references such as *projective identification, decathected objects, countertransference,* and *partially digested introjects* (whew!).

I use *children* to mean children and adolescents of all ages. If I need to define a child or group more narrowly, I use other terms, such as infant, toddler, adolescent, or first-grader. I refer to those I see in therapy as *patients* (though I appreciate the sentiments of those preferring the term *clients*). When speaking about children in general, I randomly alternate male and female pronouns to avoid the intolerable monotony of he and she, her and him.

Beginning

I

Getting to Know You

But how much farther it will reach, none can
say;
For no man yet ever saw the bottom of the
clue.

—Brother Robert Sanderson, *Sermon 23*

Was eight-year-old Danny enacting erotic, oedipal wishes for his mother? "Gee, you *really are shoving* the bottle in that box!" Or did his play reflect a wish to masturbate? "You crank and crank your handle, faster and faster and faster till *kaboom.*" Perhaps, anticipating punishment for his sexual curiosity, he staged my castration to avert fears of his own. "You aimed your bomb right for my crotch!" With a beginner's pride I detailed my clumsy and naïve attempts to solve the riddle of my first patient's behavior.

Kirin—the kindest of clinical supervisors, whose cardigan, knit tie, and suede walking shoes could have been Mr. Roger's own—listened patiently, then deliberately scratched the back of his neck. Although he must have noticed that my comments brought negligible results—I suspected discomfort with my work caused his itch—he neither advised nor criticized. "Keep trying," he humbly encouraged.

In Danny's second hour, he again deployed his makeshift rocket launcher, a dented and faded jack-in-the-box held between his knees. With painstaking slowness and torturous intent he ground out one tinny note, then another. "Ready?" he teased, halting the bent arm at its peak. "Aim." He pointed

13

the front side's once brightly colored lion-taming scene directly at me. "Fire!" He cranked wildly. Listening to the frenzied, twisted melody, I easily imagined the monkey chasing
the weasel. "Boom!" he cried out in perfect synchrony with
the blast. A short, stubby, and empty fruit juice bottle fell
several inches from my feet. Danny promptly repositioned
the glass missile atop the dangling clown's head and, with a
heave mightier than needed, slammed the flimsy lid shut—
ready for the next shot.

Undaunted, and no wiser, I resumed the hunt. Was he
searching for the nurturance of infancy—for the bottle, for
the breast? Was he angry over not being so fulfilled? Did his
assaults express that anger or some other dissatisfaction? My
wayward guesses brought no apparent relief or sense of being
heard. Nor did they bring insight or facilitate his play, which
went virtually unchanged, a sign, I was soon to learn, that its
purpose still eluded me and had not yet been served.

Upon hearing this story for the third successive week, Kirin
shifted in his chair and modestly grinned. He gulped, then
wondered aloud whether Danny might be wanting something
to drink.

"Something to drink! All that commotion for something to
drink? *Why can't he just ask* for a drink?"

"Why, indeed?" my mentor calmly reflected. He knew that
Danny, with my help, would be answering that question for
many months to come.

When I gave Danny the chance, he readily confirmed Kirin's "thirst hypothesis" and good-naturedly needled that I'd
"sure taken a long time to get it." Heard at last, and satisfied
by the juice I'd brought along for him, he no longer needed
to repeat his appeal. He shelved the jack-in-the-box and re-
deemed the bottle. New and different play developed.

I had conspicuously violated the conventional medical wisdom that galloping footsteps should evoke suspicion of horses
before zebras, that more obvious hunches should be entertained before rarer ones. Wishing to impress my supervisor,
and carried away by my sophomoric belief that anything longer than it was wide symbolized a penis, I forgot that a cigar
occasionally was just a cigar, or at least, could be a cigar in
addition to whatever else it seemed to be. That empty bottle,
while signifying much more, also plainly stood for a juice

bottle without juice, a bottle that needed filling. Imagine how Danny experienced my intrusive and overly exotic queries to his simple plea. "Might I offer you a fantasy of breast-feeding, motherly sex, or genital destruction?" "No, thank you," he probably thought. "A juice will do fine." Danny's urgent and temporarily enduring request for juice surely represented a complex of deeply held thoughts and feelings—including sexual wishes involving his own and his parents' bodies—of which he was yet unaware; but at that early moment in treatment, he primarily, concretely, and acutely experienced them as a thirst for juice from me.

"A child needs a psychologist to give him juice?" you chide. Grandmothers would agree: "Big-shot doctor therapist. From what do you know? I raised seven children, and none went thirsty for three weeks." The more economically bent might snicker, "That was the most expensive juice Danny'll ever drink." This skepticism is healthy and deserved. A child does not need juice prescribed and administered by a doctor, especially at the substantial fees doctors charge. And anyway, what is the point of this therapy business? How does a child whose life is pervaded by frustration profit from more of the same in therapy? Isn't that akin to soothing toothaches with sugar water or headaches with noise and bright lights?

In some ways it is. Frustration in therapy feels, and in actuality is, no less real than the frustration that torments life outside of treatment. In so many words, patients protest that they already have too many people in their lives who don't give them what they want. Why would they want or need another? These misgivings also anticipate a second truth: that frustration *by itself* does not cure or heal. Frustration by itself serves one function well: it frustrates. What is served by my leaving a plate of homemade chocolate chip cookies on my desk, but not allowing children to eat them? Or my furnishing an office with colorful, tantalizing toys labeled "Look, but don't touch"? Am I being shrewdly therapeutic, artificially inducing unfulfilled hunger and curiosity to be analyzed? No! I'm creating phoney and abusive experiments in which I create wanting, then deny its satisfaction.

Let's return to Danny's situation. Had I played the cruel host, secretly plotting or invoking his quest for juice? I had not offered and reneged on providing a beverage. I had not turned up the heat to parch his throat. Nor had I spurred his thirst with desertscape prints or posters of icy soda bottles sweating at the beach. And though thirst alone could have explained the first time, what had accounted for his seeking juice in our second and third hours—a search that presumably would have continued indefinitely? Danny, as other children often do, could have brought his own juice or visited the clinic water fountain on the way to my office. His choice not to suggested that more than thirst was afoot.

Kirin's wise counsel, his understated "why indeed?" helped me to see what that might be. People are as they are for good reasons and Danny was no exception. He requested juice as clearly as he was able, and wished to be heard at least as dearly as I wished to hear him. Maybe, in part, that was it. Sensing a safe, worthy place and partner (a.k.a. my office and myself), he set out to work on a most basic dilemma: How to get (his) needs known and satisfied; and the corollary, How to cope with failure to do so.

But how could Danny sense safety and worthiness in someone who had misinterpreted and not satisfied his call for drink? Because as much as he wanted juice, he wanted other things more. He wanted sustained interest in his wishes and himself. He wanted me to continually seek understanding when his play or words confused rather than to reject or blame. He wanted *my* confirmation of *my* failure to satisfy him and *my* tolerance of the frustration and anger that my shortcomings evoked in him. Though Danny felt that frustration to be no different than any other, the way in which he shared and resolved it with me was entirely new to him. He was not impressed by my interpreting empty bottle as phallus or juice as breast milk; he *was* moved by my equating empty bottles and frustration, being quenched and being understood. I may have blown the juice question, but otherwise passed Danny's test as therapist.

As was true for Danny, much of the early work in therapy deals with the child's assessment of his new therapist. This testing begins no later than the first moment of the first hour. I say, "no later," because children generally begin wondering about me as soon as they know that they will be coming. Most hold some minimal information about me, which fuels their images of what I'll be like when we meet.

When returning a parent's initial call, I commonly speak briefly to prospective child patients, saying, "Hello, is your mother or father there?" Upon our subsequent introduction, children have told me that I sounded taller, fatter, older, younger, meaner, friendlier, and even smarter on the telephone than I did in person. Months into his therapy, Hank confessed that I'd insulted him by not asking to speak to him on that first call to his home: "You spoke to my mother and my sister (who happened to answer the phone), but it was my therapy!"

Simply hearing my name can generate abundant fantasy. One boy, Richard, was thrilled at the idea of seeing a therapist by the same name, whereas Sally, whose troubles followed the birth of her baby brother, Richard, was quite displeased. Other children have been confused by my having the same name as someone they loved or who's mistreated them. Parents occasionally have revealed that I am a namesake of a beloved father or scoundrel ex-husband, associations that unsurprisingly color their expectations of me.

When children hear that I'm a doctor, many fret that I'll listen to their hearts, poke their bellies, and give them shots. "Psychologist" holds little meaning for the majority, although some are relieved to learn that, not being a physician, I cannot give medications. Others feel gypped because they are not getting a "real" doctor. Several children have imagined that I'd resemble some fictional therapist, the list including Bob Newhart as the droll group therapist, Judd Hirsch as the earthy and dramatically confrontive doctor of *Ordinary People,* sundry cinematic psychiatrists who moonlight as psychopathic murderers, and, perhaps most flattering, Dr. Ludwig von Duck, quacko-analyst. I've been asked, "What kind of shrink are you?" and "What do you shrink?" but only one has asked where I keep the heads (that joke reflecting some real worry over what I, this strange kind of doctor, did with the children he sees).

Every child is told something different about the reason they are being brought to me (except for those who are told nothing):

* * *

"You're unhappy, and I'm unhappy for you. I can't seem to help, but I want to find someone who can."

"You're going to see a nice man who talks to children about their feelings."

"I know school has not been a happy experience, and this man can help you."

"Your father and I are concerned about your behavior."

"Your father and I don't like your attitude."

"You and I need help getting along."

"Don't bug me! Ask your guidance counselor. It was his bright idea."

"You're going because you're a slob who doesn't care about anything."

"Because you're boy crazy."

"You're nuts."

I've chosen a provocative sampling from the comments I've heard. Though discerning the good from the bad may seem easy, in truth, it is not. The ways in which these warnings impair or enhance a child's attitude toward therapy are relatively un-predictable. An outrageous comment might firmly and clearly push one child toward therapy, but make a second child feel overwhelmingly defective or beyond help. More measured and sensitive explanations may calm another's anxiety about seeing me, but be discounted—along with the suggestion of therapy— by a second child as more parental namby-pambyism.

These messages often reflect, more or less directly, whom the parents judge to be blameworthy and needy of help. Con-sider this interesting mix, each of which some child has heard. What do they convey?

"We're all going to see him because we don't know what the hell is going on here."

"Someone in the family has to get help, and it's too late for us."

"Something has to change; things can't continue like this."

"Someone has to change; we can't continue living like this."

"You have to change; we can't continue living like this."

The most glaring example I know of a parent's message bearing adverse influence occurred in the outpatient clinic of a psychiatric hospital. Midway through her evaluation, a fourth-grade girl suddenly began to shriek and viciously punch her head: "I'm not staying here. You're not gonna keep me here, I don't care how bad I do. I won't live here. I'm not crazy, I'm just stupid. I won't! I won't! I won't! I don't care what Momma says." Her mother, I later learned, had talked to Joanne as they walked from the parking lot to the clinic past the hospital's playground. "Mess up today," she warned her daughter, pointing to the children playing behind the secured chain-link fence, "and that's where you'll end up."

We easily can put ourselves in Joanne's sneakers and understand her reaction. She was afraid of being condemned as punishment to a mental hospital, of becoming a motherless child. But what had prompted her mother's cruel threat? To find the answer, we, who like to think of ourselves as encouraging our children only to do their best, must defer our harsh judgment and try to walk past the playground in her shoes. Joanne's mother feared the evaluation would demonstrate her unfitness as a mother and result in her daughter's being taken away. When she saw the hospitalized children, she felt the pain of a childless mother. Her destructive words intended to induce good behavior and ensure that they stayed together, but ironically led to Joanne's panicked "messing up." (Of course she actually had not messed up, and the incident catalyzed repair of their relationship.)

When parents ask me how best to prepare their child for therapy, I tend to be reserved. After a brief conversation I know little about the family and have little idea of the best way to tell their child why he's being brought here. This is especially true when children refuse to come. It is presumptuous and foolish of me to believe that a well-turned phrase can move a child to come against his will. In those instances I've found that giving parents an opportunity to vent their extraordinary frustration with their child—over the appointment-balking in specific and misbehaviors in general—often enables them to get him to treatment by their own invention.

Although getting to know someone takes a great deal of time, the process begins during the early moments in the waiting room. Does the child appear to be clean, healthy,

physically fit, and, not to be overlooked, his own age? Does
she look like a girl or he like a boy? Is his facial expression
happy, concerned, tearful, brooding, or blank? Does she sit
tensely or at ease, rigidly erect or curled up cozily? Do I find
him in a chair, on the floor, or under the table? What activity
occupies her—homework, reading (if so, what), coloring (on
paper, a coloring book, a textbook, the wall), or playing (with
what and how)? Or is he busy unraveling upholstery, knead-
ing a cookie into the carpet, or trying to disassemble the
doorknob? Sometimes a waiting child does nothing but stare
ahead.

Has the child accommodated to the room, or has she attempted to re-create it in her own image? Children have used
a second chair as footstool, changed the volume and station
on the radio, rearranged and tipped over furniture to build
a fort. I've seen two children use the couch as a table, one
pulling up to the much larger couch, while the other, a much
bossier child with no friends, dragged the couch to his chair.
Children frequently arrive with bags of snacks and fast food
which, as every parent could predict, they eat and manage in
varied ways. Eager to meet a friend, one mother brought her
depressed daughter an hour early along with a full-course
meal in a Styrofoam doggy box. (That same mother sincerely
wondered why her overweight daughter didn't like herself,
and why she ate when feeling lonely.)

If clothes make the man, they hold even more relevance for
the child and his therapist. Are they fashionable, conservative, or bizarre? Inappropriately babyish or grown-up outfits
concern me, as do those out of keeping with the weather—
for example, surfer shorts in January and high laced boots in
July. I wonder about army camouflage suits any day of the
year. What does the insignia on that hat mean, and why is a
boy from Boston wearing a San Diego Padres sweat suit? (Because that's where his divorced father lived.) Do the emblems
suggest a wish to exclusively affiliate with either champion-
ship teams or perennial losers?

In addition to what the child's clothing implies, I am curious what it says—literally, especially in the context of the
child's age. A T-shirt mocking the sexual escapades of Mickey
and Minnie Mouse, disconcerting to see on a preschool girl,
developmentally suits a twelve-year-old boy. The "I ♡ My

Mommy," happily adorning the tops of toddlers, augurs something less healthy on a high schooler. Are the sweat shirt's printed words silly, witty, cute, sexy, hostile, derisively prejudiced, political—liberal or conservative—moralistic, or otherwise provocative? And *whose words are they?* Do they seem like words spoken by or addressing issues that matter to a child of that age? Does a four-year-old girl genuinely prefer an editorial on abortion to a silk-screened Kermit? The older the child, the greater the probability that the opinions expressed are her own.

Is the child's hair styled ordinarily or with an unusual flair—spiked, tailed, streaked with multiple colors, or dyed a color not naturally found on earth? Are there unusual ornamentations—for example, three earrings in one ear, one in the nose, or glittering stars laid into fingernails? Excessive or gaudy makeup on any girl is noteworthy, as is any makeup on a very young girl; and though more commonplace today, jewelry on boys may carry important meanings. (And always, when considering any aspect of appearance, ethnic and peer culture must be considered.)

When I have questions about the way a child looks, I tend to err on the side of silent respect. Yet there are some fashion statements that simply cannot be ignored. I did not hesitate to comment on a nine-year-old boy's sweat shirt that read "I like 'em young and raw." (I learned that it was a gift from his uncle who, although not a very positive model, was the one person who the nephew felt loved him.) I've found that children who wear outrageous apparel are not put off by my interest; if anything, they enjoy the spotlight.

I also observe who accompanies the patient. Is it one or both parents, a nanny, or a divorced father's new girlfriend? I wonder, and often inquire, what kept the child's more likely escorts away? Who sits near whom? How does the parent treat the child—babied, listened to, ignored, criticized, or abused? Does the patient or a sibling exclusively monopolize the parent? Do the family members interact with each other— laughing, talking, or arguing—or do they sit in total silence? And of course, what are the family members like individually?

When I introduce myself to the child, does she bury her head in her mother's lap, quietly say hello, or coolly inquire as to my own well-being? Is her glance averted, turned warmly in my direction, or does it coldly pass through me? Are her eyes clear and bright, or dull and cloudy? Some children quickly stand up to greet me, trying to anticipate my every move or request; whereas others proceed at a snail's pace, dramatically showing me that they rush for no one.

The list of clues goes on and on. However seemingly fascinating or pedestrian, the possible meaning of each individual clue should be neither overvalued nor ignored. Taken together and in context, these early clues begin to tell the child's story.

II

Gimme Shelter

A Station safe for Ships,
   when Tempests roar,
A silent Harbour,
   and a cover'd Shoar.

—John Dryden, *The Works of Virgil*

In a field as controversial and divided as psychotherapy, there is nonetheless remarkable agreement on the important role that trust plays. Without trust, any course of therapy is doomed to fail. But how is a child made to feel trusting, especially early in therapy? How is a child made to feel trusting in the very first hour?

"I've got another one!" Seven-year-old Cory gleefully teased a staple from the shaggy, dirty gold carpet. We had spent the past forty minutes tracking down used staples that somehow had been strewn over the rug. "That's thirty-two." She carefully placed her find deep into an oversized manila envelope that could have held another thirty-two thousand. "It's a good thing we used a big bag!" she assessed. To make sure that her prey could not escape, she authoritatively rapped the paper cage on the desk, then squeezed her face into its open end to see for herself that all was well.

Reassured, she returned to her hunt. "I better check one more time." For several more minutes she crawled over the rug, visually inspecting every square inch while

minesweeping with her hand to feel for potential
ambushers. Once satisfied that no staples remained to
set a trap for her, she jubilantly announced, "Green
light! Now I can walk barefoot"—and she safely did.

Family members had abused Cory physically and sexually,
for a long period of time and from an early and tender age.
As if that was not enough punishment, she, like too many
abused children, loved and depended upon those who had
done little more than use her for their own perverted satisfaction. (I am at present consciously withholding my understanding for the abusers.) Children are expected to tell their
hurts and woes to their mothers and fathers, but she could
not. There was no reason for her to trust anyone. Relatives
and family friends had shared in the abuse—some acting,
some watching, others knowing but looking away. In her
world, no one was safe and reliable; everyone was a suspected
conspirator.

When Cory entered my office for the first time, she worried
that I, too, would mistreat her. But she was alone with that
feeling, unable to share her worry with me because she feared
that might anger and lead me to beat or rape her. It would
have been foolhardy for her to confess her fear of being de-
voured to the wolf. How could she let me know that she was
scared and what it was that scared her?

Cory let me know through the staples. When first noticing
one on the floor, she stood above it, awaiting my reaction.
Only after I'd verbally supported her wish to discard it did
she openly devote herself to searching for the remaining staples. My initial acceptance conveyed that I took seriously what
she perceived to be a threat to her safety; my willingness to
join the hunt further demonstrated my concern for her wel-
fare. My words *and* actions said to her: "You deserve to be
protected from danger, and I will help to protect you." Her
later, appreciative comment that we had worked together to
prevent her getting "stabbed in the butt by a sharpie" exposed the underlying impetus to her anxiety and crusade. Not
only had I helped to keep her safe from the mislaid staples,
I also had not mistreated her myself, and specifically had not
anally raped her—of all the abuse, the act that she most
feared.

Had I ignored her discovery of the first staple or dismissed
it as harmless, she would have seen me and therapy as more
abuse. Had I thrown out the staple without having encouraged her involvement, I would have missed the full and important meaning it held. And last, had those staples not been
dropped, I am certain she would have found some other peril
through which to communicate her worry. Despite her de-
moralizing experiences Cory had not given up; but sadly, not
all abused children are so resilient.

> Judy sat perfectly upright, her gaze firmly fixed on her
> motionless feet, her paled fingers clenching the hem of
> her sweat shirt for dear life. Her jersey's turtleneck
> pulled up over her mouth and an outer sweat shirt's
> hood tightly drawn framed her reddened, sweaty
> forehead and two horrified brown eyes. I asked the high
> school freshman whether she wanted the window open,
> but she didn't reply. By the end of the session she had
> relaxed slightly; however, she had not responded to any
> of my questions or comments with as much as a single
> word.

Although Judy sweltered, she could not remove her hood,
so much greater was her need to hide than any to be cooler.
And as uncomfortable as she looked, I did not encourage her
to take it off. She could figure out for herself how to feel less
hot, and obviously she felt better with the hood on. Besides,
suggesting that she do what she could not would feel like
criticism. I wanted to reduce her excruciating tension (and
cool her off), but how?

Sensing that she wanted the window open but was unable
to tell me, I opened it, while noting how uncomfortably warm
and stuffy the office was. I chose my words deliberately, wanting her to hear that I was trying to ease my and not her
discomfort. I did not assume that her reticence to speak, of
which her self-muffled mouth forewarned, reflected an indifference to the room's temperature. I instead suspected that
she was unable to tell me what she wanted, that she feared
asking and taking for herself. A breeze that Judy perceived as
blowing on her behalf could not refresh and might burn.

What accounted for her being like this? She had been popular and a good student, and only recently had her work and sociability deteriorated, a change for which her mother could identify no possible reasons. According to her, every-thing was as it always had been. Gradually, I learned what had been. Unlike Cory, Judy had not been harmed sexually. Her abuse was physical and came at the hands of just one person, a person who in many ways was good to her. When feeling bad enough to drink, however, when unable to bear what she could not give her daughter and what she herself had never been given, that person tried to ignore Judy as a form of damage control—to restrain her own frustrated and angry outbursts. But being a child, Judy often persisted in asking for this or that, and for that she was frequently hit by her mother. Unlike Cory, Judy could not play out her story. Holding herself under tight wraps lest any desire unwittingly make itself known, she most needed my toler-ance for her reluctance to tell me what she needed. By a cruel irony she could not tell me herself of that need, be-cause that in itself would have been asking for what she needed.

Both Cory and Judy guarded against the bodily harm with which they were too familiar. What about children who have not been sexually or physically abused? What occupies their initial sessions?

> Glen worked as earnestly as Cory. Playing surgeon to my nurse, he called for: "Pencil. Ruler. Paper. No, construction paper. Scissors. Tape." I did not ask "Why?" or "What for?"—fearing that my questions might shut down his play—but quietly watched his left profile speed forward, backward, then forward again. Like a smoothly running coal car, he commuted between the window, where he methodically sized each of its sixteen panes, and the desk, at which he individually recorded every measurement. I did not bother to point out that they were all the same size; he could see that, and if he could not, he had his list of numbers to show him.
>
> The fifth-grader then soberly cut sixteen equally sized squares out of the opaque construction paper and taped them onto the panes, as he worked, the room growing darker and darker. After he neatened up, Glen spent the

remaining minutes with his back to me, facing the
blackened window.

Glen was more personable than this vignette might suggest.
He pleasantly responded to my comments and would have
cooperated with any request I made of him. Had I conducted
a more structured interview and led him with planned questions, he would have followed civilly. However, he quickly
made it clear that he was a boy with a job to do. I was more
than happy to indulge his initiative, saying: "It is your hour
to do as you please." Relatively freed of any obligation to me,
he went his way with the single-minded purpose of boarding
up the window with paper.

Glen had not been physically abused in any way, never punished with a slap or a spanking. His parents were thoroughly
kind and nurturant. And contrary to what one might guess,
he did not dislike sunlight or hold a special interest in the
nighttime. It was a congenitally deformed right ear lobe that
prompted his strange construction project. As a toddler, so
he recalled, he had often walked about cupping his ear in his
hand to keep it hidden. Recent plastic surgery, which successfully corrected the defect, had not brought the expected
emotional relief. He believed that others could still see the
outline of his original ear, and that he deceitfully presented
himself as he wasn't meant to be. Others' compliments on his
actual good looks did not impress him; and he discounted
more objective evidence, such as photographs and videotape,
as mere replications of his false image.

But let us return to the office. A boy shuffles forward and
backward, keeping his right side out of sight—that's clear
enough—but what of the windows? Glen hated mirrors, for
they always reflected; but he never knew with glass, for when
least expected, it might indirectly reveal him to himself or
somebody else. Having rendered the windowed wall unreflec-
tive, the room optically trustworthy, he faced the paper-
shuttered window, assured that I could see nothing but his
back. By keeping me in the dark—in more ways than one—
Glen kept his ear and himself safe.

Cory avoided harm by rounding up staples; Judy avoided
harm by withdrawing and not showing her needs; Glen
avoided harm by shielding his ear from my view. Although

their methods differed, they all defended by way of similar logics: respectively, avoid what you fear; avoid doing what might lead to what you fear; and prevent someone else from doing what you fear. With many children the defensive rationale is not so neat.

> Buddy entered like the proverbial gangbuster, greeting me with a handshake buzzer and squirting flower. For a solid hour he performed and tormented with a benumbing barrage of pranks and bad jokes: "There's a stain on your shirt. Oops, got ya nose!" "What's the difference between you and a brainless gerbil?" "I give up." "No, say you don't know." "I don't know." "The brainless gerbil would." He stumped me with the most notorious riddles. "Survivors don't die, so they don't have to be buried." "We said Ping-Pong balls. Not King Kong's balls!" During slower moments of his nonstop routine, he farted, burped, and raspberried with unabashed showmanship.
>
> As we were about to say good-bye for the hour, Buddy held out his hand. "You really want to get me again, don't you?" I noted, putting my hand forward while bracing for the shock I anticipated. "Wait!" he yelled, jerking the gadget off his finger and stuffing it into his pocket. "Have a real one." I safely shook the empty hand he now offered.

Not every fifth-grade boy has the moxie to buzz and razz an unknown grown-up. Given that Buddy knew I was a "head" doctor at a hospital clinic, his gall impressed me even more. What drove this prankster extraordinaire, or if you'll excuse the pun, what was his game?

"Where there's trouble, there's Buddy," his teacher described. "If he could just learn that he's a fifth-grader and not the principal, life would be simpler." The list of Buddy's transgressions included teasing, tattling, and seldom doing what was asked of him. He preferred activities that he judged more worthy of his attention, while ridiculing his compliant classmates as babies. He'd do anything—even take hurtful falls—to get himself noticed. Buddy's extroverted style helped him to make friends fast and lose them even faster. He was a lonely boy.

The report from Buddy's mother was not nearly as upbeat. She portrayed him as dictator of the household (which they had shared since his father disappeared during the pregnancy over nine years ago). Buddy controlled the television, meals, vacations, bedtimes, and even his mother's whereabouts. Daily necessities, such as brushing teeth and showers, usually led to tantrums or uncontrolled wrestling matches. He mercilessly berated his mother over her slightest expression of displeasure or criticism. Whenever she tried to socialize, especially when she went out on dates, he raised such a ruckus that she eventually stopped going out. The backbreaking straw, which prompted her to call me, was his running a skateboard's muddied wheels over the freshly painted walls of a room she'd recently fixed up to entertain friends.

Consider how Buddy's mother ended her initial conversation with me: "If he knew I wanted him to breathe, he'd probably stop just to spite me." The hostile reference to her son's death was unmistakable. Was there doubt whether he knew his mother wanted him to breathe, and was there any doubt whether she did? No one could blame her for wanting to kill him at times. Any mother would have been frustrated, if not absolutely worn down, by his continual opposition. And yet, in part she had been contributing to his rebelliousness for years.* Buddy sensed his mother's ambivalence about being his mother. He assumed that something disagreeable about himself had created her misgivings about parenthood, that she would have loved being someone else's mom. What he could not see was that his mother, for good reasons of her own, often did not want to be anyone's mother; unfortunately she could not see that, either, for that awareness would have brought with it intolerable self-hatred. Believing in Buddy's badness protected her from seeing what she thought was her own badness as a mother. Having learned the hard way that his good behavior did not seem to make her happier or like him more, Buddy decided that he might just as well be a bad boy; rejection for misbehaving hurt less than rejection for being himself. An obnoxiously good offense became his strongest defense.

---

*Of course, the full reasons for his defiance were much more complex, and to a great extent involved the life-long absence of a father.

Buddy's performance was hardly impromptu. His dazzling assortment of tricks and props required forethought, if just to gather and bag, and he later confessed having rehearsed his magic and brainteasers during the previous evening. His having thought about me before he came suggested that I and therapy already had meant something to him. But there was even more to his preparation. Prior to our meeting, Buddy— wanting me to like him while not knowing how to insure that—had readied himself for my rebuff. He would misbehave and I would dislike him. His zaniness represented a compromise between his wish to entertain me (win my favor) and his defense against the pain of not doing so (fully expecting me not to like him, he would push me away first). As it happened, my admiration for his tricks and acceptance of his rowdyism led not to their escalation, but to their temporary surrender and a genuine handshake.

Although we often conceive of defensiveness as something negative—something which puts off others—it doesn't have to be. Some of the nicest ways about people serve to protect.

> Lisa opened the oversized book of rhymes that she'd brought with her. "I'll tell one to you, and then you'll tell one to me," she gently directed. Though her talent for narration greatly surpassed my own, she was pleased enough with me to request that we read eight additional poems to each other. "Now," she explained seriously, "we will take turns reading paragraphs of the same poem." Our rhythm and intimacy quickening, we progressed to recite alternate lines, then words, and ultimately syllables. "Maybe someday we will read one together," she suggested on her way out.

Lisa was a good girl with good grades and good friends; she came from a good family. Having always been helpful and generous to a fault, she showed more concern for her parents than herself when informed of their plans to separate. "But Mom will be alone. Who will help her when the lights go out or the car's broke?" "But Dad will be all alone. Who will feed him?" Her parents found these sentiments curious, because her dad did not fix the cars, and they both did the shopping and cooking. Astutely surmising that she spoke of her own worries about being alone, they brought her for therapy.

Lisa neither withdrew nor repelled; she bade me sit and read poetry beside her. What defensive function did her sweet and pleasant manner serve? Lisa played the good girl to keep me from being at bay, so as not to be alone. Caught in a psychic catch-22, she could not express her upset over the divorce, for she believed that she and her badness had caused it. Over time she learned that she had not at all precipitated her parents' marriage troubles and that her anger did not have to quarantine her. As she progressed in treatment, she became less bound to doting on others to the exclusion of herself.

Like a good harbor, the child therapist offers the besieged child physical shelter, tolerance of her defensive preoccupation, and a rare opportunity to let down her guard and rest. Just as a sinking hull must be righted and secured before more lasting repairs can be made, therapy can help a child enduringly heal only after she has been spared further abuse and neglect.

III

Come Again Soon

"Be good to the child and he will come to you tomorrow."

—Unknown*

Therapy, being a self-exploration, requires that the child become a willing and invested partner in that venture. Becoming so engaged—the technical term is *therapeutically allied*—further requires that the child grow attached to his therapist. Without good feeling for me the child has little reason to endure the inevitably painful and frustrating aspects of treatment and our relationship.

But what creates that affection for me and the therapy? To begin an answer, let me first relate an incident from my days as a graduate student, that illustrates what doesn't. Throughout our four meetings, Doris had toasted me as a better listener than her previous seven therapists, and claimed that I was worth much, much more than the one dollar she paid to see me—the community clinic used an exceedingly generous sliding payment scale. In her words my assistance was "priceless"; she considered me to be the "lifeline" sustaining her. Yet after the billing office raised her fee fifty cents, I never heard from her again.

*Compiled in Liam Mac Con Iomaire's *Ireland of the Proverb*. Grand Rapids, MI: Masters Press, 1988.

Her departure did not shock me, for all along something had felt wrong. In hindsight her behavior was best explained by the "third law of psychophysics," that applies to the phenomenon of excessive tribute: For every spoken compliment there exists the opposite unspoken, but equally pressing, complaint, or to put it more colloquially, "Many an overly done toast is served in place of a smoldering roast." My patient had been unable to confess her great frustration with me, and I—being too appreciative of her praise—had not encouraged her to do so. Had I helped her to speak more of her dislike for me, she'd have liked both me and the therapy better. As it happened, she decided that protecting me from the truth was worth neither her time nor her money.

Ironically, a child's resentment of therapy is one of the surest inroads to forging relatedness. Some children gripe readily and spontaneously:

"I'd be better off watching my nails grow."
"You know I don't want to be here, don't you?"
"Don't think that I'm *ever* gonna tell you anything important or what I really feel."

They remain unaware that their declarations of resistance and privacy are in themselves wonderfully revealing. One boy, designating a summer therapy session as his last, added, "And I'm not coming on Christmas or Thanksgiving, either, and you can't make me!" "Gee," I was tempted to respond, "I was just thinking about next Tuesday. Who said anything about Christmas? That's six months away." And doesn't that warning sound a lot like someone's unsolicited reminder not to throw him a surprise party? Is he asking for one? Such vows are music to my ears and require little more than my validation: "You are letting me know, right now, how you feel about coming on Christmas." Children seldom encounter and typically cannot help but like a person who comfortably handles, and implicitly accepts, their openly rejecting or critical remarks.

Some children, however, require more help in expressing their skepticism:

"Did this meeting pull you away from something good?"
"Not really, I was just watching television."

"Television?"

"Just some stupid show."

"Being in your own home watching any show can be better than talking to a stranger."

"Yeah, I guess I wouldn't mind lying on the couch right now. I'm kinda tired."

This is commonly how a dialogue begins. The child may think, though seldom states until well into therapy, "Hey, this guy is really interested in why I don't want to be here. He might be interested in why I don't like a lot of things in my life."

Patients often are uncomfortable sharing their misgivings about me and therapy even when given my explicit encouragement. Unaccustomed to criticizing an adult to his face and perhaps genuinely wishing to spare my feelings, these children, however, may be willing to comment on something less personal—my office, for example. Instead of "What don't you like about my office?" I might ask, "If you could redesign this room, what would you do?" My request for an architectural consultation can pique the interest of reticent children, give generic voice to their discomfort, and thereby evoke clues to the nature of their aversion to therapy.

Thus, an abused girl for whom closeness meant violation wanted a bigger room. An adopted girl, who for several years had lived as an orphan, preferred one that was smaller and cozier. "Too many windows," complained a suspicious boy, worried that he'd be spied on; a second child, desiring escape from therapy and her feelings, wanted more windows. The office's warm lighting made one young girl, estranged from her father, feel awkwardly romantic, while two highly stressed children found that same light harshly bright and irritating. A wish for a cushier chair reflected the longings of a girl from a physically undemonstrative home; that for sturdier furniture betrayed an aggressive boy's realistic concern that he might break something. Depressed children have described the muted, traditional colors of my office as too dull and gloomy. Another child whose parents were divorcing nastily thought that my blue and gray chairs "clashed too much." A child's reactions to any aspect of myself or the office, such as the toys, the pictures, and the waiting room, can reveal rich information and—by way of my acknowledging and showing interest in them—help to nurture our relationship.

Given the considerable number of children who come to therapy begrudgingly, you might expect me to rejoice for those who come with bells on their toes. And sometimes I do. Experience has tempered my exuberance, however, since the speediest in are often also the speediest out. James, who had spent his second hour raving about his first, never came to the third or fourth. When a child too readily pleads for treatment every day or "forever," I watch for signs of a premature desertion. The precipitant for quitting may be, not an underlying dislike of therapy, but the intolerable frustration over having so little of it.

I've described children who are slow to open up. There are others who turn themselves inside out at the speed of light. Quite commonly, these highly stressed children dive into therapy headfirst and at the deep end. Seemingly born to play, they do not await any invitation to tour the room, and they do not waste their time on the checkers or the dominoes. Like moths to a flame, they are instantly drawn to the toys that most allow for fantasy—the puppets, dolls, and dinosaurs. Dynamic and frantic play commences—eating, fighting, exploding, biting, flying, fucking, and dying. It's all happening! Scenes, themes, and characters change quicker than I can ask myself, "What does this all mean?"

On troubling and rarer occasions, a child's thoughts and emotions are too intensely charged to be transformed into even wild play. Deprived of that relatively neutralized outlet, a life story is told in its full gore and at breakneck speed. The child may reveal family secrets, tell of horrendous abuse, point the finger at real-world villains, or elaborate primitive and forbidden fantasies. He may scream, curse, or cry—behaviors I seldom observe in early sessions. These children are easily overwhelmed by their strong feelings, especially within the stimulating, anxiety-provoking, and relatively unstructured therapy setting. They may not be able to look upon a dollhouse without imagining, and perhaps enacting, the terrors they carry inside. Their reckless abandonment to the therapy process also may reflect a so-called counterphobic defense:

rather than avoid what they fear, they rush headlong toward it.

Left to their own devices, these children are prone to reveal more than they want to or can manage, and later may experience rebound guilt and shame over the accusations, feelings, or wishes they had just publicly owned. After leaving the hour, they may feel embarrassed, concerned as to what I'll do with the information, or vulnerably alone without my support and protection. Consequently, those who earlier could not play fast enough may soon want no part of me or therapy.

Consider Joey, a seven-year-old boy who had literally run to his initial two visits. On each of those days, he created play in which an older man left his family to become a famous pilot. That man's wife and children, especially one son, pleaded with him to stay, to be a "little less famous" for their sakes. "And if you stay home, you can be a famous father, too," the boy promised. But the father, set on pursuing his own dream, walked out the door, unpersuaded. With approximately five minutes left in each session, Joey would announce that the day had come for the father's acclaimed solo flight. Everyone came to watch, that is, everyone but the son. What they all witnessed was chilling. The plane exploded into flames, then fell to the ground where it and its pilot burned to ashes. Both therapy hours ended with the son hearing the awful news on the radio, and lamenting that his father "should have listened."

On the morning of his third hour, Joey's mother called to tell me that he didn't want to come to therapy anymore. "He says all you ever do is ask him why he's mad at his father." (His father, who actually was neither a pilot nor dead, had fled before his son's birth and had never met Joey.) Though I hadn't once asked Joey how he felt about his father, he blamed me for the painful play and memories that therapy was invoking. Fortunately, his mother—who'd called simply to alert me to the situation—understood what was happening and continued bringing him during this difficult phase.

Whereas I try to loosen up withdrawn or guarded children, I try to firm and tighten up the child who can not securely repress or bury painful thoughts and feelings. Virtually a constant hostage of his impulses, never knowing what slight event or gesture might trigger their outpouring, he urgently seeks help in containing himself, in keeping his lid on. How, in real terms, can I do that? Most critically, I watch closely. Play that brings him relief and insight is better than that which only panics him. If play or talk appears to be making a child un-duly anxious, my immediate objective is to reduce that anxi-ety.

> In her third session Katrina—who believed (somewhat realistically) that her father preferred both her younger and older sisters—produced an elaborate version of *Cinderella*. According to her script the heroine took mighty revenge, insulting and torturing her mean sisters—at first, healthily, then sadistically. But when Katrina began to strangle a doll with great agitation and with her own (and not Cinderella's) hands, I intervened. "Cinderella's feelings are getting much too strong to hold onto by herself," I observed, trying to bring Katrina some awareness of her overly mounting rage.
> With relief she admitted that her anger frightened her and seemed to have a will of its own. She then returned to her play, but this time Cinderella herself did in her sisters, to Katrina's more comfortable pleasure.

And I may need to set a similar limit when the aggression comes *my* way:

> Kelly was justifiedly furious about her life predicament—being raised by an unpredictably abusive father. The dollhouse seemed to intrigue her, but she announced that she would not be using it that day, instead asking to play catch with a bear doll. At first her tosses were subdued and thrown underhanded, but they soon became faster, overhand windups. When I noted the change, Kelly angrily whipped the bear past my head. "What the heck just happened?" I asked in exaggerated disbelief. "I know what I'll do," she said, smiling, placing her left hand on her right pitching arm. "That'll keep it from going too fast."

I did not do much, simply observing Kelly's temporary loss of control and leaving the ball in her court. She came up with her own satisfactory solution, a way that worked quite well. I originally might have set a limit on her playing catch with a doll: "Bears are not for playing catch. How about using this real ball?" But she already knew that! She also had seen the soft balls in the toy chest. I assumed that her unusual use of the bears was in some way a preliminary to more traditional doll play—and a test of me. I could have externally controlled her behavior, but so what? I would not be there to govern her the remaining six days and twenty-three hours of the week. Although it may have been argued that only firm clamping down—taking away the bear, stopping bear catch, decreeing a timeout (that is, having Kelly stand or sit quietly alone for a short period of time)—could have taught her the conse-quences of her behavior, I preferred not to punish Kelly or excommunicate her from therapy for even a single minute. I gave her the chance to restrain herself and she did.

How else do I keep a child from spilling more than she wishes? When I am asked if I can keep a secret, or whether I want to hear one, I do not jump to answer, "Yes, yes." I curb my curiosity about the secret, but indulge my curiosity about the child's question:

"You wonder whether I can keep a secret?"
"You want to be careful about whom you tell secrets to?"
"What are you worried might happen after you tell me?"

This groundwork helps to nurture trust, informs me as to what is really worrying the child, and enhances the likelihood that the secret, when told, can be explored constructively and with minimal destructive backlash to her. Secrets can be big things, revealing potentially dangerous information or inner-most feelings, and therefore need to be welcomed as slowly and cautiously as suits the child.

Analogously, I am careful not to intrude on these children. One can easily ask a child who's spewing sensational material to tell more; however, it is usually more prudent to go slowly. Telling something about one's abuse does not necessarily sig-nify a willingness to share everything, and telling all may re-flect having grown up in a home where privacy and boundaries were not respected. A child may be an open book mostly because she doesn't know that it is okay to be any other way.

As a therapist, I must be careful not to become overly invested in a child's talking. Because a child responds to every question does not mean that she wants to or that it is of benefit for her to do so. And when the child who last week told all wants this week to color silently or to play tic-tac-toe, I must be patient. Her rigid attempt to prevent the previous session's eruption is to be expected and needs to be accepted. I must respect the child's wish for closure as much as that for candor.

There are countless other ways to help keep a child from baring too much of his soul. Occasionally, I deny a child's request to take off his shoes or go shirtless, and may suggest that a child who is becoming worrisomely disorganized on the floor sit up or join me in a more structured board game. And, contrary to what one might expect of a therapist, I'll sometimes distract such a child whose hour is soon ending with questions about his bike or the weather or his plans for that afternoon, in order to help him regroup and make the difficult transition back to the outside (though I must also be wary not to make the child feel ignored or pushed out).

What else convinces children to come and partake of therapy? I listen—trying not to interrupt with questions—and do not correct grammar, complete unfinished sentences, or suggest words that the child cannot find. I refrain from jumping to confront inconsistencies, especially in the middle of a story; and if they remain at its end, I query rather than accuse. I am not bothered by fleeting thoughts or tangential associations; I welcome them. The child's ideas are precious not only to him but to the therapy, itself.

> "Those new long coils of gum piss me off. And so do those big packs. Everyone thinks it's so cool to chew ten sticks at once—like big deal. As soon as the taste is gone, they spit it out. Well, not me. I chew one stick all day. Long after the taste is gone, I keep chewing it. I'm not a fair-weather fan like some kids.

One does not have to be a psychologist to recognize that there is meaning in those words. Unfortunately, much of what children say—even in therapy—is often discounted as trivial, irrelevant, or as avoiding real feelings and problems. If I had not appraised those thoughts worthy of further investigation, what paydirt I would have missed:

> "You sure are loyal to your gum, not like others."
> "You better believe it! How'd those kids like it if somebody threw them out as soon as something little went wrong? No, you're looking at a one-stick-a-day guy."

Subsequently I learned more about that boy's checkered foster-home history and the agonies of being repeatedly moved about.

I also am cautious, and do not pretend to understand a lot quickly. In fact, I make clear that our getting to know each other will take time. When, for instance, an adolescent had just attributed his school and job failure, occasional drinking, and extreme social isolation to the principal's bias against him, I did not rush either to agree or disagree.

> "Well, there you have it in the proverbial nutshell. Or maybe the pistachio shell. I think you pretty much get the drift of what I meant, don't you?"
> "I suspect it's more complicated. Could it be?"
> "Yeah, but who feels like going into it? Would you?"
> "I don't know what there is to go into."

I realized that I was being difficult, but my words were true. Until he elaborated on what transpired in his life and mind, I couldn't know.

A similar situation occurs when a child asks, "Ya know what I mean?" I've often found that I'm asked this when the child doubts herself or feels that she's not being clear or straightforward. Although I feel a great pull to nod and say, "Sure I do," I sometimes must admit that I don't know what she means, leaving to her the choice of whether she wants to try again to tell me.

I take a child's concerns seriously and let her know that I do. That is where the action is. When a parent tells me that the problem is homework but the child speaks of anxiety concerning the school dance, therapeutically speaking I'm at the hop. And, likely what I'll discover is that the two are not unrelated.

I do not read the child a riot act at the start of treatment, stating what is and is not acceptable. Nor do I set unnecessary or premature limits. When a child looks as if he might break something, I watch calmly first. I do not jump up to warn or physically intercede, but wait to give the child the opportunity to manage himself. I've found that even the most reputedly delinquent adolescent, when given my respect, mistreats neither me nor my office. And on the occasion when a child asks me what the rules are, I ask her what she thinks they are or should be. Her mandates—"No hitting," "No stealing," "No hugging"—may directly identify the impulses with which she is struggling at that very instant.

I do not falsely reassure, promising that all will be well, for I seldom know for sure that it will. I frankly tell children what will be expected of them and do not offer miracles or easy solutions. Nor do I offer cookies or chips, though many children would like me to. I do not perform magic tricks or tell jokes in order to snare for I am not here to entertain. I am reluctant to lure with artifice for fear of what will happen when the truth is found out—that we meet not to party but to do therapy.

Attachment begins early but grows slowly. There are no shortcuts. Verbal guarantees of safety or nurturance carry no more weight than those for hair-replacement systems and miracle slicers. A therapist must prove trustworthy over time. Only consistent experiential demonstrations, in times of both quietude and turbulence, convince the child. Though all children love to be wined and dined, the safety, understanding, warmth, and containment of therapy are what foster trust and ultimately seduce the child patient.

IV

What Can I Do for You?

"Say why bareheaded you are come,
Or why you come at all?"

—William Cowper,
The Diverting History of John Gilpin

In my enthusiastic rush to introduce the world of play therapy, I've neglected to tell how children come to be my patients. That matter is crucial because child patients do not arrange their own treatment; parents and other grown-ups do. Although bringing one's child to therapy can be a caring and courageous act, few parents feel either. Rather, many are certain that having a child in therapy incontrovertibly proves their failure as parents.

And who can blame parents for not running to my door? Look what awaits those who bravely venture forth. Over sufficient time their children will "tell it like it is," forcing parents to reckon with a more revealing and candid out-of-the-home version of "Kids Say the Darnedest Things." They will be exposed at their worst—their most embarrassing moments, regrettable words, and ugliest deeds. And what about the considerable inconvenience and expense? Someone has to drive the child; someone has to pay. Given these realities, that any parents call is a small wonder; yet they do. What are some of their reasons for doing so?

Deciding that walking down steps "wastes too much time," a boy jumps down a three-story stairwell. A ninth-grade girl who'd shown no reaction to her cousin's death two months earlier has lost all interest in school, food, and friends. While folding laundry, a mother finds a suicide note in her son's jeans. A jealous brother sets fire to the bed in which his mother and new baby sister sleep. Too frequently a child has been abused.

Fortunately, less dramatic complaints are more prevalent. The parents have received troubling school reports: their children are performing below their ability, not trying, disrupting the class, seeming socially isolated, or otherwise distraught. Home life is an ongoing civil war. Going to bed, getting up, and doing homework regularly lead to tears and psychological bloodshed. I've heard from weary parents unable to remember the last day their child has not thrown a tantrum. Changes in personality may worry parents, as an outgoing child has grown sullen, or a quietly obedient child has become wildly defiant. Children frequently suffer migraines and stomachaches for which no physical cause can be detected. Therapy may be sought to help a child mourn a death or cope with an ongoing divorce, and on rarer days, parents are honoring their child's request to talk with someone.

What must it be like for the parents who call me? Every clinician knows the intellectual challenge of case presentations, but imagine how much more difficult the task when speaking of your own child and problems. To fill me in parents must sift through a lifetime of personal facts and feelings, past and present. But how can anyone possibly tell their child's story in fifteen minutes? Though the glib answer is, "They can't," the more accurate reply is, "With great difficulty." Remarkably, though years of details are missing, parents' abbreviated narratives convey the essence of their child's circumstances, their words a distillate precisely reflecting the experience and history from which it brewed.

Some parents speak logically, with little feeling, while others forsake reason for sentiment. One father, who was not a physician, presented his son's situation with an efficiency worthy of a surgeon conducting rounds; whereas another, painfully flooded with emotion, struggled to make any sense at all. Both encounters told much about life with father. Given patience and support, most parents, even the quiet and distracted, can make their cases and their children known loudly and clearly.

I carefully listen to the way parents' stories unfold. Do they immediately lay their cards on the table, bluntly offering "take us or leave us"?

> "Things are a mess. No, they're worse than a mess.
> He's in trouble at school, with the police, and with us.
> I'm no better. I'm a drinker. I'm considering bankruptcy.
> You should know up front that paying you might be a
> problem. This is not the kind of case, I suppose, you
> therapists fight over."

Or do they tentatively edge their way in?

> "You're probably wondering why I'm talking so much
> about the candy wrappers and cleaning her room. Try to
> bear with me. It's not easy. I'm starting with the little
> annoying things because it's hard to talk about why I
> really called."

Parents who have misgivings about therapy may earnestly try, through me, to convince themselves that their child does not need it. When I was about to ask why one such parent had called, he sincerely added, "Oh, I remember what I wanted to ask. Do you think you should know that Eric saw a boy drown over his vacation?" That, "Oh, by the way" warned of a family tendency toward premature burial, a habit of avoiding painfully alive and unresolved experiences by putting them to rest as if dead and gone. This father did not intentionally try to deceive me. His torment over the thought that his own son could have drowned led to his truly unconscious omission.

When parents call, I continually try to assess the severity of their situations. Though most are not catastrophic, I am on guard for those that are. The more seemingly urgent the trouble, the more slowly I proceed; at no time is a careful evaluation more warranted. Some parents minimize crises, not wanting to see them or not wanting to impose on me:

"Yeah, I guess going to school drunk says something, maybe."

"That happened once?"

"No," a father answered, with a nervous laugh, "many times. But you know how seventh-graders are."

Others send up flares unnecessarily. A parent's insistence that I do something immediately makes me put on the brakes and ask to hear more before intervening. When that same parent declines my offer of several emergency meeting times because of previously planned shopping trips, birthday parties, or haircuts, I turn off the siren and flashing lights for the time being.

Humor comforts some parents through the ordeal of a call. Too ashamed to describe her son's recent shoplifting, one mother hinted that I might want "to nail down my toys" before we met. Upset and bad jokes travel well together. Consider these abundantly common one-liners evoked by my inquiring, "What's been happening?"

"How many hours do you have?"

"Got a week?"

"Just ask me what hasn't. It'll save us both a lot of time and headache."

"Are you *really* asking?"

(After a good laugh) "I'm sorry, that question just hit me funny."

"Trust me. You don't want to know."

"Let me put it this way. No one's killed anyone today, but it's only four o'clock."

One mother recited each of her four children's names, on second thought added her husband's, and later asked whether it was too late to "throw in the dog's." Why do I get so many silly answers? Because mothers of children get so many, or because my question is silly? I wonder how "What's been happening?" plays to an audience of overstressed mothers facing an endless list of demands. Perhaps it's akin to asking Bambi what's been happening in the forest. Many mothers admit they don't know where to begin and express frank surprise that anyone cares to know.

When problems have existed for months or years, I wonder why parents have decided to address them at this time. Maybe they've given up hoping that a horrible temper will mellow naturally or that bed-wetting will be outgrown. Perhaps a child's sassy free spirit, celebrated four years earlier during his toddlerhood, has evolved into obnoxious belligerence. When a boy is caught stealing from a convenience store, his passive father can no longer deny his son's habitual delinquency. A daughter's "mistakenly" swallowing too many aspirin may finally convince her self-reliant father to seek outside help for her depression. Parents may have become less tolerant, energetic, or caring, or be unable to face an imminently failing marriage. Both sadly and encouragingly, abusing parents may have come to be found out and stopped.

Sometimes parents call primarily because a teacher, pediatrician, or friend has urged them. "Yes," I ask, "she does sound worried, but *are you worried?*" After parents vent their resentment over such meddling, they often confess to having similar concerns. Progress is much surer when parents pursue a child's therapy at their own bidding rather than at another's.

Before choosing a therapist some parents want to know more about me. They may inquire about my education, training, teaching affiliation, and views on therapy. "Do you have children?" they ask, believing that someone who doesn't can be of little help to someone who does. People have asked if I specialize in guilt, anger, sadness, sex, boys, girls, shyness, disobedience, and so forth. My replying that I am not an expert on any one emotion, disorder, or type of person has turned a few away. Sensing correctly that I was the "kind of therapist who talks about feelings," one mother cordially bid me adieu, as did another who could not fathom my using toys in my work with children. "That is the problem!" she said with vehemence. "Children need less play and more reality." Whatever their nature, these queries and comments virtually always reflect loving parents' desire to find responsible and competent treatment. Entrusting your child to any caretaker is hard. Entrusting your child to a therapist, and to the vulnerability of treatment, is even harder.

Occasionally parents interview me in person before they bring their child. Early in my private practice, that made me quite anxious. In need of patients I tried too hard to please the child and her parents. Despite my best efforts, I did not always impress and win them over. One child preferred a therapist who gave snacks and soda. Some parents and children just did not like me, whereas two parents chose other therapists because their children appeared to like me too much. Many families simply decided to forgo therapy at the time. Occasionally I never learn why someone decides not to return, though it's easy to understand that those who did not feel comfortable at our trial meeting would wish to avoid speaking with me again.

Sometimes I cannot give parents what they want—a "quick and dirty" treatment, for instance. Ironically, parents who shop for speeding-lane treatment often have children whose pervasive and deep troubles warrant major highway reconstruction. Certain that I can do little in two or three sessions, I refuse with kindness and offer recommendations to clinics with staff who know more about short-term therapy. And I suggest that people who need drug counseling, marriage therapy, or family therapy go to specialists in those areas.

Periodically, divorcing parents ask me to evaluate them in order to aid their fight for custody. I refrain. My assessments do not prophesy or substantively contribute to those decisions. History, as many have stated before, is the best predictor. No personality appraisal, however healthy, can override a proven record of abuse and neglect, or demonstrate the parenting one can or does give. And what about the methodological problem of testing someone who is on a mission? How open can a parent be while undergoing tests to determine her parental fitness? Similarly, I refuse to test children for the purpose of identifying the preferred or better parent.

Rarely, I am asked to test an adolescent for the purpose of recommending suitable occupations, using vocational tests that match interests and skills to jobs. For example, according to my admittedly limited and cynical knowledge of these tests, someone who likes biology, the human body, and people rates high on the "physician" profile, while someone who likes biology, the human body, and is introverted may be advised to become a mortician. I recall receiving the results of one such testing for my mildly retarded patient. "This client is appropriate for the repair of small gasoline engines" was its singular finding. After dealing with my patient's confusion over

why that career had been suggested to him—he was not me-
chanically inclined and hated getting his hands dirty—I could
not help but wonder which of his traits had precluded his
working on large gasoline engines or maybe small ones running on diesel. Admittedly, choosing a profession is a scary
endeavor, but there must be better, less arbitrary, ways of
going about it.

When parents seem satisfied with me and I am comfortable
trying to do what they ask, can we finally arrange to meet?
Not quite yet. If a health maintenance organization (HMO)
provides the child's health care, the cost of therapy with me
will not be covered, for I do not belong to any. This applies
also to government-assisted programs, such as Medicaid,
which in my state covers private therapy only when conducted under a physician's supervision. Frustrated parents
often ask that I see their child anyway, pledging to come up
with the money to pay on their own. I discourage this, however, and urge them to find a therapist who can accept their
health-care benefits. I am cautious, knowing that parents in
crisis are prone to agree to travel distances or pay fees beyond their means. As the crisis subsides, the inconvenience
grows. When the hardship of treatment finally surpasses
its need, parents—understandably stressed or resentful over
the extraordinary measures they've taken to obtain therapy—
may end the treatment prematurely (and possibly leave the
child, especially one for whom trust is an issue, worse
off than when she began treatment). Therapy that is more
affordable and closer to home has a greater chance of enduring.

After the dust settles, there remain some children who actually come for therapy. By this time, I know something
about the reasons they are brought, but do I know fully
what the parents want from me and therapy? The answer often is not black and white. Their wishes are not one-
dimensional and do not correspond exactly to the complaints
cited on their first calls to me. Parents usually want "bad"
things fixed and "good" things fortified—symptoms allevi-
ated, trouble with school and the law eliminated, rebelliousness reduced, and conscience loosened or tightened. They
may insist that all they want is for their children to be happy.

But they may also want more, or be conflicted over what they want.

For example, some parents see me as an arm of parental law—a plainclothes cop—recruited to knock sense into their disobedient child verbally. To those parents therapy is an alternative method of control, mind control. Child psychology is something to be used on children to outwit them. The tactics are familiar: act as if you really don't want your child to eat the spinach; feign telephoning the police when he misbehaves; offer to call the local orphanage when she herself threatens to find a new home where parents will treat her better. Long ago, these parents erroneously assumed that their child's sole purpose in life was to spite and annoy them; over the years and by their own doing, that became just what the child lives for. They created the very monster that they needlessly once feared. (As some of these parents observe that my kindness and understanding seem to improve their children's behavior more effectively than their disciplining, they soften—not surprisingly, given that their considerable effort to bring their child to me must signal some wish, however ambivalent, for their child to feel better about himself.)

Although parents consciously want the best for their children, they unconsciously may have other plans. Consider the eight-year-old girl who came to my office dressed in hot pants and white go-go boots. Her mother garishly painted her nails and lips, yet refused to let her join a Brownie troop because it met in the (dangerous) evening. This mother wanted to keep her daughter safe from exploitation but, simultaneously and without awareness, she also wanted her daughter as unprotected from sexual misuse as she had been, as a child subjected to incest.

Willy's parents wanted therapy for him because of his weak effort at school, and complained about his poor study habits and "impossible" attitude toward homework. But Willy soon explained that whenever he sat down with his books, his parents offered him chores to earn money or invited him on errands to the mall. Their motivations concerning his schoolwork were more confused than they initially conceded to me, their son, or themselves. Similar dynamics apply to any sort of misbehaviors—such as disobedience of authority, abuse of a sibling, or sexual escapades—which partially gratify a parent.

Parents unknowingly may fear relief of the very same symptoms for which they brought their children. They may prefer their son's stomachaches to his showing them direct anger, or a daughter's shyness to her being more confident or socially outgoing. Many depressed mothers have not wanted an overly dependent and homebound child to grow up and away from them, just as some overcontrolling parents have not wanted their child to gain confidence in himself and his judgment. As long as Harry, a diabetic boy, avoided taking physical risks, he spared his mother unbearable anxiety over his health.

Remorseful parents may wish to compensate and make amends for ways in which they feel they have failed their children. I've worked with several single mothers, for example, who felt agonizingly responsible for their sons not having fathers. Securing therapy for their children may represent some parents' attempts to make restitution, and acknowledge that things were not as they were meant to be or should have been. By bringing a child for therapy, the parent gives her the opportunity to heal, and implicitly, the permission and space to spill the hurt and rage known to exist. One very kindly mother's asking whether I did good work with bad children revealed her great guilt and her underlying question: "Do you do good work with bad mothers?" Though she was anything but a bad mother, she believed herself to be one.

Such subterranean agendas, hidden from view, exist in all of us, and are signs of neither evil nor bad parenting. Although we may consciously strive to spare our children the same harms, inhibitions, and humiliations that we have suffered, we often succeed in doing otherwise. Inevitably and unconsciously, we promote, resist, and frankly stunt varied aspects of their development. None of us are immune from these unknown and potentially destructive influences upon our perceptions and raising of our children. All that we can do is seek greater familiarity with them in order to more peacefully live and parent in their presence.

The objective reasons that parents request therapy for their children are relatively few. However, their motivations for doing so are infinitely complex and unique. If upon first meeting I could read those meanings, I'd thoroughly understand why parents and child are as they are. But I cannot. Instead, I must settle for their more limited and laborious unraveling within therapy.

In Therapy

V

All by Myself

"Watchful over his aloneness."

—James Legge,
The Life and Teachings of Confucius

Not one of us gets all of the understanding we want, and few get as much as we need. Leroy got less, much less. Not because his parents did not try or care to give it; they did, very much. Plainly put, he was a hard child to understand and give to. As a baby he did not seek or enjoy his mother's attentions, or at least, did not show the usual signs of pleasure that mothers observe and cherish. Her gaze did not enchant his own nor did her playfulness bring him visible delight. She felt no response to her cuddles—no melting into her arms, no reaching out for more mommy. If that was not sufficiently painful, his passive indifference to her affections sometimes felt more like active dislike, as when he looked away from her or pulled back from her caresses.

Children's being able to talk generally makes home life and development easier, for they can now tell what is needed, what's the matter, where it hurts. But Leroy's language, which was delayed and eccentric, provided instead more opportunities for frustrating miscommunication between him and his parents. By his third birthday the other telltale signs of autism had appeared. His arms flapped and body spun. With hypnotic interest he watched his fingertips slowly wriggle just inches from his nose. He so desperately avoided others' eyes, they might as well have been the blinding highbeams of oncoming cars. The slightest changes in routine, invisible to most, evoked fierce tantrums and physical upset. Despite his parents' devoted efforts to know their son, much of the time they felt lost as to what went on inside him. Their own child was their greatest and most beloved mystery.

The teachers at his preschool found him no easier to manage. The most minor differences in his day—a desk moved inches by a janitor's broom or a new brand of milk at recess—could upset him, leading to disruptive behaviors. He yelled, refused to follow rules, hit, kicked, spat, and powerfully shunned others. Frightened and confused by his unusual mannerisms, classmates tended both to avoid and tease him. Under this threat, his unfamiliar ways grew yet stranger and further alienating. Leroy perplexed everyone, and everyone perplexed him.

I slept fitfully the night before we were to meet, and toward morning was awakened by a dream that I was an astronaut whose spaceship had escaped orbit. The sense was not that I wished to break away, but that the earth's gravity had grown weak and no longer could hold me secure from such a distance. Out the small hatch window I watched my childhood backyard grow smaller and smaller until it disappeared from view. Too far from earth to be heard, my radioed pleas for help went unanswered. I hurled through the dark, cold unknown of outer space, dreading that I would be alone forever.

Looking back, I find it unbelievable that I had little idea of what my dream divulged that night. As a distraction, so I then reasoned, my thoughts turned to Leroy. His two previous therapists had described him as too unreachable for play therapy. Would he talk with me? Would he play with me? Would he one day even grow to like me? Would I reach him at all? In retrospect, we made a good match. He was a child who needed someone to make contact with him, and I was a therapist who needed, for reasons yet undiscovered, to make the connection that had eluded others.

The following morning, I entered the clinic lobby, where I met a boy rather tall for his six years and looking extraordinarily frightened for someone of any age—face tensed, eyes darting everywhere except toward me, his new therapist. His habitual toe-walking, a result of neuromuscular immaturity and exaggerated by the stress of our introduction, gave him the appearance of someone crossing a bed of hot coals.

"Hello," I said, holding out my hand to shake.

Leroy pulled back. He jerkily rotated his head down toward his right shoulder and twisted his upper trunk away from me, while keeping his legs and feet planted in my direction. His body seemed to say, "I want to be with you, but I cannot." I knew that he was trying to endure, not ignore, me and our difficult meeting. His parents* spoke up to tell him that they'd be waiting in the lobby; they nodded good-bye to me. They'd obviously witnessed this scene before.

In the office, Leroy fled to the far corner, where he crouched down and squeezed his face tightly into the joint of abutting walls. For several minutes I watched his tightly huddled back heave with anxious breathing. Wishing to console him, I said, "It's not easy mee—" but he abruptly covered his ears. Though I immediately stopped talking, he continued to press his hands tightly against his head, cautiously removing them only many minutes later. His apparent mistrust for my silence was well founded, for after a few moments I mistakenly tried to acknowledge the discomfort I'd just caused him. "You don't like my talk—" He again blocked my sounds. My voice seemed to hurt him physically. How could that be? Was it what I said, or simply the noise? I spoke softly and kindly, yet my words fell like pointed arrows on tender skin. I wanted to tell him that I understood and could feel his pain, but that wasn't true; I could do neither. Anyway, he likely appreciated my silence more than anything I could say—so I said nothing. We spent the remaining forty minutes in stillness. Like animals in the wild—he not budging from his sanctuary, I not venturing forth—we surveyed each other from a distance.

I knew that Leroy would grow accustomed to me very slowly, if ever, and that each therapy hour, if coming once every seven days, would seem to him like the first. To minimize the chance of his guard hardening between sessions, I suggested that we meet twice weekly, and his parents agreed.

---

*Although my work with parents will be referred to throughout the case discussions, it is deliberately very much a secondary focus of this book, which spotlights the child and his play.

We were in business, perhaps not a booming one but a business nevertheless.

Still in his corner but facing outward, Leroy spent the next five therapy hours running a little red horse around a race-track game (chosen because it was the toy closest to him), hundreds of laps, each one identical to the last—the same speed, the same rut. What was going on inside him? Was he having fun? He neither smiled nor laughed. If he was in any way pleased or satisfied, he didn't show it. Only his occasional smelling of the game materials and spitting disrupted his seemingly joyless circular pursuit. I observed closely but did not comment; even in quiet, growing used to me represented a formidable ordeal. "He must be doing this for some good reason," I reassured myself, even if I could not see what that was. I sorely needed to believe that, for if his behavior had no meaning, what could I possibly do with him as a play therapist; and more disturbing, what meaning could others' or my own behavior hold?

While racing his pony during the sixth hour, Leroy bent over and, as had become a temporary ritual, pushed his nostrils to the game board and inhaled deeply. Anxious to take some action, I gambled and spoke, "You are smelling the game," though I fully expected his rebuff. Panicked by my verbal approach toward him, he ran his horse faster and faster around the oval. I reminded myself that this was not yet the moment to give up and put a puppet of a basset hound wearing a plaid Sherlock Holmes hat on my hand. I pressed the puppet's black felt nose against the board and made loud sniffing sounds. Leroy dropped his little plastic animal to watch intently, then put the side of his head down to the floor in order to look directly into the furry dog's eyes. Awkwardly he uttered, "You smell stuff"—his first words to my puppet and me.

I'd have rejoiced at a mere parrot's mimic, but he'd varied the phrasing, taken my words in, and acted on them. Someone was in there! "Yes, I do smell stuff," Schnauzer, as my puppet came to be called, thrillingly affirmed. Weeks later, I made that dog detective further explain that he smelled in order to learn more about his world. "I smell things happen to me," Leroy concurred. These exchanges with me, however lean, implied that he could do therapy, too.

For weeks Leroy continued to seclude himself. At first I merely noted this: "You are playing in the corner." Our sharing a common world had to begin somewhere, somewhere simple. I did not speculate aloud as to why he needed insulation. To suggest that he was afraid of me or needed to be left alone was dangerous. If he did not feel that way, he'd see me as intrusive *and* insensitive to him. And if I guessed right, I'd blow his cover. Hiding would no longer provide escape and I'd appear to be a mind reader, making both therapy and me as unsafe as he feared.

Gradually Leroy elaborated this play and expanded his territory. By kneeling behind chairs at opposite ends of the playroom, we lived in separate houses with explicitly defined and inviolable boundaries. For several hours we stayed at our respective chairs, doing little more than knocking on their wooden legs and seats to verify that the walls of our houses were intact. Leroy spoke rarely and only to remind me that I was not to venture toward his house. As his play evolved, he gave us cardboard mailboxes to receive correspondence. Our letters tended to be concrete and simple:

"The floor is gray," he wrote.
"Yes, the floor is gray," I wrote back.
"How do you know?"
"Your first letter told me so."

In addition to giving him the minimal contact for which his mail appealed, my written observations confirmed his view of reality. Yes, I intended my letter to validate implicitly, the floor is gray. I also see a gray floor. We see the same floor; we see the same world.

Most of our initial contact was nonverbal or by note. When Leroy attempted to tell me something, he'd writhe, squint, and sputter—a word here, another there. I wanted to free his tongue and hear his words. Like a younger, unaccused Billy Budd, he tried to speak his mind but he could not. Was there any greater frustration? "You want to tell me something, but it's so hard to," I'd counsel. "We can go slowly. I have lots of time to listen." Leroy would walk away, settle himself, and return to speak his mind in bits and pieces.

Curiously, Leroy's capacity to voice his concerns was dramatically enhanced when he was alone. After a receptionist erro-neously told him that I was not back from lunch—although I was in the next room with my door slightly ajar—he spoke expressively of my assumed absence. "Egads! Where ever could he be? He knows I am here waiting. This worries me, it does." When I appeared, he fell silent, unable to share the feelings he'd just articulated away from me. Talking directly to me put him at risk of being misunderstood, punished for what he said, or having his wish go empty.

"But I'm safe," I longed to say. "I'm your friend. I won't hurt you." Had I thought he'd have believed those words, I would not have hesitated to say them. But Leroy knew better. He knew that even those he loved inevitably misunderstood, and that *their* failings hurt most of all.

To say that Leroy enjoyed sameness is like saying that plants enjoy sunlight; he needed it to survive. We began and ended sessions virtually to the minute. In one rare instance of my being late, he worried that "the clocks [were] not well." Ques-tioning the integrity of a timepiece was safer than confront-ing me as the tardy perpetrator. He noticed when one of dozens of pencils in a cup was gone, or when a lamp shade had been tilted slightly. "What happened?" he asked, bracing himself for the bad news he anticipated.

Early on, I naively tried to accommodate his rigid need for order and attempted to restore the office exactly as he'd left it at each previous meeting. I failed miserably, unable to fore-see which turned flowerpot or worn piece of chalk might trig-ger his hurt, because those small differences were negligible to me. My capacity to perceive change was significantly less acute than his. Our work proceeded at a snail's pace.

"The out-of-place crayon troubles you. You'd like every-thing to stay the same." "Yes," he softly affirmed with a dis-tressed brow. Together we would try to reestablish things as they had been, while sharing just how much these deviations in his environment shook up his world.

Leroy steadily showed greater interest in the puppets and, like exploring young toddlers, investigated them with his body and unadulterated senses. He rubbed, smelled, and, less fre-quently, licked them. In times of stress, he soothed himself by rhythmically stroking softer puppets; in calm he rested his cheek upon them quietly. But eventually he put them on his hands to make them move and talk.

A large number of puppets helped to regulate how close we came to each other. In an extreme example, Quacky (a hard white rubber duck with a yellow beak) would call Mrs. Cow (a feminine, fleecy beige cow with a pink felt tongue, pretty eyes, and long eyelashes) to request that Baby Cow (a small, fuzzy pink-and-gray spotted beige calf with little horns) deliver a telegram to Schnauzer's mailbox. When I once short-circuited this scheme by forgetting one of the messengers, Leroy angrily threw down his puppets and retreated to the chair in the other corner, his "house." Over time his interpersonal fragility lessened; our interactions became more direct and employed fewer puppet middlemen.

Though hardly a novel feeling for me, confusion acquired peak-experience status in my work with Leroy. We shared a land but not a tongue. More often than not I was unsure what he said or did, and felt lonely and incompetent. If I could not convey some basic understanding, what did I have to offer? Initially, perhaps to counter my own bewilderment, I convinced myself that Leroy had a message for me, however hard it was to comprehend. I needed to learn his language, and to some extent he needed to learn mine.

This surely was the case when he first told me that "Japan blew up." He waited for me to reply, but I didn't know what to say. Uncertain whether I'd heard right, I asked to be sure. "Japan blew up," he pronounced more clearly. That country had never before come up in his play or talk. I associated to the bombing of Hiroshima, though that made little sense in this context. Leroy continued his seemingly unrelated play until the hour's end, when he repeated it for the third time.

"Tell me about Japan's blowing up," I urged Leroy with little expectation that he would.

"Japan blew up," he patiently restated.

He was trying to tell me something, though I had no idea what. I wasn't worried that I'd blown my last chance, however, for an important message tends to be sent until it is heard. It returned in three weeks, but this time "Japan was sad." When I queried whether the sadness had anything to do with blowing up, Leroy warily backed away, staring at the corner of my clock. Following the trajectory of his stare, I saw the answer—

a small gold oval sticker with black letters, "Made in Japan." I finally understood and could respond. "When our time runs out, you feel blown up and sad?"

"Like I'm broken," he corrected in a whisper. He made perfect sense in his native language.

Feeling safer with and closer to me—feelings ironically promoted by my willingness to let him be as remote as he needed to be—Leroy dared to give us telephones. As did most children, he claimed the real phone—a broken one that I'd found a neighbor throwing away—and assigned the plastic toy one to me. Like our letters, our calls originally were descriptive, brief, and occurred only at his initiative.

> "Hello?" I picked up.
> "Hello," he tentatively replied.
> "You called me."
> "How did you know?"
> "The phone rang."
> "I made it ring, didn't I?" Leroy smiled broadly.
> "Yes, you did make it ring!" I smiled back.

Though Leroy still was unable to articulate his feelings, his phone play hinted what they might be. More frequent and longer calls meant he was feeling less anxious and less needy for distance between us. His "accidentally" disconnecting us, hanging up with a slam, or telegraphing unsavory vocal farts signaled obvious displeasure with me. Ultimately he endowed our homes with front doors, and our mutual visits grew more common and comfortable.

Although our relationship was firming, allowing Leroy to control it was not always easy. He could invite closeness, then detach instantaneously—for example, by requesting, then refusing to accept a letter from me. With my toes resting on his threshold, I was tempted to push my way fully into his door. But I had to remain patient and go slowly. Entering his world, however wondrous and seductive, was a serious journey to be taken patiently and carefully. Rushing might lose ground or take us to places Leroy was not yet prepared to be, especially with me.

Puppets assumed increasing responsibility as vehicles for Leroy's communication. His choice of puppets became more determined, rather than based on an indiscriminate need for more and any objects to stand between us. He cast specific puppets in the roles of specific impulses or feelings, and like a Hollywood film director he interrupted play scenes to bring in the mad shark or bad wolf. His experience of himself as a mass of fragmented and disparate feelings was shown vividly when he attempted to jump on my lap, a most unlikely and bold move for him.

I was shocked and pleased that the boy who earlier had been afraid to leave the corner had now come so far out. Momentarily wishing that love in itself could cure, I briefly considered giving him a bear hug but I then broke the news: "You can't sit on my lap, but you can pull a chair right up next to mine."

Leroy stared at me. "Why not?" I imagined him asking. "I thought you liked me." But instead of speaking, Leroy frantically stuffed all of his puppets—an angry wolf, a hungry pig, a scared baby cow, and six others—beside me, into the space on my chair that he'd wanted for himself. He achingly explained that the "hole hurt his eyes [and so] he fill hole with puppets." By sitting with me symbolically in the form of his nine puppets, he fended off the hurt of my rejection. His reliance upon many different creatures to play his single self corresponded accurately to who he was. No one puppet could integrate and hold all of his feelings, because he himself could not.

Leroy, like many younger children, was not thoroughly convinced that the puppets on my hand were not somewhat alive. In his mind they inhabited the wonderland existing between the animate and the inanimate, between the real and the imaginary. Although he understood intellectually that the puppets were not real—if you asked him whether they lived, he'd say no—he related to them as if they might be. Superficial observation suggested that Leroy was simply engaged in the nature of puppet play, their coming theatrically to life when played with. Closer scrutiny, however, revealed his thoughts about the magical powers of my hand inside the puppet.

He asked many very serious questions about what life was like for the puppets who lived with me, and expressed a sincere wish to come join us. In a striking example, Leroy instructed my puppet to be a contestant in a game requiring discovery of prizes hidden behind different doors. He whispered to me the number of the door that held the prize, then directed me not to share this information with my puppet. When I inquired whether Leroy wanted me to make the puppet guess correctly or incorrectly, he criticized me for asking such a stupid question. How could I possibly influence the puppet's choice, he puzzled, unless I broke my promise not to tell it where the prize was?

Leroy steadily grew more attached to me. His written instruction to "bring [him] a pencil back" after Christmas break showed an awareness of the sessions we'd miss, as did his February postcard greeting, "Be back Friday," sent from Niagara Falls. Increasingly he tried to obtain a snack, physical affection, and extra time from me—little of which came. My failure to gratify these wants frustrated him tremendously and led to great anger. Though I judged my withholding of those wants to be therapeutically sound, I felt cruel and stingy. Leroy, however, did not give up trying to "get" from me and did not become irreversibly detached, signs that his feelings were becoming more tolerable to him and that the therapy was working.

On a beautiful spring day, the kind on which we all know to what a young man's fancies turn, Baby Cow wrote a love letter to my Schnauzer, brazenly asking for one in return. I wrote back:

> Dear Baby Cow,
>   I wonder if the letter you want is
>   —I LOVE YOU—
>   Is that the letter you want?
>   Schnauzer

After Leroy read my letter, he furiously ripped and threw it into the wastebasket.

"What is it?" I asked, knowing full well what it was.

He did not answer but boycotted me, sitting on the opposite side of the office. I wondered whether I'd been too harsh, whether I should have just sent him a love letter to nurture the closeness he was letting himself want and feel. I feared that I'd gone one step too far, that I'd lost him. Having made my choice not to send a love letter, however, I had to wait to see the results of my actions. Fortunately, I did not have to wait long.

Leroy walked to the pail slowly, retrieved the pieces of the letter, and taped them together. With a red pencil he crossed out all of the words except for three.

"You made Schnauzer's letter say, I LOVE YOU!" I exclaimed.

Leroy's face glowed. He'd rejected me in revenge for my rejecting him, and we both had survived.

Although we had been meeting for ten months—a very short time for a child like Leroy—there were many indicators of progress, and not just within therapy. He was getting along better with other children and communicated more easily. He threw tantrums only infrequently and showed much less flapping and other unusual behavior: He even looked at me occasionally. His IQ, measured as considerably below average twelve months earlier, was now assessed as above average! His language skills, in particular his reading, had grown strong. Although these gains exceeded our hopes, the news was not all good. My internship year was ending, and so would Leroy's therapy with me.

Leroy was angry at a reminder that our year was ending. "You told me in July. Let's play." His annoyance that I'd discredited his memory betrayed the true source of irritation—only twelve weeks of therapy and me remained. He ran to climb inside a cabinet from which, once satisfied that he'd found a good hiding place, he came out to collect an armful of animal puppets and dolls. For many minutes he worked to fit himself and the toys into that small space. Once everybody was in, he shut the door and there he stayed for the remainder of the hour. I listened to Leroy speak to the puppets, his brethren-in-felt. "We're okay. We're not alone," he reassured them in a small and scared voice. "We're all here. It's okay, Quacky, don't cry. Don't be afraid, Wolfie. We have each other. We'll be fine." Leroy sought comfort, for he was being left, yet he could not rely on me—I was the one leaving. In the safety and darkness of his "cave," he comforted and protected his creaturely soulmates and they him, just as he once had felt and wished to be comforted and protected by me.

Leroy subsequently withdrew and played much more on his

own. For days he enacted verbatim scripts from the *Mr. Rogers' Neighborhood*, vehemently resisting my attempts to join him. "Mr. Rogers is there every day," he pointed out.

"He *never* goes away?"

"No, never. Just never."

For the final two months of therapy, Leroy re-created game shows he'd seen the previous day, with scripts that eerily resembled the originals. "Can you tell our studio and home audience about the lovely prizes that await them? Why, it's a contemporary design home entertainment center!" Leroy wanted closeness, but real people were complicated, dangerous, and—as my leaving was reminding him—undependable. In contrast, television personalities were constant—always looking the same, on the same channels, at the same times. He could love their two-dimensional images without having to smell, feel, or relate to them in any directly human or bodily way.

Leroy brought a book that he'd written about game shows to his last few sessions. That document, from which he asked my puppet contestants countless factual questions about game shows, became the bible for our "Game Show Trivia Game Show." "Who hosts *The Newlyweds Game?*" "What show is hosted by Gene Rayburn?" Leroy worked hard to distract himself with these obsessive questions, but he could not dodge his feelings. When I mistakenly gave the name of a host who no longer was on television, Leroy abruptly ended the game and spent the remaining minutes alone in the cabinet. In the following and last hour he explained that the host was mean for dying and leaving his loyal viewers. After I said good-bye, Leroy wrote that he'd miss both Schnauzer *and me*. Believing that *our* show had been permanently canceled, we both knew who he thought the mean host really was.

When autistic children were first studied, their disorder was blamed on "refrigerator" mothers who were described as overly ambitious, overly intellectual, and coldly unresponsive to their children. Gross biases and misinterpretations tragically led to these faulty conclusions. The mothers of those early cases were indeed bright and successful, as were most mothers who had the awareness and means to pursue help for children with special needs at that time. They indeed also appeared somewhat cold and unresponsive, as would most mothers who found their basic maternal instincts and invest-ments profoundly unsuccessful and unreacted to by their chil-dren. Who would not be sobered by and defended against that experience? We can only imagine the guilt and self-hate those mothers suffered.

Recently we have learned that autism is essentially neuro-logically based, of varied unknown causes, and of widely varying severity*—ranging from the classic and severe cases we immediately think of through much milder forms. We now know that the autistic child comes into the world with relatively compromised capacities for social and language development, and that much of who that child becomes can be understood as ways that he compensates for and copes with those innate vulnerabilities. We also know that parent-ing a child who may be unresponsive and rather incompre-hensible poses an enormous dilemma for parents, especially the mother. This is not to say that the mothering of an autis-tic child is any less important or influential than for any other child, or that bad mothering does not make mat-ters worse; only that it does not typically—if ever—cause autism.

Although this enlightenment has rightly changed the treat-ment for most autistic children from the psychoanalytic to the behavioral, there are some brighter, more socially able, and more mildly affected children, such as Leroy, who can use language and fantasy sufficiently well to benefit from tra-ditional play therapy. Behavioral theory could not adequately explain the complexities and variations of Leroy's play and his relationship with me. His flapping and spinning faded without my having concretely rewarded his not making or punished his making those movements. Although I did not direct his play to address language, by spontaneously setting up mailboxes, phones, and front doors, he ensured that we communicated more and more. Behaviorists might have pre-dicted Leroy's being overwhelmed in an unstructured play environment. And yet, of his own accord and creativity, he

*As conceptualized by J. Bemporad, J. Ratey, and G. O'Driscoll in their article "Autism and emotion: An ethological theory," published in the *American Journal of Orthopsychiatry,* Volume 57, 1987, pp. 477–484.

established a play world that targeted his needs, meeting him where he was developmentally, better than any that a therapist could have engineered for him. In fact, given his massive dread of being controlled by others, I believe he would have found a more highly structured environment to be overly demanding and threatening rather than safe and inviting. He cherished the regularity that we shared and I supported *because he had initiated it*—because, having grown up around him in the course of therapy, it directly provided what he needed. He would have less valued, if not resented and resisted, regularity that I'd arbitrarily imposed on him, and had based on my early assessment of him rather than in response to what he slowly showed me in therapy.

A more behavioral approach also would have failed to acknowledge Leroy's experience as an autistic person. Though a behavioral strategy may have improved his behaviors, it would not have confirmed his pervasive experience of being frightened, misunderstood, and rejected—feelings quintessentially defining who he was and with which he was generally alone most of the time. That some think such children are psychologically less needy or less capable of benefiting from emotional sustenance and understanding is as baffling and upsetting as it is unfair and simply wrong.

When I received a call from Leroy's mother the following spring, I was surprised and joyful. He was finishing his year of therapy with a current intern, and she, knowing that I was now licensed as a psychologist, wanted me to treat him again. We were being returned to the airwaves! Though my anxieties about resuming our work were considerable, they were dwarfed by Leroy's own. Martin, his current therapist, described how the news spurred Leroy to play out *Star Wars* scenes in which Han Solo—representing myself—was defrosted to rejoin the crew with Luke Skywalker. But this dream come true was not one hundred percent pure; it was contaminated by a fair amount of nightmare. Leroy worried that I had changed and wondered whether I would still like him, and what would happen to his new therapist, a man to whom he was very attached.

Though he ran into my office for our first—and now onceweekly—meeting, he didn't mention his return or his latest therapist's departure. Instead he withdrew, looking quite sad. He quietly drew a detailed map of a Boston subway line that was being replaced by a new one running several blocks away. For months Leroy meticulously diagrammed the two lines, deliberately drawing them on separate sheets of paper, then made up a game show based on trivia about them. "What comes after Essex station?" "Is Dover underground or outside the tunnel?" Aware from his dedicated mapmaking that he cared very deeply about his subject matter, I strove to learn the facts. My correct answers delighted him; however, my errors depressed him and led to his concluding that I did not care enough about his interests and him.

In time Leroy taped the maps of the two lines side by side, until he'd assembled one big map showing both lines and the corresponding pairs of old and new stops. Over many more weeks he built three-dimensional paper models of stations, and played out my Schnauzer and his puppet friends going between them. His commuters found themselves in a painful dilemma: choosing the familiar old line meant missing out on something new and exciting; forsaking the old line was disloyal and, should the new one collapse, left them with nothing. By Leroy's estimation, losing the original line enraged the public, even though they enthusiastically welcomed the streamlined newcomer.

Weeks into our second year back together, Leroy brought in a local magazine's picture story about the two transit lines. This memorial pleased him much and moved him to determine that most people wanted both lines kept open so that they could ride whichever one they wished. "Even when they're on the new line," he explained, "riders like knowing the good old Orange Line is still there."

"Like you wish Martin was still here?"

Leroy grimaced. Even though he'd spent some fifty-odd hours playing this out, the truth stung. "I wonder if he knows about the new Orange Line?"

"You'd like him to."

"Yes," a shaky voice affirmed. "Maybe I could write him about it." But he didn't. For almost fourteen months, and through the coincidental renewal of a subway route, Leroy had worked to make sense of his confusing transfer back to me from a therapist whom he also loved.

Having confessed his longings for Martin, Leroy turned his attentions to his confusion about my whereabouts for the past year. I remembered the story of a friend's father finding his lost dog on the other side of Boston two years after she'd run away. The two enjoyed many days of blissful reunion until one peaceful Sunday dinner when his master suddenly yelled, "So where the hell were you all this time?" Leroy too wondered where the hell I'd been and why I'd left him after our first year. But he could not ask me, even in play, until I proved that I was back for good.

There was no question that therapy was helping, but much more contributed to Leroy's progress. His mother was a devoted advocate for his educational needs. Both parents vigorously supported Leroy's own eagerness to participate in all kinds of activities that fostered social and physical development—Scouts, soccer, bowling, and dance. His religious faith, especially belonging to a church community, also highly enriched his daily life. And of course, his body and nervous system grew more mature daily.

Looking at Leroy standing proudly, almost a foot taller now, it was hard to believe that we'd begun over four years before. Leroy leaned against the fireplace mantel, singing mournfully, "Holy Mary, Mother of God ... forgive us sinners now and in the hour of our death...." Though the words of the rosary were familiar, I asked what he thought he sang. "Salve Regina," he told me somberly.

"Salve Regina?" I was not at all lost as to the meaning of his comments. He had spent much time over the years talking with Regina, the clinic receptionist, while waiting for his hour with me. He'd tell her about his schoolwork, his new toys, and his worry about me. But Regina was out sick that day.

"You miss her."

"Where is she?"

"You're worried about her."

Leroy turned toward me. "Have you received commu-
nion?" he asked with trepidation.

"You're scared that I have not?"

"Yes, he is." His reference to himself as *he,* a regression to
his earlier unusual use of pronouns, was a tip-off to his great
stress.

"What's *he* afraid of?" I asked.

"If you die, you'll . . ." He spoke the last words so softly I
could not hear them.

"If I die, I'll . . . ?"

"If you die," he blurted, "you'll never get to heaven." With
his lower lip trembling and eyes opened wide, his face was a
study in terror.

"And we won't be together."

"Yes." His eyes welled. They gazed—not over, under,
around, or through—but into my eyes with love.

Leroy felt Regina's absence as if she'd died, and it stirred
his ever present worry that I—and the parents he loved even
more—could die, too. The comforting belief that we'd all be
reunited in an afterlife strained under the duress of his present fear of loss. This wish for us always to be together underlay his more immediate and perennial torture—why we
were not together more in this world. Through months and
months of tedious, painful work Leroy had begun to understand just how hard it was to feel closeness, and once felt,
how terribly hard it was to let go. He *both dreaded and needed
his aloneness,* though he was needing it less and less these
days.

By our mutual consent, the account of Leroy's therapy ends
here. By the book's publication, we'll have completed our sixth
year; it is likely we will continue together for many more. I
suspect that one day I'll hear a knock on my front door, but
I will not find Quacky or Mrs. Cow. It will be Leroy. And
when I ask with delight what brought him here, he won't reply, "Route 332," or "the Orange Line."

"I just wanted to see you," he'll be able to say—and more
preciously, he'll be able to feel.

Though some communicate and socially relate more easily
than others, no one's inner world can be taken for granted

or easily entered. Coming to understand another person's experiences proceeds slowly, and only through careful observation and patient inquiry. Leroy taught me, better than any teacher or text, this basic principle, which guides psychotherapy with all people, whatever their capacity to speak, think, feel, and play.*

*I wish to make explicit mention of two works that particularly enhanced my understanding of and capacity to enter Leroy's world, as well as that of every other child and adult with whom I've worked, autistic or otherwise: Rudolf Ekstein's classic *Children of Time and Space*, New York: Aronson, 1983; and Bruno Bettelheim's *The Empty Fortress*, New York: Free Press, 1972. Despite Bettelheim's misblaming of mothers (a natural, even if misguided, outgrowth of his profound appreciation for a mother's influence on her child), the shortcomings of his research methods, and recent bad press, he generated more than one man's worth of brilliant insights into children.

VI

Lost and Found

"The God to whom little boys [and girls] say
their prayers has a face very much like their
mother."
— James M. Barrie

Look upon this worn and browned photograph:

It is a winter market scene in turn-of-the-century London.
Christmas greetings and prices of long ago are soaped on the
store windows. Peddlers push their carts and shopkeepers ply
their trade along a snow-flurried, cobblestoned street. A young
couple walks arm in arm, oblivious to the hectic commerce.
Just off-center in this bustle stands a small girl of about three
or four, dressed in a plaid woolen coat and cap, her muddied
leggings making her appear broader and shorter than she is.
With both hands against her right shoulder, she tightly holds
onto her braided ponytail. The passersby, busy with their own
affairs, do not seem to notice or care that she cries.

Why does she cry? Most observers would guess not that she's
misplaced a doll or bag of toffees, but that she is lost and wants
her mother. Why do we so naturally equate a lost child with a
missing mother? Perhaps the best person to answer that question is a lost child, or in Ashley's case, a child who once was lost.

"It was the best thing you ever did!" the five-year-old
crowed, having said little else during our initial meeting. Her
mother, who had been questioning whether she'd done her

daughter any good, teared at this heartfelt vote of confidence. The self-criticism addressed her adoption of Ashley, the remarkable story of which she'd just told.

Against her family's will and without either their emotional or financial support, Beth had traveled by herself to South America, to the part-police station, part-orphanage where Ashley's mother had abandoned her. Subject to an unusually demanding adoption procedure, made even more rigorous by an ongoing state of martial law, Beth had been required to remain there for several months in order to learn Spanish and fulfill a trial phase of living with the then two-year-old girl. That probationary period was aptly named, for it was indeed trying. Ashley was strong willed and furious, she spoke no English, and most of all, she did not seem to want a new mother. For their first few days together—days that surely must have felt much longer than ordinary days to the new mother in a strange land—Ashley refused to eat or sleep, and cried endlessly, not in complaint, but as if irretrievably dejected. Beth recalled her profoundly discouraged sense that the adoption was not going to work, saying, "She was so terribly unhappy. I just couldn't imagine that she'd ever let me be her mother."

They returned to America physically and emotionally exhausted: Ashley suffering from tuberculosis and a variety of parasitic infections; Beth, though not ill, feeling the effects of having gone so far away for so long for such a momentous event, and coming back with enormous responsibility and very little money (she had taken several months' leave without pay from her job). Haunted by relatives' pre-adoptive forewarnings and inflamed by their more recent but equally critical I-told-you-so's, Beth's self-doubts and anxieties grew. The new single mother and only child were severely stressed, but—as Ashley had just certified— they had each other, and that was the best thing of all.

In our final few minutes together, Beth described her daughter's present troubles: her defiance of authority; her occasional running away from preschool; her biting, hitting, and spitting at both children and teachers. She made clear, however, that the primary reason for seeking therapy was to help Ashley cope with her having been orphaned and adopted. We scheduled once-weekly therapy sessions and said good-bye.

Throughout the rest of that day my mind drifted to Beth. Knowing firsthand the challenge of raising children in even the most conventional circumstances, I contemplated the commitment she'd assumed. It seemed to me leviathan, virtually unfathomable. I envisioned myself thousands of miles from my home in a one-room apartment with a child of a different culture and language who wanted her original parent, not me. I questioned whether I'd have had the character and stamina to do what she had done.

I also wondered about Ashley. Had her desertion been a crime of negligence committed by a callous mother who did not want her, or an act of love, a reluctant surrender by a depleted mother who wished only that her daughter have more than she could give her? This little girl already had borne more than a lifetime of pain and hardship, and so, I suspected, had Beth. Though they had not shared Ashley's infancy, they had been through so much else as mother and child. For the moment I fended off my concerns over Ashley's life as a baby—life too early to be recounted verbally by her, but that would surely be implicitly remembered and revealed in the course of our relationship.

When Ashley and I began play therapy the following week, she wasted no time in making herself at home. Before I'd shut the office door, she claimed the small area of carpet between the side of my blue wing chair and the dollhouse— a heavy-duty plywood structure sturdy enough to withstand the earthquakes and drunken brawls that girls and boys (even those secure in their manhood-to-be) inflicted upon it. Ashley stared at my face for a minute before she observed accurately, with a smile, that I wore glasses "just like" she did. Her pleasure over our being alike was a good omen.

Turning to the house, Ashley gingerly pulled out and closely examined a small wooden table. She softly placed it upright on the floor, then did the same with the kitchen sink. As she removed the furniture, she grew less timid and was soon flinging chairs and beds everywhere. "There!" she yelled, having emptied the house except for several small brown bear dolls that lived there.*

Carefully, Ashley made a grown-up bear wearing a purple

---

*I use animal dolls (with which children easily identify) because they generally keep fantasy play safer and more fluid than human figure dolls do, by providing greater psychological distance and disguise.

calico dress precariously seat a pink-smocked little bear on the passenger side of a yellow metal jeep, then climb behind the wheel, and speed off at breakneck speed. A few seconds and one sharp turn later, the mother's driving had catapulted her cub out into the woods. "She's alone. She's lost," Ashley mumbled, sounding dazed and looking lost herself.

"All alone?"

"Someone lost her, but she doesn't know who. She's waiting to be found again." Quickly regaining her bright eyes, Ashley had the mother ride back to the scene of the accident. "Get in!" she invited her daughter. "Oh, boy!" the girl exclaimed and jumped onto her mother's lap.

We both were relieved and joyous that the mother had recovered her abandoned daughter, but this good feeling could not last. Ashley, who was studying the board and playing pieces of a game she'd found, suddenly threw the directions booklet down as if it was a hot iron. "I don't like this game anymore."

"You don't?" I picked up the paper, assuming that she'd been frustrated by instructions too difficult to read or follow; I soon saw, however, that they were written wholly in a foreign language. "Spanish?" I asked.

Ashley tightly closed her eyes. "I don't see it. It's not Spanish! I don't like it!" Opening them, she kicked the box at me, unable to find respite even in a child's game. Far from being defeated, she did not retreat but came right back at me, sticking a foot-high tyrannosaurus rex in my hand. "Be nice," she requested pleasantly.

"Hello," my dinosaur greeted.

"No, you're mean now. Be mean!" she ordered harshly.

I made it growl.

"No, you're not mean." She spoke gently. "Be a nice dinosaur."

Again I spoke cordially on its behalf, and again Ashley sharply pushed me to act unfriendly. What was the meaning of her to-and-fro game, reflected in her alternating tone of voice? I tried out my theory.

"Sometimes the dinosaur treats you nice, but sometimes he treats you mean. Sometimes he shows you Spanish."

"Yes!" Her roar confirmed that she'd felt lured into a false sense of security with me, then unsuspectingly clobbered with a reminder of her hurtful, Spanish-speaking past in South America. Having let me know of my transgression, Ashley resumed her play. She tenderly blanketed a tiny baby bear in the jeep's rear cargo space, and seated its mother nearby to watch over the infant. When our time was up, she raised the baby so that its eyes met mine.

"I wonder whether you just told me your life story?" I asked, following Ashley's unspoken direction to make eye contact with the bear, not with herself.

"I know that, silly. *I* did it!" the baby replied. Ashley tucked the bear back into its four-wheeled cradle, then she happily rejoined her mother to leave.

Seven days later, Ashley took up exactly where she had left off, an encouraging sign that she cared about and was able to remember our previous week's work. Playing a devoted mother bear she wrapped its child in a small bearskin rug to keep her "good and warm" and patiently fed her so that she would not "get hungry stomachaches." At bedtime they lavishly hugged and kissed before falling asleep together.

Until this moment I had had no reason to speak, but the action stopped. Ashley stared blank-faced at the two bears lying side by side in the doll bed; something on her mind or in her heart prevented her from playing or talking. I could have asked what made her desert her play or what she felt or thought at that very second, but she probably would not have responded. I instead observed what she'd been doing. "Ashley," I called to get her attention, "that mother took such good care of her baby."

Ashley jumped onto my lap. My appreciation of her play had touched her deeply, sending her fantasies of intimacy reeling. What was I to do? She wanted my closeness and affection, the same cozy attention she, as mother bear, had given to the baby. But was that in her best interest, or might it confuse or harm her? I knew that no amount of holding, though feeling good for the moment, could make up for what she had missed getting from her blood mother, nor could it neutralize the traumas she'd experienced. If I instantaneously gratified her wishes for physical love, however seemingly reasonable for a child of her age, I'd defuse the painful impetus to her therapy. Temporarily satiated, she would lose the immediate incentive to explore and grieve her painful longings, and leave therapy neither wiser nor stronger than when she came. Moreover, what would sitting on my lap mean to her? And if I permitted that, why—she might soon wonder— couldn't she have a hug or a kiss?

Disheartened and sobered by my clinical conscience, I exclaimed, "You're sitting on my lap!" in hope that I'd bring awareness to what she was doing and eliminate her actual need to sit there. She snuggled farther into my lap, obviously having not read the same child psychology manuals as I. "I know how much you want to sit here, but I won't be holding you on my lap," I persisted. When she still did not budge, I lifted her passively uncooperative deadweight onto the floor.

Her eyes filled with tears. Unwilling to take my abuse (so it felt to her) lying down—another indication of her resilience— she dropped seven bear dolls into my lap, then threw them back on the floor. "They're garbage," she declared. She did the same to three "stupid" dinosaurs, and to a handful of puppets that she called "garbage *and* stupid trash!" all the while laughing without any happiness.

"Wait a minute." I deliberately paused. "I wonder if . . ."

"What?"

"I wonder if *you* felt like garbage and trash when I wouldn't hold you."

Ashley circled the room, screaming, "Stinky, smelly trash! I'm stinky, smelly trash!" With forced laughter she collected all of the animals that she'd chased from my lap, sat against the far wall with them on hers, and shouted, "We don't like you, *either.*"

"Either?"

"You heard me. We don't like you, either."

"Does that mean I don't like you?"

"Yes, you don't like us."

"Because of my lap?"

"Shut up! And we don't even want to sit on your lap, so don't even ask us to. We never wanted to sit on your stupid lap anyway. We always never liked you."

"*When* did you *begin to always never* like me?" Like her own, my awkward and illogical grammar captured her emotional dilemma.

"You know when, stupid," they catcalled.

"When I didn't hold Ashley in my lap?"

The animals hooted and howled at my question; their barn-yard jeers said it all. They had cast me out, tit for tat, because I'd done the same to their honored play mistress. Whereas both our time for that day and our brief honeymoon were over, our real relationship had only begun.

But real does not necessarily feel better. When I next greeted Ashley in the waiting room, she hid behind her mother's legs and softly refused to come with me. "Something to do with last week?" I asked. Ashley dramatically sobbed and stamped her feet as Beth gently guided her, without a fight, into the office. As soon as I had sat, Ashley lobbed a soft, floppy doll—the kind that comes with its own adoption papers—onto my lap, then ran behind my chair. "Who is this?" I asked over her not-so-stifled giggling.

"Sharon. And you can't throw her off because she's a doll." Ashley knew what she was talking about.

"*She* can sit on my lap?"

"Yes, but"—Ashley ran around to snatch Sharon back—"she doesn't want to. She doesn't like you. She doesn't like you because she's *my* best friend."

"Sharon didn't like what I did to you last week?"

"She doesn't like you because you made me get off." Her anger and its source accepted by me, Ashley carefully lay Sharon down to sleep on the seat cushion next to me—a not-so-small peace offering. A tiny baby from an Indian village play set immediately caught her eye and led to a frenzied search for its mother. Upon finding her Ashley squealed and slid the infant into the papoose. She soon interrupted this symbiotic ecstasy by putting them both into a canoe, explaining that the baby was "gonna get lost." She looked distressed, but then appeared to have a light bulb of an idea. "I know," she said, grinning. "*You* be the baby!"

"What should I do?" I inquired. Over the years I'd learned to give children the chance to direct their play rather than confuse it with my own characters and plots. As a rule, less of me encouraged more of the child. Ashley had no qualms with my request for her input. She instructed me to cry and act very, very scared.

"Help! I'm afraid. Help!" my baby called. "Help!" Ashley thoroughly enjoyed watching my baby figure fall overboard during the torrential storms she sent its way. Raging floods and wild winds carried the baby farther and farther from its family; each catastrophe brought Ashley immense pleasure. When she sensed that the hour was over, she chained the baby to its mother. "Now they can't get lost," she declared. She had made sure of that.

Now, Ashley was not a mean person. Her substantial sadism was generated by and defended against even larger feelings of helplessness. She controlled the baby's fate to reverse in fantasy what she actually had experienced, thereby becoming a powerful victimizer instead of the powerless victim she had been. Through this play she began to master and overcome the profound trauma she had suffered.

Ashley saw the threat of loss everywhere and in everything. For almost an entire session she searched through hundreds of dominoes to find the one "good" domino that carried the full nine dots on both sides. "No dots are missing," she glowed. "Everybody's home!" According to her, the object of board games was to herd the playing pieces together. "Hurry up! Hurry up! Get back with us," she chastised any that strayed. Even a framed print of a rowboat in still waters was not immune from her perceptual apprehension—its lack of passengers a reminder that a favorite teacher had left her school. When I asked how this made her feel—a satirized therapy question of some actual utility—she grabbed a sheet of paper and quickly drew a circle with dotted eyes, nose, and upturned mouth. Holding that mask up to her face, and through her feigned crying, she asked me to guess what she was up to.

"I don't know," I thought aloud. "I hear crying, but I see a big smile."

"I'm happy!" she insisted angrily.

"Your happy mask hides a sad little girl."

Ashley now cried for real. Her teacher's departure had summoned back feelings from the original loss of her mother. She hastily drew her own version of that boat, including a mother-and-daughter crew, which for our remaining minutes she obliterated by dragging a black marker back and forth over it. As we all know, and Ashley was learning, there is no pleasant way to encounter something that saddens to the core.

Though we'd been meeting for only a couple of months, the past was returning fast and furiously, often to Ashley's dismay and displeasure. But who could know the distance and depth to which a game of her playing doctor would take her? After having examined and prescribed rest and relaxation to the furry, abundantly maned lion puppet she'd assigned me, she made her identical but smaller puppet telephone me. "R-rrrrring. R-rrrrring."

"Hello?" my larger lion answered.

"Daddy, Daddy, help me," the little lion squeaked. "I was left at the zoo. I'm scared and all alone in a cage. I'm locked up all alone."

"What happened?" I asked, marveling that Ashley could possibly be remembering the details of her desertion.

"I was left here and they locked me up. Come help me. Hurry, please! Call the police."

The police indeed informed me that she had been left in the middle of the night by some unknown person. I obtained the station's address, and rushed off to find my child. When as daddy lion I rescued my baby, I was greeted by hugs, kisses, and somebody else's name.

"Mommy, Mommy, Mommy!" the little lion cried. "I missed you so much. She left me here all alone. She just left me here." For some time Ashley's puppeted hand nuzzled hard against my own.

"Mommy, Mommy?" I thought. "Wasn't I just Daddy, Daddy?" Instead of confronting this discrepancy—"Gee, I thought I was your daddy"—I assumed that her change of my identity was no accident. "Who left you here?" I asked the baby lion.

"My mommy left me."

"Your mommy?"

"My *other* mommy."

My heart jumped. Her biological mother, or more precisely, her biological mother's *absence*, had come on the scene. Was this to be a dramatic breakthrough, a turning point of her treatment? I wondered. Ashley, however, immediately damp-ened my eagerness to explore this new material, exclaiming that she was "all done with this silly stuff [and that it was] time to clean up." What had prompted her retreat? Was she too sad, or too something else? Or had my interest in her other mommy seemed excessive and perturbed her? I relied on my judgment to trust Ashley's own, that it was time to put memories away, not take out more of them.

After cleaning up, she played the mother bear, putting her baby bear to bed with a softly hummed lullaby. Ashley seemed not only unmindful of my presence, but happier than I'd ever seen her.

Foolishly I spoke—"The baby and her mother are so happy!"—expecting my observation to please Ashley very much.

But she did not like my talking at all. Instead of basking in my comment, she hummed louder. Her soothing bedtime song grew boisterous and attacking. "La, la, la, la, la. . . ."

Regrettably—and probably as a result of my feeling excluded—I had interrupted her blissful fantasy of a mother and child, a fantasy that could promote healing by itself, without my intellectual explanation. My talking had ruined the magic of the moment. How could she enjoy her daydream while I was calling her back to class?

When alone in her crib, an infant who has known early maternal satisfactions and pleasures consoles herself by conjuring up her mother's image and the associated bodily good feelings—the warm fondling, the gentle swaying, the relief from painful hunger—that her mother's real presence has repeatedly given her. This happens in the same way, though much more profoundly, that one avoids feeling a few degrees of winter's cold by remembering a Caribbean vacation gone by. Those motherly memories serve as an eternal wellspring of good feeling and self-sufficiency throughout the child's life, especially when hurt or deprived.

I wanted Ashley to have been so nurtured, which would have made her mother–baby fantasy a reminiscence, a recovery of something lost. I preferred this, my own fantasy about Ashley's fantasy, to one in which she imagined a symbiosis that had never been; that was a much bleaker past, with a less hopeful future. But I had no more time for self-reflection; a jeep was heading straight for me. It screeched to a halt just as the front bumper touched my pants leg.

"Growl! Growl! Growl!" Ashley roared.

I looked down. A spiked dinosaur stood in the driver's seat; a small bear slept on the rear seat.

"Everyone thinks the dinosaur's growling," she whispered.

"It isn't?" I whispered back.

"No. It's the baby," she snickered, still in a hush.

"The baby?" I repeated in playful disbelief.

"The baby?" She turned on me as if she'd never heard the word before I spoke it. "The baby? Why, babies don't growl. Only bad dinosaurs growl. Babies," she screamed, *"don't get that angry!"*

I considered reflecting her feeling that babies don't growl and get angry, but, as she had convincingly demonstrated, they sure did. I carefully chose my words to convey understanding for her fear that showing anger could lead to something bad—most likely, her abandonment. "Babies *don't like to* growl and feel so angry, especially at people they love."

"Yes," she endorsed heartily. "They don't!"

As it always does, early loss had dealt Ashley a double blow. After she'd lost her mother, who was there that she knew well and trusted to help her cope with the pain and anger? In the best of worlds, a mother helps her child learn to manage such unsettling feelings. By tolerating and validating the child's envy and anger, for example, the mother fosters the child's own acceptance of these in herself. And by caringly being held through inevitable moments of rage, the child grows more able to manage those feelings herself. But Ashley had been relatively deprived of this support, and consequently had a greater need to disown and become a stranger to such aspects of herself.

When several months had passed, Beth and I met to review her daughter's progress in therapy. I learned that Ashley was more cooperative, less clingy and combative, and generally appeared calmer and more contented. I also learned that in about seven months Beth and a boyfriend (about whom I knew little) were going to have a baby. By her mother's report Ashley was excited but was not sleeping well. Since hearing the news, she each night had climbed into her mother's bed, rationalizing that the baby got to sleep there. Feeling understandably guilt-ridden, Beth had difficulty keeping Ashley in her own room, though she recognized the need for consistency and boundaries, especially during the pregnancy. She predicted that Ashley would likely have further reactions, including the fear that she again might lose her mother. I could not have agreed more and told her so.

Though Ashley did not mention the words *baby* or *pregnant*—it was clear they were on her mind. For several sessions she rearranged the furniture to "make more room," without explaining why space had become a valued commodity. She also zealously reordered the toy box, which she condemned as overly crowded. "There are just too many toys, especially little ones. Too many toys. Don't bring any more in here!"

The pregnancy first came up directly after Ashley had used the bathroom in my house (the office in the adjacent, converted garage did not have one). Visiting my bathroom was a big deal for most children. After all, they often fantasized about the life my family and I led; here was their chance to see for themselves what really went on inside my home. Some children saw pretty much what was there and contrasted that with their idealizations—"Gosh, you have dirty dishes in the sink, just like we do"—though most saw much more than existed—oversized television screens, mountains of toys, and huge bowls of treats. Often they reported sighting child tracks—toys on the floor, children's books, half-eaten cupcakes on the table—as evidence that I had sons and daughters. Most fascinating, their fantasies caused some to recall having seen, out of the corner of their eye or down a darkened hall, children who had not been present in my home. On the contrary, one boy, totally unaware of his wish to have me to himself, did not remember actually bumping into my son. As did the majority of children who went into the house, Ashley milked the excursion for all she could get—slowly surveying my living room, kitchen, and mudroom. She uneventfully walked out of my house, but reentered the office on her hands and knees, barking like a dog.

"You visited my home and now you're crawling on the floor and barking," I observed.

On the floor in a three-point stance, Ashley shook each bear at me with her free right hand, while growling in a voice befitting its size and gender.

"Why is everyone growling at me?"

"You know why."

"Because I made you leave my home?" It was the lap-sitting issue revived in disguise.

"Growl! Growl!" the bears angrily replied as they assaulted my shoes—toes scuffed bare from playing on the floor—with little bear kicks and jabs. Ashley handed me a play phone, sat down next to me, and suggested that I call Sharon (the doll that had sat on my lap), her best non-living friend. The line was busy; I'd been set up. When, at Ashley's chuckled urging, I tried again, she picked up the phone and told me, "Sorry, wrong number. There's no Sharon here." Having tried hard to frustrate the heck out of me—as, I assumed, she somehow felt I had done to her—she was delighted with my melodramatic goshes and shuckses, wholesome expletives playfully intended to show that she'd gotten to me. "Try Rudolph," she suggested. I truly was surprised when he answered to say that Sharon was home, but that she was much too mad to talk to me.

"Gee, Rudolph," I asked, "do you know what she's mad about?"

"You woke her up. She was dreaming. But you woke her."

"She was dreaming?"

"A dream come true. She was in a dream come true." Ashley's pupils seemed fixed on some far-off vision, as if she was the one dreaming.

"What made it such a dream come true?" I inquired in the tranquil voice I'd use to say good night to a child who was tottering on the edge—about to fall asleep, about to catch a second wind.

"Nothing." Rudolph's friendly tone turned hostile; Ashley frowned grimly. "You ruined her dream and that made her mad. Ask her yourself. You woke her up. And she's a grouch. She's a monster when she wakes up." Having expressed enough of her anger to come closer, Ashley dropped her boy voice to speak naturally. "Hello?"

I put down the receiver to ask Ashley, as an aside, what I should do.

"Ask me if I'm mad."

I picked up the phone. "Are you mad?"

"No, I'm not mad," she replied sweetly.

"Did I ruin your dream?"

"Yes," she spoke a bit less sweetly.

I knew what I had to say, but did not like the fact that it was going to hurt her. "Ashley," I sighed, "was your dream come true ruined when you left my house?"

She dropped the phone and slumped to the floor, her knees

drawn to her chest. "I could live here and sleep with the puppets. I don't take up much room. Look!" Ashley folded herself to show me just how little she could become. "Really, I don't." But when I did not take up her offer straightaway, she—fighting fire with fire, desertion with desertion—promptly retracted it along with her longings for my love and attention. "But I don't want to live here anyway. I don't like it here. I don't even like coming here. I'm gonna have my own room and the baby's gonna have a room and my mother's gonna have a room. We're all gonna have a room. I'm not afraid to sleep by myself. I like it."

I shook my head in opposition.

"I do, too, like it!"

"Ashley"—she turned from me so that I spoke to her back—"you don't like sleeping alone at all. Not at all." I did not have to speak quizzically, for I was certain that she hated to.

"No," she softly agreed, "I don't." Her honest, undefensive words signaled that her distress had lessened. Before this day, she had been so intensely worried about being displaced by the coming baby that she could neither speak nor play about it.

Good news in therapy is not always good news at home. Ashley's opening up with me was making waves at home. She became more demanding and as her trauma enlivened—as was necessary for its eventual resolution—less able to be soothed. She occasionally hoarded food in her bedroom as she'd done long ago, and talked of missing her real mother. Beth lamented that it was hard to bear the brunt of Ashley's anger for her biological mother—"After all, I've been the reliable one. I'm the one that stayed"—but not as hard as hearing Ashley speak of her loyal love for that woman. I described how no words could readily allay Ashley's fear that someday she would again be abandoned, a fear painfully expressed in her asking Beth: "Will you always be my mother, even when I'm dead?" And besides, with the birth of a sibling, wasn't she going to partially lose (and now have to share) her mother? Fortunately, Beth understood from her own therapy experience that there was no easy way through these feelings. Regardless of how much love and support others gave her, Ashley was the only one who could truly come to terms with her own frightful worry; no one could do it for her.

Increasingly preoccupied with the pregnancy and her mother's changing body, Ashley drew little circles spiraling wider and wider to cover four sheets of paper taped into one. Clay-ball babies, fattening like avalanching snowballs, outgrew their tiny cribs. She continued to address her dislike of sleeping alone by building cardboard-block bedrooms that housed individual beds for our respective puppets. Over many weeks the separating wall shortened, then disappeared, the colored beds inching together until they formed one shared by both puppets—a revelation of her wish to sleep with and be as close to me (and her mother) as the baby growing inside of Beth.

Ashley's gift for play impressed me, especially for a child who'd been betrayed so early in her life. Many children would not have been able to play out such despair and anxiety. Additionally, she was relatively trusting, emotionally alive, and very invested in people, qualities that were the psychological proof of the pudding. What accounted for her strong spirit and refusal to give up on herself and others? Though it will never be known for sure, Ashley may have been "well enough" mothered for her first two years. Beth recalled being told that Ashley may have been breast-fed for her first two years, and that her weaning may have followed the birth of another baby. If the birth of a sibling originally had resulted in Ashley's expulsion, how, I thought, could she not be wary of Beth's pregnancy?

Her history further came to light on the first snowy day of the new year. I was reading with my door ajar when I overheard Ashley enter the waiting room. "Why doesn't he clean his office?" she asked her mother with annoyance.

"His office is clean," her mother answered.

"No, I mean *that!*"

"Oh, that's snow. That's not dirt. That's someone's snow from their boots, just like we brought in."

As I laid my book down to greet her, Ashley ran into the office, slamming the door behind her. She jumped into a desk chair and instructed me to sit. "What's that?" she asked, pointing to a manila folder on the desk.

"You don't know what that is?" I was fully aware that she knew it was a folder to hold another child's drawings, just like the one I'd given her.

"Nothing!" she said, as she was wont to say when disliking my comment or where it seemed to be leading.

Impatient with her indirect but clear hostility, I asked a mildly nosy, rather useless question: "I wonder what nothing looks like."

Her response—"Like a cloud. Not like a baby"—reminded me that she had good reason to feel bristly.

"You don't want to see a baby."

"No, I don't." Ashley opened a can of clay. "I'm gonna make a duck." Midway through making what appeared to be a very pregnant bird, she squeezed its stubby neck into something much longer and skinnier, then poked its end against my face. "S-sssssss," she threatened.

"Why, it's not a duck, it's a—"

"Snake!" she yelled before quickly stuffing the clay back into the container. With a wooden block she hammered the lid back on as if caging a real and dangerous serpent. Ashley then ran to the toy chest to pull out a plastic map that depicted a blue ocean teeming with sea creatures. She named a red plastic scuba diver as the photographer; however, rather than snap their photos, he criticized them. "You," he berated, "are bad, very bad fish."

"What makes them such bad fish?" I queried.

"Because they are hungry," Ashley replied for herself.

I recalled the story of her having stockpiled food at the orphanage. "What do they want?" I asked, expecting to hear of wishes for unlimited sweets, but cakes and candies were not what Ashley and her fish wanted.

"To be picked by a fisherman. Every fish wants to be picked."

"Every fish wants to be picked?"

"So they can go home with someone. Every fish wants to live with a people."

"But what are the pictures for?"

"So the fisherman can pick out the fish she likes best to take home."

"Ashley," I pursued as not much of a long-shot, "did they take pictures in South America?"

She fell against the chair. "How did you know?"

"Your playing told me so," and it indeed had. I envisioned the lonely children lining up in front of the camera—some still smiling their hardest to win a home, others simply feeling too hopeless to try or care anymore.

Ashley curled up on the floor, under her jacket—shivering. Being orphaned feels cold and exposed even in a tropical climate, even when being remembered in a cozy office at room temperature.

"Did everyone—did all of the children—find a home?" Of course, I knew they hadn't.

"No, some kids stayed there. It was sad 'cause everyone didn't get a home." She cried quietly. "I want to go home now. I do." But she did not budge.

"Ashley," I spoke softly. "Are you worried about your home now."

"No, I'm not!" Ashley threw off her coat and sat up. "I don't feel bad at all!"

"But," I continued, her eyes red and swollen, "you look very sad."

"Wrong. Wrong! You're wrong. I hope you see thousands of kids. Thousands and thousands"—her voice grew louder and louder—"and thousands!"

From plastic fish to her fellow orphans to my patients. Thousands and thousands of them. They were all the same— all competitors for the love that she wanted exclusively. There may not have been thousands of other children vying for her mother, but there just as well might have been. To Ashley that one growing baby felt like thousands.

It was time to stop, but Ashley—in her typical fashion—had quickly bounced back. She held a growling tyrannosaurus in my face. "You should clean your office," it growled.

"Ah, you must mean the snow in the waiting room."

"Growl! Growl! Clean it up for Ashley, *right now!*"

"Because Ashley doesn't like to think about other children coming here?"

"Yes-sssssss!" Ashley shrieked for the dinosaur she threw with a high, happy arch into the toy chest. Her smile broadened farther upon discovering that the whitened footsteps in the waiting room had melted away.

She had little notion of the unwanted footsteps she would hear the following week.

"Congratulations!" Beth offered a week later, in the waiting room. "Was it a girl or a boy?"

"A girl." I asked how she knew, for I had not told any of my patients that my wife and I had been expecting or had had a baby.

Beth explained that she'd seen a second child's seat in my car, and anyway, she and Ashley had noticed that my wife was pregnant some months ago.

Ashley buried her head in Beth's lap. "I don't want to go in." Her mother coaxed her through the door; Ashley then lay belly-down on the floor and colored for about twenty minutes, ignoring me and everything that I said. Finally, so it felt to me, she tossed me the wolf and big lion puppets, and placed the alligator and baby lion on her hands. We each waited cautiously for the other's first move.

"What should I do?" I asked, intentionally breaking the ice, for time was flying by and Ashley was quite upset.

"I don't know. You're the doctor."

I reminded myself of the scene in the waiting room and of the shocking news she'd just heard. "Are you guys mad at Dr. Bromfield?" my wolf asked her puppets.

I'd stepped on a mine. "We hate Dr. Bromfield! We hate Dr. Bromfield! We hate Dr. Bromfield!" Her alligator and lion cub chanted loudly and rhythmically. Although she repeatedly changed the lyrics—"Dr. Bromfield stinks. Dr. Bromfield stinks. Dr. Bromfield stinks."—their passion and triple refrain held constant. "He is trash. He is trash. He is trash."

So barraged, I found myself understanding why some children are willing to do anything, even misbehave, to get themselves noticed. Ashley's tirade and insults felt much better than the cold shoulder she'd previously been giving me. I could easily stand the hate behind her words, for I knew it was fueled by even greater love.

"... We hate Dr. Bromfield. No one likes him. No one likes him. ..." Her words softened and bit less.

"He's a crumb, a crumb, a crumb." She was tiring.

"By the way," my wolf asked, "why does everyone hate Dr. Bromfield?"

"You know why," she accused.

"I do?" She nodded. "Oh, you mean because of—"

"THE BABY!" she yelled. "The baby, the baby, the baby, the baby, the baby, baby, baby, baby, baby, baby. ..." The words shot from her mouth like machine-gun bullets, while her puppets begged her to stop. "Oh, no, don't stay that word," she made them plead in vain. "Don't say that B-word, please!" But she was untouched by their calls for compassion and soon resumed her torture: "Baby, baby, baby, baby, baby, baby. . . ."

When the chorus faded, my wolf pursued. "By the way, why does the baby get everyone so mad?"

"Because," she replied, in no need of further priming, "he helps her and feeds her and reads to her and dresses her and tucks her in at night and gives her baths and holds her and plays with her. . . ." She attacked in hope of stopping her tears. "We hate Dr. Bromfield. We used to like him. We don't like him anymore. We hate his baby. His stupid, stupid baby. His ugly, ugly baby. His stupid, ugly baby"—but she cried anyway.

Though our time was up, neither she nor I nor the puppets on our hands budged for several minutes. Having her eventual—and first ever—request for extra time granted by me, she lowered her hands to her thighs. She closed her eyes and began to sing the same melody as before, only much more slowly and softly. "We want more time. We like it here. We like Dr. Bromfield. We don't want to leave *ever.*" That one word, besides breaking the tempo of her chanting, signalled her giving up the day's battle against me, and her willingness to now acknowledge the tremendous longings she was feeling.

Ashley had tried to see my baby as stupid and ugly, as everything that she believed would make me not love my new daughter, and the same reasons for which she erroneously imagined that she herself had been abandoned. (Lest we forget, she had presumably also lost a father along the way, and was more than acutely aware and envious that my daughter would have what she did not—me.) Moreover, she could more easily dispose of and not miss an ugly, stupid therapist than one whom she valued. But she could not avoid seeing the truth. As much as she hated those who had given her up, she loved them even more, and wished that she had never had to leave them.

Soon after this juncture, Ashley—who had shown continued and considerable improvement within and outside of treatment—decided she did not wish to continue. After several weeks of volcanic tantrums and determined refusal not to return to therapy, Beth reasonably decided to give Ashley a break for the time being. Though we could have speculated on the meaning of the resistance, we both judged that Ashley had done much grieving, and perhaps needed a respite to prepare for her new sibling (a brother, whom, I have been told, she welcomed heartily, or as heartily as any older sister can). Whatever underlay Ashley's wish to stop therapy, she had succeeded in *leaving me first* (and maybe that was the key), more able to love and be loved by Beth, her lasting mother, and others.

Until we grieve for the pain and resentment of loved ones lost, we cannot fully attach to others. Until our feelings of hate and betrayal are given rein, our love and trust are bridled. By fundamentally being like a good mother—holding, accepting, and forgiving—therapy allows the child, and her mourning, to come and to go.

VII

Out of Control

"If I can hold my head above water, it is all
I can."
—Henry Fielding, *Joseph Andrews*

"A thousand miles an hour!" Capturing the unanimous attention of our fifth-grade class was not easy, but even the most
jaded among us listened intently and in disbelief to our teacher's words. "It's true. The earth rotates at a speed of almost
one thousand miles per hour." One girl pirouetted until she
fell back against her seat. "No, much faster than that," Mr.
Backus corrected. He startled us further with the fact that the
earth revolves around the sun at over sixty thousand miles an
hour, much faster that the hottest Corvettes cruising our
neighborhood. "Yeah, so how come we aren't all dizzy and
falling down all the time?" one skeptic asked on behalf of
everyone else. Another child ran around the room with a
spinning globe, while the rest of us marveled that any person
or thing could possibly stay put in one place. Partially in jest,
partially in earnest, we tried to feel the celestial motion by
sitting quietly with our eyes closed. In spite of our unusual
group effort at self-control, no one was able to sense the plan-
et's movement or hear its whiz.

Lamentably, there are children, however, whose inner and
outer worlds move so rapidly and tumultuously that they
might as well feel the earth racing through the galaxy. Abra-

ham, or Bram as he liked to be called, was one such—very bright, very troubled—child. This ten-year-old boy was referred to me after he'd drunk a bottle of over-the-counter cough syrup in a halfhearted suicide gesture. He later described not really wanting to die, but being angry that his mother—in a moment of fury over his having sprayed whipped-cream obscenities over her birthday cake—had threatened to take a vacation without him. "I just wanted to *show* her," he explained, instead showing everyone else how severely his feelings could cloud his judgment. The emergency room physician found no physical damage and wisely recommended therapy.

Bram lived with his mother, who'd been separated but not divorced from his father for over twelve years. Dolores Hunter was a likable, though rather controlling and intrusive woman. She tended to indulge her only child's every material whim and confide in him—about her financial, bodily, and even sexual woes, as if talking to a husband or lover. At other times she contemptuously belittled and rejected him.

According to Dolores, Bram's father was a housepainter, specializing—on the rare occasions when he worked—in high-risk, high-paying jobs such as church steeples and peak work, "the stuff no one in his right mind wants to do." Louis Hunter treated his son, with whom he presently had sparse contact, cruelly. While teaching Bram to play checkers some years ago, for instance, he prominently had displayed a running tally of their scores—exceeding one hundred victories to none, in Dad's favor—on the kitchen message board. He feared that playing any less than his best would make his son soft and unable to withstand life's misfortunes. A self-medicating diabetic, he had often insisted that Bram, against his will, witness his injecting insulin into his own thigh, and on at least two occasions forced his son to push the needle's plunger. Although these incidents in themselves were troubling, they were mere signposts to a more chronically traumatic childhood.

Bram's behavioral difficulties were not new. For years he'd been an underachiever in school; his reading and math skills were about a year behind that of most children his age, despite his superior intellect. Both his academic and conduct grades ranged from mediocre to abysmal: "Seldom listens, uncooperative, distractible, speaks out of turn, disrespectful, lazy, smart-alecky, provocative, has few friends, temperamental, controlling, condescending, unruly," and so on went the list of behavioral descriptors compiled by his nursery through fourth-grade teachers—adjectives that all applied equally to his behavior at home. He slept poorly and regularly felt fatigued. His daydreams, which could be frighteningly "gruesome and ugly," did not help to relax him. Yet he had never received any special educational or psychotherapeutic help.

When Bram first noticed me entering the clinic lobby, he twisted around the waiting room floor lamp, which he manned like a windsurfer, and kicked his mother's leg off the magazine table. "Knock it off, sonny!" she warned before replacing her foot, only to be hit again. "Whoa. Give it up, baby," he crooned back. Then, to his mother's embarrassment, he explained, with unmistakable insincerity, how he was just trying to curb his mother's bad habit of putting her feet on other people's furniture. Off and running, they loudly debated who was the ruder of the two, until Bram initiated a tug-of-war using his mom's earring. "Ow! That's my ear, if you don't mind," she snarled with a grin that made me, and probably Bram, wonder whether she really minded.

Their hostile play continued down the hall and into the office, where Bram promptly and provocatively attempted to make himself look calm—legs crossed, elbows on the chair arms, and chin cradled in his interwoven hands. He smiled arrogantly at his mother; she looked daggers back at him. While she searched her handbag for a cigarette, Bram crept in his wheeled secretary's chair toward hers, first finger pressed to his lips in warning for me not to ruin his prank (though I would not have anyway). There was no real danger in what he did, and I'd have prevented nothing that likely didn't happen all of the time at home. My task was to know them better, and presumably this game of predator-hunts-its-unsuspecting-prey was showing me something important about their relationship. Bram darted a pinch at his mother's arm.

"Goodness, what ever is wrong with you?" she asked with loud exasperation, before suddenly remembering that I was there, quickly lowering her voice, and changing the subject. "I can't believe you wore that wrinkled shirt."

When Bram noticed her face flush, a response to his pulling his T-shirt into two pointed breasts, he smiled at me, then
nonchalantly goaded, "Gee, I don't know. She seems upset
about something, doesn't she?" His mother's plea that she was
"at the end of her rope" evoked only his sadistic offer to buy
her "twenty feet more so that she really could put her troubles to rest."

Mrs. Hunter sat up and straightened her dress. "We are
wasting this poor man's valuable time. I'm sure he has better
things to do than listen to us fight. And if he doesn't, I do."
Her condescending words betrayed the obvious hostility that
she restrained. Was she expecting me to be the limit setter,
the disciplinarian father who'd teach Bram to be respectful
and obedient? She turned away from both of us in disgust.

A heavy silence signaled the end of the party. No conceivable question of mine could have revealed the nature of their
relationship as effectively as did my letting them be. For what
remained of the hour they continued to bicker, though she
was no match for his enthusiastic and verbally tenacious com-
bat. I learned that they fought like this—in her words—"only
every waking hour" of each day. Bram added that even during
sleep her presence could "haunt his sweet dreams into a
nightmare." As they departed, Mrs. Hunter teasingly asked,
"We're quite a pair, don't you think?" Unsure what she meant
by *quite*—unusual, eccentric, sick, dazzling?—I stated the one
thing of which I was sure, that they seemed to be quite a close
pair.

For a mother and child to enjoy each other's company and
humor is a good thing, but there was an unsettling quality to
their joking. Their behavior appeared to suit siblings or flirt-
ing teenagers better than it did mother and son. I wondered
whether our meeting had overstressed them or had put them
on good behavior. Had I witnessed the worst or was today's
session as good as it got?

Most likely, their way of relating in that initial meeting had
something to do with meeting me, with being in the presence
of a third—in their minds, an evaluative—person. I wondered
whether my drained, unhappy feelings after they'd gone reflected how they had felt upon leaving. Perhaps their competitive, got-to-have-the-last-word performance revealed not
simply their mutual dislike, but their wish that I—an imag-

ined husband and father—not give more to or like the other better.

In Bram's very first hour I saw that my relationship with him would be intense. He ardently strove to understand and negotiate what I was to him and he to me. At his behest, I played an Indian, surefootedly guiding his exploration of an unknown frontier and rescuing him from a poisonous snake and deadly quicksand—both which he referred to as "she." He wanted me all-powerfully and knowingly to safeguard his well-being and lead him through this play, his therapy, and life; however, this illusory comfort soon panicked him. "How do I know you're not really an impostor?" he grilled, in fear that I'd exploit—for my profit and to his harm—the early trust he'd shown me. I conveyed understanding for his worry and suggested that only by watching me over some time could he judge whether I was genuinely trustworthy. Warmed by my straight and sincere answer, he asked whether he would have to come see me forever and would have to bring his children into the sessions. Having known me for less than two hours, he already feared sharing me with his own children twenty-some years down the road. When I announced that our time was up, he dealt with the loss of good-bye by claiming that he was happy "because he never really liked coming."

For many weeks Bram rigorously tested me. Would I keep him from breaking things in the office? Would I keep him safe? Would I kick him out? Though my office contained no valuable or fragile items, Bram uncannily detected every breakable material in the room—the clock's crystal, the glass covering pictures, the light fixtures, and my eyeglasses. A small crack in one windowpane caused him to imagine my unforgiving treatment of the child he assumed had broken it. "You probably yelled at the poor kid till he cried. I bet you'll charge him twice what it costs to fix it." He was obviously not accustomed to receiving fair treatment or the benefit of the doubt. Bram ate clay foods, and danced in front of the window, daring to jump through the screen. "What do you care what happens to me?" he asked. "I'm nothing to you." Though his comments and gestures were provocative, he required neither actual physical limits nor verbal prohibitions. My respectful relying upon Bram not to hurt himself, an attitude very dissimilar from indifferently ignoring him, made him feel valued as more than nothing by me, and as a result, less self-hateful and needing to hurt himself. "You trust me, don't you?" he said in slow and accurate recognition.

During this period I learned more about Bram and his mother—from his mother, whose own issues frequently surfaced while discussing her son's. After she had spontaneously endorsed the confidentiality of Bram's treatment, she described how her mother had regularly searched through her drawers and read her diary, and questioned my "middle-class obsession with privacy." While she tried to talk about Bram's school situation, she continually recalled her own struggles with teachers. And when complaining about being Bram's slave, she mourned not having someone to take care of her. She described how Bram had been born—a difficult delivery, requiring "forceps and steam shovel," which Mrs. Hunter attributed to his reluctance to "leave a pretty grand place." With tears she imagined how much he had loved being inside her, and how much he loved her, though how much *she missed having him there* was more obvious. She recalled no health problems or major separations; in fact, Bram and she had never spent a night apart.

Dolores talked at length about her ex-husband, an alcoholic and occasional past wife beater. She claimed that while she hadn't cared what he did to her, she regretted that Bram had witnessed the violence. Insistent that she held no grudges against Louis, she voluminously listed his inadequacies as both a husband and father. Allegedly, he didn't pay child support and never remembered to buy Bram birthday or Christmas gifts. She okayed my request to invite him in to meet me, though she bet her last dime that he'd never come.

I wondered whether Mrs. Hunter's pessimistic prediction was motivated by her ex-husband's proven deficiencies or by a wish to keep him from Bram. Over the years a number of parents, married and divorced, had persuaded me that their spouses were unable, uninterested, or unfit to share in their child's therapy and life, and in several cases my blind acceptance of that fact had led to avoidably compromised treatment. When I called Mr. Hunter, he scheduled an appointment and seemed appreciative of being consulted. I looked forward to meeting him and giving him a chance, to be the first person in a long while to acknowledge his importance in Bram's life. Maybe that's all he needs, I fantasized hopefully. Maybe he'd been waiting to be welcomed back into his son's life. But he didn't show up for his appointment. I became one more person that Louis Hunter had let down.

Wednesday came again, and so did Bram. I was surprised that he gave me a friendly hello, as just last week I'd suggested—in reaction to his mother's telling me that they habitually slept together—that his mother stop letting him crawl into her bed at night. He hadn't made one word of complaint over that proscription then, so I'd anticipated some delayed backlash. However, without much ado he put on a brown bull puppet with white horns, sleepy brown eyes, and a yellow ring through its nose; on his other hand he took a fuzzy pink pig with big black eyes, long eyelashes, and a wonderfully squishy snout.

"Hey, Baconface, how 'bout a date?" Guido, as Bram named the bull, asked in a street-tough voice.

"I wouldn't go out with you if you were the last bull in the world," the pig sneered back in a higher, huskier tone.

"Oh, yeah. Well, I didn't really want to go out with you anyway. Who'd want to go out with an ugly pig?"

"Who'd want to go out with a stupid, lazy cow?"

The puppets shook their heads violently as they carped at each other. The insults flew for over a half hour, until the bull finally pounced on the pig. The battle escalated. Bram's hands rapidly beat on each other, while he excitedly provided the soundtrack of biting, sucking, howling, and wounded noises.

As fascinating and alive as the play was, I reminded myself that simply venting feelings does little to help a child understand or manage them. In an effort to learn more about this display of aggression, I selected a friendly, wrinkled-faced bloodhound puppet to inquire, "What's going on here?" Both Guido and Baconface abruptly pulled apart to stare at my bloodhound.

"What's your name, beagle breath?" the pig asked in a most intimidating manner.

"Hey, look who's here," Guido called out. "It's the busybody dog sticking his nose into everybody's business."

"Yeah," they both mouthed, "get lost, pooch. Can't you tell when you're not wanted?"

"Get lost?"

"You heard us! We've been fighting like this for years. Ya think some dog punk can come in just like that and mess with us? Now get out of here and let us fight in peace!" Guido threatened, while the pig proudly and affectionately stood by his side. Guido's message was not wasted. Inspector Hound, by way of my control, backed off.

Through the puppets Bram had safely expressed his passionately mixed feelings for his mother. Guido beat and ragged on Baconface, knowing with confidence that any retaliative abuse or rejection given him would be in play; this differed from his own anxious dread that expressing anger toward or wishes to separate from his mother would, in reality, lead to equally real abandonment. Simultaneously, he did not want me or therapy to disturb the privileged and close relationship he shared with his mother. "Break me from these (loving and otherwise) chains" was his more grown-up plea; "Back off, Jack" was his more regressed warning. When I suggested that he might be angry over my suggestion that he sleep in his own bed, he cynically asked whether I next would be sending them to live in separate homes, expressing again both his wish and fear; he could not evade his ambivalence.

Given how psychically connected Bram and his mother were, her call to me later that same afternoon was hardly coincidental. By her perception, Bram was behaving worse than ever at home. He asked for more and more, and yet trashed whatever she did for him. "I'm not dragging him to therapy so he can abuse me like his father did," she said. Her seeing Louis in Bram worried me because her son was not a grown, abusing, and abandoning husband. She risked generating an evil prophesy for him to fulfill. At the same time, neither did I blame her for not wanting to be mistreated. She announced that she would give his therapy three more months, and emphasized that the reprieve was solely at the suggestion of her therapist and not her own idea. I wondered to her whether she might be having some misgivings about the separation that therapy might bring about. I did not specifically mention the sleeping arrangements, though I more generically hinted at her likely upset over the loss, saying, "It's not easy for a mother to let her son grow close to another person, especially a relative stranger." She did not respond; nor did she terminate Bram's therapy.

The unchallenged closeness that Bram and his mother had shared for years carried a steep price. She could not always differentiate her own needs from her son's. If she was cold, Bram needed a jacket. If she was lonely, he must need a hug. She gave Bram more attention than the average child received, yet his true needs often went unrecognized and unmet. Sometimes the attention in itself was damaging, as, for example, when they shared baths or she told him of her menstrual experiences. Though these intimacies immensely gratified Bram, they also psychologically burdened him. By his age many boys have discovered that they cannot have their mothers sexually and exclusively; Bram had not and still believed that he could. That was very scary, especially with no father present to kick him out of the parents' bed. Being the man of the house satisfied Bram's fantasies of omnipotence and grandeur, but left him feeling perilously unlimited and out of control. Paradoxically, such power did not facilitate his growth, but instead hindered his separating from his mother. How could he leave someone with whom he was so fused and who needed him so much? (Although his therapy helped, Mrs. Hunter's own therapy, not discussed here, with a social worker I knew moved this developmental process along at least equally.)

Despite his being a little king at home, Bram did not think very well of himself. The depth of his self-deprecation became clearer in his play with plastic dinosaurs, notably his picking on one brontosaurus, a big, fat green herbivore with a long neck and a small skull. "What a dufus head!" Bram degraded. "He must be the stupidest dinosaur that ever lived. No wonder he died off. He didn't deserve any better."

I was dismayed by the enormous self-hatred and terribly harsh conscience conveyed by those few simple lines. How could he feel so stupid when his IQ was so high? Although I was not sure of the answer, the dilemma bore resemblance to the thin girl who sees fat in the mirror or the generous parent's self-perception of being neglectful. What we see is profoundly influenced by what we feel. A black mood can darken everything, even on the brightest of days.

The tyrannosaurus rex, assigned to be the bronto's teacher,

rang the school bell. Bronto waddled in late. "And where were you?" the teacher asked sternly.

"Duh, I don't know. Must've got lost."

"Lost? Why a lowly worm could find its way to school."

Bram made the bronto laugh dim-wittedly at the insult, as if unaware that his teacher had ridiculed him.

"And stop that foolish laughter! What are you, two years old?"

The teacher dragged the embarrassed pupil to the front of the room, where, by way of simple questions that the bronto could not answer, he made his student the laughingstock of the class.

Bram then put three identical doll beds together to make a large table on which he lay the bronto. He molded a clay helmet around its head from which he ran strings to a wooden block. "This won't hurt a bit," the dinosaur teacher whispered into the frightened student's ear, before he bellowed, "Crank it up!" Bronto writhed and screamed, "Oh, my head. It hurts. It's exploding. It's on fire." Bram ran to the desk and furiously drew an X ray of the bronto's head, which looked more like a computer circuit board that had blown a fuse. "His brain's broken," the teacher tactlessly diagnosed. "I'm afraid he'll need more electric treatments."

"How terrible," I sympathized in a quiet voice, hoping that my empathy for Bronto would comfort Bram.

"Anyone that stupid and bad's got it coming to him," Bram quietly responded before explosively pummeling the dinosaur's head with his fist. "I hate you! I hate you! You and your sick, crazy brain." Noticing blood trickling from his knuckle, he flung the toy against the wall and fled out the door. I was unable to catch him as he ran out of the clinic in the direction of his house.

I agonized over whether to call him or his mother. Bram unquestionably felt great hatred for himself, probably the most horrid feeling of all. Seeing the blood confirmed his worst primitive fears, that his anger and everything else inside him would just pour out and destroy the world and himself. What could I have said over the phone to help? He had wanted to leave. Telephoning would serve mostly to allay my own anxiety, and I feared it might humiliate and intrude on him. If he had to tolerate those awful feelings so much of the time and all by himself, the least I could do was sit tight with them for a week.

When I received a call from Mrs. Hunter the next day, I braced for her chiding. However, she had called to change Bram's appointment time and—by the way—told me that he seemed to be feeling a little better about himself, especially after the last session. I was reassured and reminded that his playing out of those horrible feelings likely indicated that they were lessening and becoming tolerable enough to acknowledge and communicate.

Bram's fear of being crazy, coming up again and again, reflected tremendous apprehension that his feelings and impulses might get the better of his mind and body. He sometimes feared that our sessions would evoke a breakdown, and blamed therapy for giving him those feelings in the first place. This supported the argument, not unpopular among clinicians but of which I was skeptical, that therapy is often so stigmatizing to a child that it is of questionable usefulness. In most cases I've found that children like Bram, whom therapy makes feel stupid and insane, have felt those ways long before their therapy began. If anything, therapy offers them a chance to share and alleviate those profoundly frightening anxieties, which up to that time they have withstood alone.

Obviously, self-control was a major issue for Bram. The slightest frustration evoked indiscriminate angry assaults, both verbal and physical, upon his mother, peers, and teachers— whoever was handiest. To think before he spoke, to think and speak before he acted, were both unnatural to him. Bram addressed this weakness through months of playing with a fancy black sports car that he brought and left in the office.

"Maddog," the "fastest car in the world," had three speeds: "super-fast," "super-atomic fast," and "Holy shit, how do you stop this thing or we're all going to be dead meat!" Bram's early play consisted predominantly of its repeated crashing to destruction. Nothing could keep the car or its driver safe. It defied traffic rules, ran lights and stop signs, and once ran down a child. No police car, speed trap, or road block could catch it. Bram steadfastly denied that the car's uncontrollability, a clear symbol of his own, frightened or even bothered its driver. Soon after a gory crash, however, from which he barely got out alive, the driver decided that something had to be done. "Until Maddog is a better car (translation: until I am a better, more self-controlled boy), we're going to have to build better roads for it," roads that partially symbolized the psychological buttressing he felt from me and therapy.

Bram created external supports to control from the outside what Maddog and his pilot could not control from the inside—just as therapy and I helped to keep his play and impulses in check. He constructed big "concrete" block walls alongside sharp curves to keep the speeding car from skidding off to disaster. Electric elevators were installed under roads so that downhill slopes, on which the car accelerated too much, could be reversed to go uphill. Road surfaces were covered with speed bumps and "sticky tar." Souped-up police cars and helicopters now succeeded in pulling Maddog over to ticket his reckless speeding.

Gradually, the driver, seeking to gain better control of his car and himself, brought the hot rod into a garage to have its engine slowed and brakes enlarged. He also purchased super-wide high-traction tires, a more responsive steering wheel, and extra mirrors. Ultimately, Bram brought a modest sedan to drive sedately around town, while he assigned Maddog to be the car he drove only at the racetrack.

But of what importance was becoming a safer driver on play roads? Was Bram showing more self-control outside of therapy? Improvement was discernible at school, especially in his coping with aggravations and setbacks. Outbursts were less frequent, briefer, milder, and more easily gotten past. His effort and grades had risen relatively rapidly to nearer his potential, though he had catching up to do. Yet there had not been much change in his propensity to provoke arguments and fights over the slightest cause.

We were into our seventh month of therapy when I sat comfortably at my desk, enjoying the cool summery breeze that blew in from the ocean. I also was looking down the long barrel of a plastic colonial musket, replicated with impressive authenticity. "Move and I'll blow a hole right through the middle of your head," Bram drawled in his thick Boston impression of John Wayne. Though my life was not in danger, I needed to think quickly—clinically, that is.

When Bram had arrived with his toy rifle, he first had shot at the far wall. After an appraisal that indicated I was not upset, he targeted the nearer wall, then the desk, and the chair. I sensed the inevitable, yet did not want to inhibit him prematurely or to steal his chance for self-control. But he had upped the ante. If I did not impose some limit, the barrel soon would nudge my chin. Did it matter if it was only play?

"Get on the floor and beg for mercy," he said. The tip of the gun came closer. "I mean it! Move!"

Bram needed to know that his own physical safety was secure with me. No child wants to be hurt, especially by an adult designated as trustworthy. He also needed to know that my well-being was equally assured. A child, especially one grappling to manage his impulses better, understandably feels uneasy if I am unwilling or unable to protect myself from his assaults.

Memories of an early case flashed by, handled at a time when I assumed that my primary role as child therapist was to play hard and well. I had thrown myself wholly into one boy's untamed game of cowboys and Indians, running from bush to rock and firing my gun with both gusto and sound effects. That unrestrained fantasy regrettably culminated in my being trapped—both therapeutically and in pretend—on the edge of a precipitous cliff, where my patient shot me in the heart. I vividly recollected his panic when I clutched my chest with a groan and toppled from the desk to the floor. It was several weeks before he would play anything beyond an overly civilized game of checkers. Although my dramatics catalyzed the immediate action, they ironically retarded the play and therapy of a boy for whom thought and deed were not clearly distinguishable.

"I'm just gonna stand here and watch you sweat. Maybe I'll just let you starve to death, nice and slow," Bram mused with a convincingly sinister scowl.

"Set the limit while you are feeling relaxed," I counseled myself. I knew that I shouldn't wait too long, for my words would sound irritated and disciplinary. I sought to redirect his play to safer channels, not to punish him.

"Well, what's it gonna be, you or me?"

"Bram," I spoke evenly, "it's not okay to point the gun at me." His rifle dropped to his side, but not as swiftly and deeply as his spirits. He told me that I'd ruined his play, stressing that he wouldn't have really shot me.

"What if you just happened to feel like doing more to me?" I asked, having seen many children resurrect, mutilate, bury, and even sleep with "dead" dolls and toy soldiers—undertakings they safely could not have pursued with a living "dead" therapist.

"You mean like filling you full of buckshot or cutting off your legs or maybe dragging you out to the desert for the hyenas to eat?" he asked brightly, apparently intrigued by this new world of possibilities.

"Yeah, something like that," I agreed. "Could you possibly use a puppet to be me?"

Bram's eye sparkled as he meticulously applied a tiny blue-and-white striped clay necktie to a father bear's chest. "This is you," he declared resolutely. He stood the bear in the middle of a circle of readied soldiers. "For crimes against humanity, Dr. Bromfield is condemned to death." For several minutes my namesake cruelly was executed, bouncing up and down as bullets riddled its dead body. Using a tiny play scalpel, the commander then sliced a clay Dr. Bromfield into sandwiches for his men. "Nothing like a good firing squad to work up your appetite," he chattily narrated while making the macabre sandwiches. I could not help but smile when the troops threw up their meal—represented by little pieces of colored clay—the remains of which they in turn flushed down the toilet. Curiously, as his play grew increasingly morbid, his mood lightened. Ultimately, the men decided to buy themselves a decent lunch at McDonald's.

Although my limiting Bram's direct shooting of me protected me physically, my doing so primarily functioned to protect him psychologically. Using a doll to represent me transferred his fantasy into a safer, less restricted theater of expression in which he did not have to fear hurting me. He was able to show me in a clear and graphic way, not permitted by more direct play, how therapy made him feel as angry and unfed as did his life at home. More valuably, he'd discovered a way to express the deep rage that he felt for and from the people he loved—including that which he presently felt about my having set a limit on how he used his rifle and me in his play and therapy.

As often happens when I treat children in one-parent families, Bram was using me to help separate psychologically from his mother. Receiving certain attentions and rewards from me allowed him to give up needing to get them solely from his mother. As he learned to relate to me and others, his life was no longer so delicately dependent upon her as his only re- source. As a consistent and reliable ally I also helped him to tolerate being in more conscious conflict with her. After all, consider how scary it is when one is not getting along with one's boss; how much scarier it must be when an only child is at odds with his only parent. In many ways, as often does a father in a two-parent family, I acted as a buffer to the original, intense relationship with his mother.

Major news events can give me a broader gauge by which to measure one's child reactions against those of others. When the space shuttle exploded, I observed many different re- sponses, though the majority of children experienced some variation of despair and anxiety at the thought of such trag- edy. Bram described a more unusual sensation: he described pleasure that it had happened. His only two regrets were that he hadn't videotaped the catastrophe so that he could watch it over and over, and that they hadn't shown slow-motion close-ups of the astronauts dying. Could he really be so heart- less, so uncaring?

The answer lay in Bram's relationship with his father. Iron- ically, Mrs. Hunter had called me the previous week to tell me that Bram had wet his bed, something he hadn't done for several years. She had no idea what the reason was, though she added that Bram's father recently had snuck out of town for good without saying good-bye. When I next saw Bram, I didn't ask him any questions about the shuttle, his father, or his peeing accident; he had no need for additional stirring. But I carefully watched as he anxiously taped jumbo paper- clip skis and a paper diamond-shaped kite to a father bear doll. The kite in turn was tied by a string to a small toy air- plane. "We're going for a ride," he spoke with dead serious- ness to me, the bear. He explained that we'd be flying toward the tallest mountain in the world (for our purposes, the rounded back of my chair), its peak covered by snow—hard, frozen, slippery snow. "And you know what's going to happen on that snow?" he slyly asked.

"I don't suppose we're going to fly over it inside a nice, warm plane?" I joked awkwardly. That was a technically bad comment to make. Had he been less driven, it might have made him feel guilty and altered his play. My question was not consciously intended to discourage his play, however sadistic it might become—and it looked pretty certain that it was going to be very, very sadistic. It came from deeper, from the place which I could not control any better than Bram could control his own—my unconscious. He was fantasizing something terribly painful and destructive, *in my direction*, and I felt it. My words revealed an unconscious wish to be safely in the plane, to sidestep the hate that was headed straight for me. Fortunately, however, my comment did not derail his work. Bram, having lost none of his conviction, sneered at me.

"Sure," I continued. "You aren't worried. I'm the one who's losing all control. Do you have any idea what that feels like?" I hoped to draw him out, but he was not yet ready.

"Ah, my little man," he addressed my bear, while checking to see it was securely tied, "you are entirely at my mercy." Making the sounds of a plane taking off, Bram ran around the office, dragging my bear in dizzying circles above the ocean, within inches of an imaginary John Hancock Building. "When you get home," Bram yelled to the bear hanging below his plane, "I want you to tell your mother that we did something educational, so I'm taking you to the Statue of Liberty." He slowed the engines to hovering speed, so that the torch burnt my bear's rear end. "Oh, gosh, I'm sorry. I forgot to tell your mother to have you wear anti-flame pants," he caustically sympathized, while hosing the bear's behind with water. "Oh, and waterproof, too."

"I think you *like* scaring me," I screamed above the roaring jets.

"I do, you little shit. I love to scare little shits, more than anything in the world." Bram suddenly flew his plane above the white-capped mountain and cut me loose. Though the plastic doll fell only a few feet, it landed with an audible thud. Bram's eyes watered. He somberly walked past the play telephones to the real one on my desk, which he dialed, holding the clicker down. "Hello," he said, speaking in a monotone, "are you sitting down?" With his back to me, he did not wait for me to reply. "I have some bad and some good news. The bad news is that your son died." I readied myself for the humorous punch line that never came. "The good news is that you'll never have to see him again." The part-suicidal, part-homicidal tension lifted; the killing had been done. I did not have to ask whose father Bram had called.

"Bram," I asked very softly, "you know what my little bear felt like, don't you?"

Bram fell back into a chair and told very sad stories about the ways his father had mistreated him. He spoke of his father's motorcycle racing and rides on the back of his dad's bike. "He got mad at me because I stuck my nails into him. I didn't mean to hurt him, I was just scared." He also told about watching his father work on an icy roof. "He thought I wasn't helping him because I was lazy. I wasn't lazy!" Bram was angry. "I didn't want to be there when he fell off." His voice grew louder. "Who wants to watch his own father get killed? Only somebody who's crazy!"

Bram could barely stand the painful feelings against which his tremendous anger, in part, defended. He needed a distraction pronto and found one in a large black ant he sighted crossing the alcove. "Look! I think it's one of those African killer ants. One bite and you're dead." He knelt on one knee about a foot from the insect. "Look at that sucker! He's a monster bug. I wonder where his poison bags are?" As the ant approached, he jabbed it with a pencil. "Hey, ant, want a headache? Here, anty, anty," he invited in a falsely sweet voice. "Come on. I won't hurt you." He played with the ant harder and harder—tapping it with the pencil, chasing it from behind—until it stopped playing back. "Come on, you lazy good-for-nothing, get up and play." But the ant did not move. Bram flipped the ant with the pencil point, trying to poke a reaction out of it. It lay stomach up, motionless. "You can't be dead," he accused. "I hardly even touched you. I hardly even touched him," he insisted, looking at me. "Dumb bug deserved to die." Bram viciously stamped on the insect, then ground his heel into the carpet. "It's your own fault. That's what happens when you go to places where you're not wanted. That's what happens." He picked up his sneaker bottom and stared at the shriveled black mass stuck to it.

"You're feeling bad for him?"

"It's no big deal. It's not like he was somebody's mother or father." His face twisted in pain. "I think he was an old, sick ant that was going to die soon anyway. Yeah, that's why he got so lost away from his dirt pile. His brain is probably tired and he gets lost a lot. I'll bet he would've died today or tomorrow even if nothing happened to him. Kid and parents ants move faster. He didn't look like he had any relatives. If he did, they would have been walking around with him. But he was all alone. Boy, that's a relief."

"You're trying hard not to feel bad."

"It's not like I tried to hurt him." Bram averted his gaze, though clearly he sought my pardon. "I planned on taking him home to the woods after I left here, after I got him some sugar for his supper. He could've had my dinner if he wanted it." He continued to stare at his ant-bloodied sole.

"I didn't want him to die. I didn't kill him on purpose. Why are you looking at me like that? Quit staring at me! You'd think I murdered someone. It was just an ant. A crummy little ant. People spray bugs all the time. I was just playing with it. Why would I bother an ant?"

"Because maybe that feels better than other things."

"Yeah, like what? Like what?" Bram asked as if he did not truly want me to say what they might be, though I did.

"Like being a boy who feels as small and helpless as a lonely little ant."

Bram burst into tears. "I'm not an ant. Why'd you call me an ant? I'm nothing like an ant. Just nothing." After several minutes of sobbing, he asked again.

I explained that I hadn't called him an ant, but that I'd observed just how much he did not want to feel small and helpless, feel like he was in a place where he was not wanted, feel like he deserved to die.

After a few minutes Bram carefully lifted the ant's remains onto a tissue. As he looked at its body, he spoke but not about *it*. "I'd like to *put him* on the back of *my motorcycle*. Every time he'd hold onto me I'd bash his hands with a hammer and break all of his fingers. And when he burned his leg on the muffler, I'd laugh. And when he cried," Bram swallowed a sob, "I'd call him a baby in front of his friends and see how he liked it."

"And then," I spoke in an affirming tone, encouraging of his healthy revenge fantasy, "he'd know just what it feels like."

"I'd make him so scared"—Bram pounded his fist on the

floor—"he'd pee in his pants. That's what I'd like to do. That's what I'd like to do more than anything in the whole world." His voice grew softer and, I surmised, forgiving. "More than anything in the whole world."

Over subsequent meetings, Bram further explored his relationship with his father, coming to understand that his bravado posture—just like his father's—was a way not to feel small, unprotected, and unloved. He seemed to recognize that he was at some risk of being like his father, of taking not just his children but himself onto icy roofs and the backs of motorcycles, into unsafe, self-destructive situations. With his hand on my dictionary, he pretended to take a solemn oath to be a good father, vowing to buy a family station wagon in which everyone could ride safely and happily. And instead of bringing his children to wait outside his therapy, he decided that he would just bring them in with him, to show them off to me. "I'll be proud of my son!" He also swore never to take a dangerous job that would worry his son. "Hey, maybe I'll do what you do. What's the worst that can happen, somebody torturing you in make-believe?"

The winter had been mild. We were midway through April and had suffered neither a major snowstorm nor a prolonged cold spell. Spring approached. The days brightened, the trees budded, and the baseball season was a week away. Though not as dramatically as the magnolia and chrysalis, Bram also had blossomed. Mrs. Hunter saw him as more cooperative and easier to please. They fought less. As of our last conversation she could not recall a major clash for months. She found him more pleasant to be with and happier with himself. In sum, he showed greater self-esteem and restraint. School went well, too. He made the honor roll and had earned a small reputation as a playground peacemaker—albeit, in a somewhat grandiose and busybodying manner.

Our relationship had also strengthened. His recent choice to skip a museum outing rather than miss our meeting was a good sign, suggesting greater trust and investment in me and his therapy. He had virtually stopped challenging the limits I set. And he had begun to see me as an ally who could help him to help himself manage overwhelmingly strong feelings and solve the formidable problems in his life. He had begun to use me as a therapist.

* * *

We live between two worlds: the more commonly shared outer one and a more idiosyncratic private inner one. Although the outer world is more consensual and colloquially referred to as reality, both are real. That is why our inner life—so much more difficult to share with others—can leave us feeling so genuinely alone, crazed, and beyond others' comprehension. Therapy can help a child to reconcile these two realities, and to live more harmoniously and relatedly between them.

VIII
Picture This

"Thoughts that do often lie too deep for tears
[or words]."

—William Wordsworth,
Intimations of Immortality

I'm leery of the claim that a picture is worth a thousand words, for, like some pictures, a thousand words do not always say much. Then again, a picture can be worth a few very telling words or say what no words can. More often a picture says what a child cannot.

Walk down any elementary school corridor during the month of November, and behold the drawings of the country's first Thanksgiving. Beside each classroom door hang twenty-odd scenes of the English refugees, in brown suits and buckled black hats, celebrating with the more colorfully dressed native Indians. At first glance these pictures all appear similar and faithful to our traditional image of the historic scene at Plymouth Rock (an image, incidentally, derived mostly from the fantasy of nineteenth-century artists), but take a moment to look closer.

Who is that Indian girl, in beautiful headdress, proudly saying grace next to the comparably feathered chief? Why does that settler child, whittling a spear, watch the festivities from afar, alone on a stump? What loved one does that masted ship, its stern on the horizon, carry away from a frowning, singly teared boy who waves from the beach? Does that platter

113

of peanut butter sandwiches on the banquet table reflect a child's wit, a high regard for that particular food, a wish to avoid drawing more difficult entrees—or does it symbolize a day expected to be less than bountiful because of a family's financial hardship or emotional stinginess? And how about that satirical portrayal of turkeys dressed in puritan clothing, happily eating a roast pilgrim complete with an apple in the mouth—or the neighboring Santa Claus, having come a month early, replacing the cornucopia's squash with gaily wrapped presents? Although we can only guess what these pictures tell, we can be certain their underlying themes are uniquely varied and personally meaningful to the young artists who created them.

Just as in school, children commonly draw in therapy. Nine-year-old Christina, however, used artwork to express herself more exclusively and poignantly than any other child I had met. A fourth-grader, she had been recommended for therapy by school staff, who saw her, in addition to being very cooperative, competent, and dependable, as overly anxious and driven to perfection, doing well what she knew she could do but reluctant to take risks when less certain of herself. Her parents observed and were concerned about these same traits at home, and contrasted them with the less inhibited, more free-wheeling spirit of four-year-old Jessica, their second daughter.

In our beginning minutes together, Christina did not respond at all to my invitation to explore the office and the toys, but, upon my suggesting that she could draw—and with a confidence so different from her otherwise tentative demeanor—she grabbed a sheet of paper and bucket of markers. Although she appeared to feel awkward with me, she obviously was at home with art. Without any guidance from me, she drew a smiling girl with pink-bowed blond hair, a green party dress, and matching shoes.

Typically I'd have asked Christina all about her drawing— What did the girl think and feel? Why was she smiling? Where was she headed?—for my inquiries about children's pictures often led to interesting revelations. For example, in past cases I had discovered that a very muscular he-man felt rather puny inside, as did the boy who crayoned him. A delicious-looking, gooey hot-fudge sundae, for which my play character drooled, turned out to be a picture of an inedible plastic model; this fakery ably conveyed one boy's experiences of living with parents who, he sensed, cared more about how they looked than how he felt. Thirteen-year-old Ella blushingly admitted that her penciled sketch of a fat-cheeked head perched atop a swollen A-framed body showed how puberty really made her feel—an image, she complained, her parents and friends could not understand or believe given her petite, graceful body. And in a most tragic case of neglect, a cheery forest scene became chilly when I learned that the tiny black hole in a tree held a baby squirrel left to "starve and rot" over the winter. Although I was sure there was also much to unearth in Christina's art, I assessed that even the dimmest penlight or gentlest remark might scare her off, and I was not willing to risk the only avenue of communication we currently shared.

But I could think whatever I wished about her drawings, as long as I eventually exercised my clinical reason. Many times I'd observed that the allegedly deeper meanings both novice and seasoned therapists believed we saw in drawings frequently revealed more about ourselves and our wishes to impress each other than they did about our patients. I'd seen more than one trainee, presenting a case conference, graciously suffer indelicate implications that they had overlooked a picture's significance. "Yes, indeed," a faculty member would pontificate, "the *black* lines and their jagged edge strongly suggest—no, indicate—a morbid expression, perhaps a suicidal inclination." "But," the student demurely countered, "I only had one marker, a black one. And its tip was split." Having myself been guilty of reading too much into a single drawing (and most everything else), and not ready to conclude much about Christina's, I silently noted how markedly her own restrained posture differed from that of the relaxed, open-armed little girl she'd drawn.

Christina neatly placed that paper aside, then proceeded, in as regulated and ordered a manner as that verb denotes, to draw a large golden ball traversed by bands and giving off rays, both of dark red and orange. When she noticed that only ten minutes of our session were left, and with a worried face, she slowly filled in the surrounding space—and the remaining time—curlicuing yellow, pink, and blue seagulls. Her peaceful border, and its cooler shades, contained the more energetic, discordant sun burning within. At the end of the hour I handed Christina an empty manila folder to decorate as she pleased and to be *her place* for storing her artwork in my desk.

As a rule I ask children to leave the things that they make (in therapy) with me. This helps to demonstrate concretely that therapy occurs within the office, and that it can hold their drawings, fantasies, impulses, and actions—basically, themselves. Our undiluted sharing of the pictures fosters their investment in me and their treatment. Keeping artwork with me also enhances confidentiality and prevents damming of art's expressive function. I've found that children often draw less freely when they expect their parents to see their pictures, just as they speak less candidly in their parents' presence. Such children work hard *not to show what they do not want their parents to see* or know, and sometimes they even decide it is simply easier and safer not to draw.

Of course, there are exceptions to the rule. Some children demand to bring their creations home, to hang on refrigerator doors or their bedroom walls. I have encouraged other children, who lack the support and caring they need in their lives, to take home what they have made with me. More than one child has described sleeping more soundly or deciding not to hurt himself after some object from his therapy, some tangible piece of me, reminded him that someone cared.

Christina eagerly personalized her folder with a fancy signature surrounded by brightly hued flowers and balloons. Before she filed her drawings away, however, she expressed a wish to show them to her mother, who sat in the waiting room. Unsure what motivated her request, yet understanding that we had just begun to negotiate our relationship, I did not ask for her reasons. After receiving her mother's praise for her work, she methodically placed it, sheet by sheet, into her folder.

A week later and with neither a smile nor word, Christina handed me a cute, spunky bunny mask that she'd made for me on her own time. I curbed my natural desire to rave over the appealing gift, for I did not know why she had given it to me. I had no idea whether she liked me, wanted to please me, sought my admiration, tried to appease me lest I mistreat her,

or—as is often the case—all of the above. If I gave her excessive acclaim now, what horrors would she imagine when
sometime in the future I didn't give any? Or what if next
month she wanted to draw something ugly, or messy, or
naughty? She might feel obligated to draw only pictures she
deemed to be sufficiently pretty or well executed to deserve
my flattery. Not wanting to encourage what I thought might
be an already inflated tendency to care what others thought
of her and what she made, I merely noted her thoughtfulness
and thanked her. She smiled briefly, then—the succeeding
silence having renewed her serious and tense mood—she sat
down at the desk to draw, again showing no interest in the
rest of my office.

She worked on a portrait of three boys. Their faces completed, she obsessively embellished the picture's background
and frame. Open white space seemed to bother her, and required her filling it with detail. Was I observing a trend? Did
the frame, like the seagulls of her previous session, provide
her some reassuring boundary or mooring? I essentially followed her lead, watching quietly and holding my questions
until she'd laid the markers down. When she was done, and
I asked, she explained that the smallest boy yelled for what
he wanted, and that the middle one stuck his tongue out.

"At me?" I asked.

Christina laughed wholeheartedly. Like most of us, she
found good-natured acceptance of her hostility gratifying.

"But the oldest," I remarked, "he's just smiling politely."
With a nod and a less cordial, more genuine smile, she agreed.
I did not explicitly suggest that any—the needy, the angry, or
the compliant—of these boys might relate to her. Obviously
they all did; she'd drawn them. Our time up, Christina again
showed her mother what she'd drawn and received her praise
before putting her pictures away in her folder.

At the onset of our third hour, I responded, "How about
your family?" to Christina's asking me what she should draw.
This oft times was an informative exercise. Were family members placed in separate rooms, together in one room, or just
plain too close to each other—in the same bathroom or bed?
Did they share an activity or were they off by themselves? Was
a significant person omitted, or someone unexpected included? Were they at home, on vacation, or in some imagi-

nary setting? And I habitually compared the child's family drawing to her others, especially those she'd drawn of herself alone. An inferiorly drawn family picture can indicate trouble at home, as it did for one girl who had been chronically belittled by her mother. Her portrait of herself in a park was not only brighter, but was remarkably better and more smoothly drawn than that of herself—despondent, angular, and slovenly—sitting in her parents' living room. Just as children can act differently with or without their parents, so can their artistic self-representations reflect the family "weather."

Christina drew a picture of her family, smiling and sportily dressed, walking on the beach. A bright yellow sun shone above the blue water and orange sand. Was this her family, I wondered, or how she would like it to be? Four aspects of the picture most struck me: Christina's relative overlap with her father (not that she was very far from her mother, either), the heart on her sweater, the menacing wave rolling in from the right side, and the splendor of the setting. I commented on these points, but Christina did not reply. Once more she shared her work with her mother, once more she was complimented, and once more she stored it away.

Our fourth meeting followed our short-lived custom. Christina went directly to the desk and drew an unusually stylish picture of a happy woman in her finest walking-through-the-park-one-day apparel, including an elegant bonnet and parasol. As I looked at the picture, I could not help but see Christina and her mother, both of whom appeared impeccably dressed even when wearing ordinary sweatsuits. "Christina," I asked, "does that lady care very much about the way she looks?"

She said nothing, but—responding to my push for her to tell me more—promptly drew something most unusual, a more visually in-depth view of that same woman's face. This close-up included flowers on the woman's scalloped collar, green eyes, and most affecting of all, streams of distinct tears falling over her cheeks and toward her now frowning mouth.

"She's very sad," I observed quietly.

"That's why she wears pretty clothes," Christina explained before she carried the two drawings out to the waiting room. Her mother was still flattering the first and gayer picture when she uncovered the second. "Oh, my," she exclaimed, presum-

ably caught off guard by the pain that had suddenly surfaced in her daughter's art. Having successfully revealed some of her own unhappiness as well as that which she perceived to be her mother's—in part to testify to her experience, in part to test what her mother could tolerate—Christina never again brought pictures out of the office for parental approval.

When Christina devoted her next hour to making well-planned, attractive, and colorful geometric designs, I initially thought these reflected a rigid reaction to her feeling that she'd shown too much of herself in the previous week's portraits. But in fact, she was not at all distant or closed down; she was more at ease and genuinely enjoyed that day's projects as I'd not previously seen her do. Drawing a lady in tears evidently had provided relief that was as real as if she herself had cried.

Christina started to show interest in the toys, or at least, standing straight as a flagpole, had peered into, but not touched, anything in the toy chest. After several minutes of silent deliberation, however, she decided not to play, instead comically drawing a rabbit's snow carnival, her most playful creation to date. Perhaps Christina wasn't ready to have some wild and crazy fun, but her bunnies sure were! I wondered aloud about the one hare that peeked out from the squarish igloo, the only one that did not frolic in the snow. Christina described that the female bunny was too shy to do what the other bunnies did, though she was amused by what she saw. She did not, as I might have expected, condemn the others for having such fun. Was she comfortably accepting of their greater ability to have a good time, or was she unwilling to show me her anger at them? And what about that partially shaded sun? I thought of the parasol. It appeared that Christina had one eye out for rain clouds, Mother Nature's and her own.

When Christina returned for her next session, she did not touch the art supplies. From clay she made a snowman—a replica of the bunnies' own—of three white balls with blue eyes, orange carrot nose, and a red grin. A blue top hat, buttons, and matching scarf completed this classic winter gentleman. I learned that years ago Christina had made a similar snowman out of real snow with her father, but that such happy times were not as frequent as she'd have liked. Once upon a time, at least, she'd sought more closeness with her father. It was too early to know whether she wanted more now (though my hunch was that she did) and whether she held misgivings about their relationship.

In the process of therapy, tensions routinely mount until they find insightful release, thereby clearing the stage for the issues that wait next in line. We were somewhere near the peak of the immediate conflict, where the going gets rougher, steeper, and slower. And Christina had literally stiffened, smiling less and not venturing from the desk. Fortunately, her drawings, embodying what transpired inside her, continued to provide me a window. There was, for instance, a drawing of two feet and a cry for help sticking out from a sand dune. Rather than talk about this intriguing picture, and to avoid her feelings and myself, Christina vigorously dotted in hundreds of sand grains. At my suggestion that maybe she felt as stuck (with her feelings) as did that person she'd buried at the beach, she drew a violent thunderstorm with angry lightning and an unmistakably mournful downpour.

Both Christina and her mother arrived at the next hour dressed more informally than usual. They, as Girl Scout and chaperon, would be leaving for a camping trip directly from therapy. But Christina did not look at all happy, though she denied feeling troubled by anything. She dragged some paper over to herself and belaboredly drew a sprightly scene of five girls being photographed in the woods, Christina representing herself at the far end of the line. The message was clearer than transparent. When I noted that she might be angry about something, she enlarged the heart on her pictured sweater. She grasped the symbol of love as proof of her goodness and as a magical antidote to the fury she hated to believe existed within her.

Having laid back long enough and assessing that she could handle more, I quickly sketched my own version of her picture. My pigtailed girl grimaced, unapologetically displeased with her second-rate place in the photograph. Christina laughed out loud. I then drew a second variation on the theme, in which a larger, victoriously beaming heroine stood smack in the middle of all the Girl Scouts and stretched her arms to block their faces. Christina laughed even louder, until I spoke.

"You don't like sharing your mother with the other girls."

"No," she sadly affirmed, "I don't." She felt guilty over her feelings, self-critically believing she should just be thankful for what she had, in this instance, that her mother was going on the trip.

Christina's discomfort with her own anger continued to predominate sessions and her artwork. She drew erupting volcanoes and fiery dragons that devastated surrounding villages, as well as colorfully detailed patterns intended to fend off the rage that she strained to squelch. But her feelings could not be so simply smothered: a long, jeering tongue snuck into her smile picture, and pasteled spirals became fireworks.

To find out more about her intolerance for her anger, I drew a girl looking into a blank mirror. "What does she see?" I asked. Christina, onto my ploy, defensively drew an empty circle but then, feeling the pressure of my waiting silence while still calling my bluff, added a neutral, straight-lined face that precisely reflected my original. Foiled, I hastily penciled a cartoonish thought balloon over the head and pursued: "What does she think about when she looks in the mirror?" Christina initially drew a less than open smiley girl, then angrily scratched it over and instead drew her first (in my presence, that is) angry face.

"She can't feel pretty and angry at the same time?"

"How could she?" was Christina's most honest reply.

But anger was not the only feeling that Christina did not like to feel or have others see as part of herself. She also didn't like to feel wanting, lonely, or envious (all which she self-critically translated into being greedy, whether for things or attention, and which she feared would further make people not want to give them to her). Until she felt that her feelings belonged in herself, she would not be able to feel that she belonged anywhere. In response to her somewhat barren, unnurturing still life of a fruit bowl and elegantly set empty plates, I drew a huge plate of chocolate chip cookies. She laughed at my crumbs, my public show of mess, on the table. When Christina drew a girl happily struggling with a difficult arithmetic work sheet, I drew a boy dejectedly scowling at his fourth-grade math lesson, daydreaming about the days of one-plus-one. And when she drew a teacher asking whether the class liked the complicated word box, I drew back a goody-

two-shoes who answered, "Oh yes, teacher," while really thinking, "Grrrrrr, sometimes I hate hard work!" Her final picture
of a goofy cat in a pile of unraveled yarn encouraged me.
"He likes making a mess!" she blurted with glee. "And," she
was almost admitting to me and herself, "so do I." She had
gotten my message, and was making progress.

I had recognized some time ago that Christina had pretty
strong feelings about her younger sister, who at the end of a
session a few weeks earlier had run in, grabbed, and played
with the toys that her elder sister had never dared to enjoy.
In a calm huff Christina lifted Jessica across both arms and
carried her—rather like a baby but more like a naughty cat—
out of the room. I tried to discuss the incident with her at
that time, but she could not do so. Now, a month later, her
powerful picture of a girl yelling, "Stop!" at her younger sister
would speak for her.

"What's going on in that picture?" I asked.

"Jessica stepped on my jigsaw puzzle. She messed it all up.
I'd like to mess up her room sometimes!"

Christina tried to express her frustration but grew too angry to speak. I suggested she draw more about how she felt,
and was quite surprised by what she did.

She had drawn what was either a very large picture of a
regular-sized baby or a regular-sized picture of a very large
baby. For some reason that distinction seemed to me crucial.
Christina explained that the child was the neighbor's new
baby with whom her mother had been playing that afternoon.
I probed for any jealousy, but that was denied vehemently. "I
just love *little* babies," she proclaimed.

Aha, that's it, I realized. "What about *big* babies, Christina?
What do you think about *real big* babies?"

Christina realized, too. "Oh, you mean like Jessica."

I nodded.

Having grown slightly more accepting of her anger, she
vented resentment that her sister (so she perceived) could do
and get whatever she wanted. "She doesn't clean her room,
she doesn't listen to my mother, and she's greedy."

"She doesn't try as hard as you to be neat and unselfish?"

"She doesn't try at all."

The issue came to a head about a month later, when her
mother congratulated me on the birth of my baby. Positively

dumbfounded, Christina listened but said nothing. Her face tightened; she was very close to crying. In the office, she sat at my desk, saying nothing and doing nothing.

"What is it, Christina?"

Her brow squeezed tighter.

"Is it my baby?"

Neither looking up nor responding, Christina drew a woman's, a man's, and a girl's head. She then dropped the marker and pushed the paper away, upset.

"It's very upsetting, isn't it?"

She nodded, still fighting not to cry.

Courageously she took a second sheet of paper. This was the only time she'd ever restarted a drawing; I knew she must be very, very distressed. Christina again drew three heads, then added three bodies. The woman asked the man whether he had a child, to which he replied that he did. Last, she drew what was in the girl's thoughts—a "no babies allowed" sign.

"You not only don't want me to have a baby. You don't want me to have *any* children, do you?"

She nodded weakly, then having gained some strength, drew a much peppier scene of a dandy bumblebee about to pollinate flowers. I ignored the obvious hint of how babies are made—the birds and the bees of nature—and focused on the even more conspicuous blue versus pink flowers. "Is there something you want to ask me about the baby?"

My question embarrassed her, but not enough to dampen her curiosity. She demurely asked whether I'd had a boy or a girl.

"A girl. It was a girl."

"Good!" Christina beamed. "I like girls."

At her next session, Christina needed some priming to resume her work. Having been more let in on her situation with Jessica, I asked whether Christina would be willing to draw a picture that showed what her life was like before and after her sister's birth.

She agreed that my idea was a good one, but qualified her enthusiasm, saying that she'd need to draw two different versions. In one, her mother, busily caring for a new baby, no longer had time to play with her. In the dramatic second, Christina's bedroom—formerly having been furnished with a toybox, lamp and framed picture of a sunny sailing day—was drawn now as toyless, lampless, and decorated with a picture of a dark house on a rainy night. I could not imagine a more palpable image for the feelings of being displaced by a sibling's birth, of the feeling that one's golden age is ended when the new baby's begins. Her wonderful then-and-now illustrations served as a springboard for her much needed complaint of the attention that babies in general, and that Jessica in specific, took from her.

"Life was better then," she recalled, "before Jessica." Christina had lost something, and not just in her imagination. From her emotional perspective, the issue was not whether she had continued, after Jessica's birth, to receive as much love and attention as she was given as an only child, but that she now had to share the kingdom (and the parents) that she once ruled and monopolized.

With her burden of self-hate eased, Christina began to show some of the wants that she'd before only been able to ridicule her sister for having. She drew pictures of candy, jewelry, celebrity sunglasses, wonder bubbles, and even unconventional silly pictures that simply made her happy. In her life outside of therapy, she'd begun to assert herself more and realize that she could have *all sorts of feelings,* and still be a good girl. Although she now spends more of her therapy hour talking and playing, she continues to express her deepest feelings through her pictures.

The special role that drawing plays in child therapy derives primarily from its value in facilitating expression. By providing an alternative to talk and play, drawing expands the communicative repertoire shared by child and therapist. And no less than talk or play, drawing invites and enhances the intimacy, disclosure, and self-discovery essential to therapy.

IX

The Ants in My Pants Are Really Bees in My Bonnet

"Teach us to sit still."

—T. S. Eliot, *Ash Wednesday*

"It is infrequently sighted in Britain, but in America is seen under every bush."* These words refer not to the yellow-headed blackbird, but to Attention Deficit Disorder, or A.D.D. as it's become popularized. The *DSM III-(R)*, the official manual of psychiatric diagnosis, considers the disorder present when a child shows several signs of inattention and impulsivity, including difficulty concentrating, seeming not to listen, not completing tasks, frequently changing activities, acting before thinking, and calling out in class. Unquestionably, A.D.D. was the childhood disease of the eighties. Did its impressive debut reflect advances in detecting a real and widespread condition or a fad of the sort that so often plagues medicine and psychology? Is it neurological or emotional in origin, and how should it be treated? This controversy served as the backdrop to my therapeutic encounter with seven-year-old Eddie.

*Quote confirmed in personal communication from Lionel A. Hersov, M.D. of London, 20 December 1990.

At the time of his referral, Eddie was failing the third grade. He concentrated poorly and could not organize himself or his work. His papers were sloppy, incomplete, and did not follow directions. Confused by his teacher's words or diverted by a distant car horn or barking dog, he missed most of what she said. Unable to persist at his individual work in class, he daydreamed and baited his classmates with silly sounds or a pestering foot. His teacher, who hoped that extra attention and a closer watch might help him to focus, moved his desk next to hers, but that only humiliated him and led to angrier and more vigorous outbursts. Though recess and playground provided escape from classroom demands, their relative lack of structure and supervision were more than Eddie could handle. He ran wildly and instigated fights, earning regular trips to the principal's office and occasional suspensions from school. Testing conducted as part of a school psycho-educational evaluation documented an attentional deficit.

Understandably discouraged, fatigued, and having seen a similar child respond favorably to the drug Ritalin, school staff strongly urged that he be medicated. But his mother, opposing that idea, sought the advice of her trusted pediatrician, who supported her misgivings and encouraged a trial of play therapy. "What's to lose?" he prudently asked, reassuring her that there'd be plenty of time for medicine should the situation not improve.

Although it now had been almost two years since Eddie and I had begun meeting, I had seldom heard him express himself so directly. I was taken aback by his sudden uncharacteristic disclosure, and moved by his profound sadness—sadness that I had suspected to be there but which up to this moment had been hidden from view.

"He was my best friend, my very best friend."

I barely heard the fading second refrain. We both looked at his drawing of a very long and appealing dachsund that wore a blue-and-red Boston Red Sox baseball cap identical to Eddie's. I wondered if this was a picture of Mandy, the beloved pet that had been put to sleep a few months before we met. He'd mentioned her only once before, while trying to convince me that his mother should buy him a German shepherd "because they're smart and tough and loyal and make their puppies lucky because they got good dog daddies." Was Mandy the best friend of whom he spoke?

While he filled her black outline in with dark brown crayon, he talked about his grandfather, too. "I used to help him fix things around the house. I guess he didn't mind having me around. I guess he must've kinda even liked me." His tentative wording—"I guess he must've kinda even"—revealed his self-doubt that he could be as lovable as he remembered his grandfather made him feel. Since Ellen Welch and her two children had moved back into her parents' home, following several years of hardship while living on their own in California, Eddie and her father had become good buddies. They played, talked, fished, and, what Eddie liked most of all, ate bagels together "every single morning." Joseph was more like a father to his grandson. "I knew it was gonna happen," Eddie lamented. He told how he'd predicted, in his mind, that something awful would happen to his grandfather while on his annual Florida vacation. "I didn't want him to go. He died on the day I was gonna see him again. He shoulda stayed home. I just knew it. He shoulda. I did. I did know. I think his heart stopped beating or something." I suspected that Grampy Joe might have been his best friend.

Eddie also had talked about his father, who'd left him when he was a small boy. "I guess he kinda drank too much. He didn't mean nothin' by it." I heard a story about a subway ride he and his sister had taken on a rare visit to their father some years ago. "He was drunk and sorta didn't know where he was goin'. We had to find our own way, 'cause when he asked people for directions, he didn't understand what they said. He spent the twenty dollars we were goin' to eat with on beer." After his sorry tale Eddie forgivingly, and probably with some acuity, explained that his father intended no harm, that he couldn't help himself. He tried to complain about the ways he felt mistreated; however, he inevitably devoted his attentions not to himself but to schemes by which he might give money, gifts, and help to his dad without injuring his fatherly pride. Was his father the best friend of all?

I'd waited a long time for him to talk so freely. Frustrated by the years of relative silence, curious about his thoughts, and fearful that such openness might never come back again, I wanted to seize the moment, ask about everything, and know more, lots more. How old was Mandy and what was she like? Did she sleep at his feet and run to meet him at the door? Would she wait under the dinner table to gobble what he slipped her in his napkin—the foods he detested, the meatloaf and the brussel sprouts—so that he could earn his dessert? Was she the one who consoled him when he was sad and lonely? What exactly did he miss about her? I had even more questions about his grandfather and father, but kept all of them to myself. I'd sent too many snails scurrying back to their shells not to have learned the havoc that my untempered interest could wreak.

Time was up. Eddie sketched the dog a few more gray whiskers and as an afterthought scribbled a large bone in her mouth so she would not go hungry while in my desk drawer. He then carefully placed the picture in his folder. At the hour's end, and perhaps to reward my self-restraint, Eddie told me what a good friend I was and that he hoped I understood why he could never like me like a father.

When Mrs. Welch, a divorced single mother, had first contacted me, Eddie rapidly was depleting whatever good feeling was held for him at home and school. His unrelenting behavior had pushed others to the edge. I felt myself resisting enormous pressure to intervene swiftly and in a big way. There were plenty of good reasons for Eddie to be preoccupied and despondent, but that did not prove whether his emotional distress primarily resulted from or caused his attention deficit. Like all of us, Eddie was a product of genetics and environment, biology and psychology; the relative influences of each were unknown.

Eddie and I first met in a local school's guidance office, used as an evening satellite clinic by the community mental health center where I worked. It was not a good setting for play therapy, especially with an active and distractible boy. Layers of memoranda, opened letters, and other personal paperwork covered the large steel desk. Smaller files and dozens of cardboard boxes, labeled "PSAT SCORES" and "JUNIORS FINAL GRADES," were piled in front and on top of the gray five-drawer cabinets that lined the walls on either side of the desk. Along the fourth wall a long cafeteria table supported a computer system and rack of college catalogues. All potential space, however small or out of reach, was occupied by school materials—bundles of standardized test booklets and student records, rubber-banded bales of sharpened and gnawed No. 2 pencils, and strange-looking machines designed to measure hearing or administer vocational and military fitness exams. In this moderately sized room, less than four by six feet of free floor remained, and that was further reduced by a large rolling desk chair and two smaller unfolded chairs that had been borrowed permanently from the lunchroom.

The therapy space—in addition to the therapy and therapist—ideally should welcome and accept its guests, its patients; that certainly was not the case here, where to move was to trespass. Everything that caught Eddie's eye was off-limits: the thumb tacks in the cork bulletin boards, the knife-like letter opener, the expensive mechanical drawing set, and the glass paperweight that when shaken displayed snow falling on a village scene. Nor could Eddie open the countless intriguing drawers and cabinets or play with the computer and the other contraptions. If curiosity truly killed the cat, Eddie would have expired in our very first hour, and through no fault of his own.

But its untouchability was not that stuff's sole torment; there was just too darn much of it! Like young children on Christmas Day who flit from toy to toy before choosing to play with the empty boxes, Eddie was overstimulated. He needed a place where he could open his eyes and not everywhere see things upon things, or hear them silently scream, "Choose me! Open me! Play with me!" Eddie came to therapy for respite from the clutter he felt inside, but here he found an external world more cluttered than he. Where could he go when he needed to contemplate nothing more than a plain gray carpet or a blank wall? Where could he go when he longed for the inside of a box, when all the boxes in this room were full?

What's more, there was very little room to move. There was no expanse of tabletop for drawing or rolling clay pizza, no empty floor for playing ball and rolling about. Eddie tried his best to show off, but his somersaults and slam dunks were blocked by furniture and inhibited by his fear that he'd inadvertently whack the monitor or topple one of the wobbly stacks of paper. Most troubling of all, there was insufficient space for Eddie to manage being with me—to come close, to retreat, and to shuttle easily between the two. He sorely missed having the room to communicate nonverbally what he could not yet put into words.

From the onset Eddie moved constantly and said little. When he wasn't busy shooting Nerf-ball baskets or bouncing a tennis ball, he doodled with my pen, diddled with his clothes, and practiced balancing on one chair leg. "School's fine," he claimed, despite teachers' reports and grades over-whelmingly to the contrary. "Good!" was how he described an after-school program that was considering expelling him and another boy for their reckless caribou-butting duels and to-the-death wrestling matches. When queried about himself or his life, Eddie typically replied that he didn't know or care. If the matter touched an especially sensitive area requiring fortified denial, he bragged that he didn't even care that he didn't know. Tasks he could not do were "dumb," the teach-ers who assigned them were "mean and stupid."

We spent most of the first seven months playing small-scale games of basketball with a green tennis ball and a large brown metal trash bucket set on top of a chair. Eddie spoke mostly to explain rules, confirm the score, or generate on-court ex-citement by bantering, "Way to go" or "In your face, Momma." He endlessly redesigned our makeshift gym to al-low for more accurate jump shots off the chair back and mi-nutely longer running dunks. To his credit, the limitations of the room did not dampen Eddie's healthy urge to strut his stuff—his exceptional athletic skills, which were truly some-thing to be proud of and without which he would have been more socially isolated.

During halftimes or between games, Eddie built domino knockdowns—or, I should say, tried to. He typically planned unrealistically elaborate designs, such as double figure-eights or concentric spirals, but seldom could erect more than four or five pieces before accidentally felling them. After two or three equally frustrating trials, he'd fling the dominoes back in their box and condemn them and the desk for being crooked. Even outside the classroom he felt frustrated, incom-petent, and in need of something or someone else to blame.

Although Eddie did not explicitly express any fondness for me, I noticed little signs that he was feeling some connection. He supportively praised my shooting, especially when it was mediocre, and brushed up against me even when there was plenty of room to pass by me. He also had begun offering me pieces of the snacks he sometimes brought with him. When playing dominoes at the desk, he swung his foot back and forth to tap my own.

And yet reports from the outside world were bleak. His school performance was poorer, and fighting with peers had escalated. His home life also had deteriorated. His grandmother was losing patience with him, and his mother feared that she and her two children would be forced to find somewhere else to live—at that time a financial impossibility. Mrs. Welch had doubts about the efficacy of therapy, and wondered against her better judgment whether medication—for which school staff was again campaigning—was the only solution. I needed to be wary of my own prejudiced and provincial tendency to underrate the benefits of medicine, while overvaluing those of psychotherapy. If indeed drugs might promote Eddie's concentration and self-esteem, why was I reluctant to give them a fair chance?

My single most compelling objection was that absolutely no one in the world understands how the same amphetamines that speed up adults' metabolism slow children down and enhance their concentration. In itself this ignorance is not a horrid thing; the benefits of many miracle drugs, to which most of us owe our lives, were discovered by accident and usefully applied for years and years—indeed, some herbal extracts, for centuries or millenia—before the mechanisms of their actions were identified. However, several factors make the case for amphetamines different.

In life-or-death situations, cure is willingly accepted today; side effects can be worried about tomorrow. Attention deficit can be a significant disability, but it is not life-threatening. The benefits of its pharmacologic treatment must be weighed carefully against the risks. Although using these drugs to treat poor attention may be safe, it represents a fairly new therapeutic application. Often a drug's long-term effects, especially on children, require decades of follow-up to be determined. In the world of drug testing, a lack of documented side effects usually can be interpreted to mean nothing more than *the good news is that there's been no bad news so far.* And in fact, some serious bad reactions (to Ritalin) have been documented.

Second, we don't know much about the ways the brain operates except that it is extraordinarily complex. I am highly skeptical about any drug that acts so powerfully upon the central nervous system. Who could be surprised if a chemical known to dramatically influence structures and processes as fundamental as the brain stem and concentration turned out to effect in addition, more lasting, broader, and untoward changes?

Third, for patient, physician, and researcher alike, the most satisfying drugs are those that seem to address the root of the problem, as penicillin does by killing specific bacteria. In the majority of cases, however, improving a symptom by medicine does not prove the cause. Antidepressants can lighten the mood of people who have suffered real losses worthy of depression. Tranquilizers can calm neurotic jitters that derive from psychoanalyzable internal conflict. The fact that Ritalin or an antidepressant improves attention—a most valuable topic of study occupying much current research—may or may not say something about the underlying reasons that a child cannot focus. Rarely, if ever, does it say everything.

And what about the psychological side effects? Children, like the patient who referred to the Ritalin tablet as his "little white straitjacket," often viewed their medication as a sign of their badness and need for external governance. How can a child develop a capacity to control himself while being given the prescription's strong message that he cannot? I've heard of children unable to take credit for success, feeling that the medicine should take the bow. These drugs also can generate a dangerous halo effect at school, whereby good days are attributed to the pill and bad days motivate teachers' questions as to whether the child took his medicine that morning. Somehow, being on Ritalin can lead others to forget that the child is affected by what goes on around and inside himself no less than his peers or his teachers. Of course, not every child experiences these conflicts, and many can work them through in therapy while taking the medicine.*

Besides wondering about the efficacy of Ritalin, I also was

*Keep in mind that my perspective is but one. There are many clinicians, educators and parents who testify to the benefits of drug treatment for A.D.D. And of course, there are many families whose resources or motivation preclude other therapies, making medicine the sole treatment option.

wary of sanctioning Eddie's being prescribed medicine based on a diagnosis that I did not agree warranted a singular disorder unto itself. Attention is a very important aspect of personality and functioning, but nonetheless only one. Why not elevate other phenomena to disorder status—such as "Intolerance of Frustration Disorder (I.F.D.)," "Unable to Delay Gratification Disorder (U.D.G.D.)," or "Inability to Withstand Any Strong Feelings Disorder (I.W.S.F.D)"? In all fairness, the conception of A.D.D. represents an admirable attempt to define, reduce, and ultimately make manageable a vague and broad category of problems (formerly subsumed by other undifferentiated labels of equally limited usefulness, such as "Minimal Brain Dysfunction" and "Hyperkinetic Syndrome"). But in my modest clinical experience I'd seen many more children with the symptoms of A.D.D. than I felt deserved the diagnosis, and found them to be a very mixed group defying unification, even if they shared some innate vulnerability toward distractibility.

Some of them lived in a constant state of fatigue, hunger, sickness, or stress. We all know how those conditions when experienced even transiently can interfere with our own ability to concentrate. Other so-called A.D.D. patients came from abusive homes. A child who is continually on the lookout for danger hardly can afford to lose herself in a book or school project. Becoming totally engrossed requires trust that no one will attack while your guard is down. A child's skittish vigilance to everything in the environment—often judged to be nothing more than an unfortunate impediment to learning—may serve a much higher and invaluably adaptive need for survival. Still other patients came from chaotic homes. Their personal radar scanned the environment not for physical harm or molestation, but for instability and unexpected change. How much can a child care about Dick and Jane while wondering if she'll see her mother or father that day?

I'd also seen many distractible children come from intact homes characterized by a different kind of chaos: life lived at a torrid pace. Their days were a frenzy of back-to-back practices and lessons that they—rolling out of slow-moving cars à la James Bond—barely got to on time. For these families, being in two places at one time was the norm. The parents were as active as their children, and as a group they routinely packed into their weekends what for most of us would be seven-day vacations. As they grew to trust me, many of these parents spontaneously wondered whether their driven and not so pleasurable zest for life partially served to ward off painful and depressing feelings that arose whenever they slowed down.

Seeing attention deficit as a biological problem treatable with a magic bullet lets some troubled families off the hook— to their own detriment. Some parents cannot or prefer not to deal with alcoholism, abuse, or other dysfunctions that pro-foundly retard their child's ability to concentrate. For some parents, unconscious fear of the pain and self-examination of therapy motivates their eagerness to embrace a neat, medici-nal solution. Others simply are not interested in explanations based on psychology or family conflicts, and see nothing that justifies the expense, inconvenience, or stress of psychother-apy.

While working to understand which—if any—of these formulations applied to Eddie, two limited interventions pro-vided some temporary relief. The first was when Mrs. Welch, a soft-spoken and very kindly woman, roughly criticized her discipline of Eddie as inconsistent, unfair, and often doled out in great frustration and anger. When I urged her to tell me more, she revealed that her fear of disturbing the peace in her mother's home was handcuffing her parenting. "How can I set a decent limit," she rhetorically asked, "if I have to worry that Eddie might cry or throw a tantrum? How will he learn that I mean what I say?" On her own she decided that she just would have to do what she thought was right as Ed-die's mother, and that her own mother would either accept it or not. I agreed, though I knew that sticking to her resolution would be stressful.

Given Eddie's recently exacerbated school troubles and having a clearer sense of who he was, I visited the school to learn more about his life in the classroom. I was pleased and relieved to find that the school staff, in fact, were quite fond of him. His being likable, an intangible quality that cannot be defined, was keeping others interested in Eddie even when he acted ornery. Although they were indeed concerned about his inability to concentrate, they were most troubled by his attitude and behavior. For much of his school day he was extraordinarily defensive, rejecting, and unreachable. I readily empathized with their plight—for there was virtually no sure-fire way to handle Eddie without difficulty—and attempted to convey what his experience might be like. I described how his pushing away of others was mostly to protect against his own exquisite sense of being defective. However tactfully given, teachers' comments made him feel intolerably stupid. Even checking over his own careless work made him feel pathetic and inept. He erroneously believed that smarter and worthier children don't need any help from themselves or others. "Don't take his mistreatment of you personally," I implored. "When he's already beaten himself up, it's hard to bear the gentlest boo from others."

While reports from school and home brightened slightly, Eddie seemed more unhappy in therapy. He initiated very competitive games during which he mercilessly teased and insulted me. Together we figured out that Eddie was trying to humiliate me, as he so frequently felt others did to him. He described desperately wanting friends but not knowing how to make them. Sometimes he wanted to be liked so badly—usually by a kid who had bullied or rejected him—that he'd give away food, money, or a prized possession. These attempts to buy friendship always failed. "I don't get it," he said. "I act nice to everyone else, but they treat me crummy."

I did not yell, "You must be kidding! Your mother and principal have told me the truth. I know you insult and start fights with kids all the time. Admit it, don't you?" I was not trying to set up a confrontation between his story and some-one else's, in this case mine. That kind of "oh yeah?" adversity pervaded and brought little benefit to his days outside of therapy. I sought to incite a therapeutic confrontation *within himself*—to make him judge how what he actually did compared with what he liked to believe he did.

"Eddie, I wonder if you treat other children as well as you think you do."

With an embarrassed smirk Eddie told how he'd "super-shined" an apple before giving it to a friend. When I said I didn't understand the joke, he explained that he repeatedly had spat on the apple to get it so clean. With wondrous insight and near hysterics, he gurgled that he could just as well have handed the kid a cup of spit and saved the apple for himself. "No wonder," Eddie chuckled, "he whipped the apple at my head."

"And you thought he was just being ungrateful?"

Eddie nodded and smiled.

It was hard for Eddie—as it is for all of us—to be truly kind to someone who was getting the good things or happiness that he wanted for himself. Over many weeks, Eddie learned more about the fact that his anger involved envy, and he began to recognize how frequently he provoked others' bad treatment of himself. Slowly but steadily he fought less and held onto his friends longer.

That spring—about a year after we'd begun to meet—I left my job at the local clinic to join the staff of a teaching hospital in Boston. Eddie and I continued our work together at my private office, one that differed in every conceivable way from the one he'd known. We were never locked out or made to endure inhumane extremes of temperature. (No child opens up when feeling too cold to remove his hat and parka.) The office generally was quiet. There was no telephone; I did not share patient hours with callers, nor was there any need to subject the children and myself to endless ringing or the click-and-whirs of an answering machine. The room was also visually calm. A desk and floor lamps supplied mellow lighting. Walls were covered with a soothing small print wallpaper in blue and beige, overhung only by a diploma and three sedate prints. The ceiling and woodwork were painted eggshell white. Toys, of which there were a limited number, were kept relatively neat in a plain cedar chest. Only art supplies and a basket of dominoes were on the desk—no heaps of work papers, no professional books. Although I'd tried to furnish the office tastefully, to accommodate both children and adults, I'd avoided furniture and accessories that were overly precious. The wing chairs and carpeting were highly durable and stain resistant. The lamp and clock were inexpensive, hardy replicas of more valuable antiques. I did not have to worry about any damage caused by muddy feet, crumbs, or tantrums; I could not be both a curator of things and caretaker of children.

Initially Eddie reveled in the extra space. He created a larger basketball court and freely paraded his gymnastic prowess. Between activities he would let himself fall to the floor, roll around or cozily curl up. He took mini-naps on the stuffed chairs, and built a clay fast-food restaurant on the desk. In short, he loved the office.

He also began to show interest in symbolic play, though pretending was not second nature to him. There are some children whose play so thoroughly takes on its own life that nothing can derail it. In the heat of fantasy they can ignore what is and safely imagine almost anything they wish. Such children easily can pretend a tissue is a baby's blanket or a domino a hospital stretcher. In contrast, Eddie abruptly stopped playing whenever he observed the laws of external reality being broken. When he discovered that a miniature cement mixer was disproportionately smaller than the pickup truck, he impulsively wrecked the elaborate play construction scene he'd worked hard to set up, and berated the company for manufacturing inaccurate and mismatched toys. He was equally sensitive to whether I adhered to the play's authenticity. If he wanted my father bear to come down to the kitchen, that bear had to descend on every stairway tread. Eddie demanded perceptual realism in his play, and felt utterly frustrated and disappointed in its absence. At those times he lost not only the simple pleasures of play, but the potential psychological benefits that playing out his feelings in make-believe might have brought.

A few months after we'd switched offices, Mrs. Welch announced that she'd been accepted into the training program of a prestigious realty company. She was very excited about this wonderful opportunity for professional achievement and financial security. She also worried about Eddie. She—as did I—had no idea whether he could endure her being home less, especially for the month-long sessions held in other parts of the country that the job occasionally required. What a dilemma. If she declined the offer, she and her children were doomed, at least for the time being, to a dependent existence in her mother's home. If she accepted, she risked overwhelming her already stressed son. She hoped dearly and with no small amount of trepidation that the long-term rewards—being able to live on her own with her children—would justify the short-term sacrifice; unfortunately, she would not know until she tried.

When Eddie heard the news, he denied caring. But his play

said otherwise. "I know everything in this room," Eddie boasted. "Test me, go ahead. Ask me with my eyes closed. I bet I know this room better than any other kid." And he did know. He knew in part because I seldom added new toys and rarely removed old ones. This constancy lent immense power to the play environment. Because changes were unexpected, they acquired great significance when they occurred. Eddie noticed when a bear doll that he'd left sleeping in a lower-level bedroom now prowled the attic, and when one of two dozen little trucks lost a windshield. "Who moved it?" "Who broke it?" "Who stole it?" "And," he pursued, "how come you let them get away with that?" His questions did not ask as much as they told of his fear that other children were punished less, treated better, and loved more than him. But, as we'd soon discover, his jealousy ran even deeper and closer to home.

Guilt-ridden and worried that her new career would bring catastrophe to the family, Mrs. Welch diligently prepared Eddie and his world for her upcoming training program in Toronto. She carefully chose a responsible college student, whom her son liked and who liked him, to stay at her mother's house with the children. She alerted the school to the situation so that they could better understand and manage any backsliding that occurred. And by arranging for Eddie's transportation to therapy, baseball practice, and a birthday party to which she knew he'd be invited, she maintained the structure and routine upon which he typically depended. Despite her fears, all went smoothly. She received sterling evaluations and, to everyone's surprised delight, Eddie coped remarkably well with her absence.

But rather than glowing with pride, they arrived to the session following her return looking battle-worn and on most hostile terms. While Eddie sulked in a chair, Mrs. Welch told how they'd been fighting over his desperate wish to quit therapy. Just before they left home, he had thrown an explosive tantrum to help state his case. Feeling frustrated, angry, and helpless—that unsavory emotional mix familiar to every parent—she confessed being at her wit's end. "He's getting too big to be wrestled into the car. Besides, being physically dragged to therapy can't be good for him, can it?"

Although I knew, I requested that she describe how Eddie

had done while she was gone. After detailing his admirable behavior, she speculated whether he might now be letting out his feelings about her trip. "No, no! I'm not," Eddie yelled. "It's not about nothin'. I just don't wanta come here anymore. I don't need therapy. I just don't like comin' here no more." He cried, but did not move from his seat. I suggested that Mrs. Welch return to the waiting room.

Once his tears dried, Eddie smiled, then walked to the doll-house. He repeatedly made a small bear doll in shorts beat up a taller bear, dressed in a flannel shirt and overalls, because the bigger bear had stolen his girlfriend. "She's mine, you big creep. Keep yer grubby hands off her," the little one warned. "Get your own girl, *stranger!*" Finally the bigger bear grabbed a girl bear, and together they drove off in the jeep. "I'll get you for this!" the forlorn bear yelled. "I will, ya know!" I suspected that the "girl" was Eddie's mother, but who was the interloping brute? Eddie spent the last few minutes covering a piece of paper with little black stars. "Ya know, I'm not mad about my mother going away. I'm really not."

"You're not?"

"No, that's not what I'm mad about at all."

Having unloaded some of the emotion he did not feel safe sharing in his mother's presence, Eddie left the hour with a bounce in his step. His mother gave me a questioning look but only said good-bye.

The following month was not a good one. Eddie grew much angrier and was at odds with seemingly everyone—his mother, grandmother, sister, other children, and school staff. He continued to fuss about coming to therapy each week, but would readily play and leave happy; however, that good feeling did not carry far beyond my front door. The school was suggesting medication again; everyone—including myself—questioned what I was doing. But I soon was saved by the news, given to me by Mrs. Welch in a parent-guidance hour and which she was trying to keep confidential, of her romantic involvement with someone she'd met at work. The puzzle was coming together.

For some time Eddie had not been able to discuss his feelings about the situation, though his play did. For example, he freely enacted armies fighting over their territories and *queen.*

"You don't want to lose your queen?" I observed.

"No, she's *mine*," his general gallantly proclaimed, "and I'll give my life to keep her." This was not a schoolboy's casual affection; I was dealing with earnest, devoted love.

When his mother and James, her fiancé, announced their engagement, Eddie could no longer keep his terror at bay. He became a tyrant at home, refusing to give James the time of day; he also resisted therapy. The needier and lonelier Eddie felt, the more vigorously he rejected everything and everybody. We were all at a loss as to what steps to take. Fortunately, Eddie and human nature showed us the way. For over twenty months, Mrs. Welch had respectfully stayed out of Eddie's therapy. Although she and I periodically met to review matters, she had come into the office during his hour only once. But now Eddie asked that she join us. Playing the host in a room for which he felt some ownership, he gestured for her to sit in my chair, which directly faced his own. I settled for a smaller gray chair off to the side—and out of what instantaneously became their line of fire.

"I hate you. You stink. You stupid butthead. I hate you. I don't need therapy. Why do I have to come here? Why do I have to keep on comin' here? You're such a stupid bumhead, stupid. Why can't I quit? Why can't I just quit?" Sometimes he looked sad, sometimes he smiled. Mostly he angrily insisted that he did not have to come back. My wondering whether he was upset about the wedding plans only brought back denials, though much more soft-spoken and civil ones than those he gave his mother.

I listened but did not intercede. My mind raced to find the meaning of this unleashed rage. Was I encouraging him to become a woman abuser? Would this lead to more uncontrolled rancor when they left, or open wounds that had been healing slowly? If I felt that his assault represented nothing more than an indulgent release of frustration, I'd have stopped it immediately. But I sensed that Eddie was doing something necessary and ultimately beneficial for both him and his mother.

"You butthole. You smell, you really do. I don't know how you can stand being you. You really are a loser. Why can't you just leave me alone, huh? Huh? Huh! Why can't ya? Don't think I'm comin' to your wedding, either. Loser. You're such a loser."

Mrs. Welch tried to reason with him: "Eddie, I know there are things bothering you. Let's talk about them calmly." But he rightly had no need for logical discussions about ideas; it was feelings that drove him. Mrs. Welch was in an awful fix. She could either be the recipient of Eddie's hurting words; or fight back mean. I seldom spoke, and mostly to encourage her to maintain the saintly restraint she was showing.

"You really are. Look at you, you're just a butthead. You can't even fight back. Look at you. You just sit there like such a—such a butt-sitting jerkhead."

Although Eddie's attack grew louder, it was becoming more confused, futile, and lonely. His words softened and sputtered. His mother and I looked at him, both knowing just how badly he felt.

"What is it, Eddie?"

"I don't know," he cried. "I really don't."

"You don't want your mom to get married?" I knew he didn't, of course, but it had to be said aloud.

Eddie strained to ignore my comment, but he couldn't. "Why does she have to? I don't want her to. I like the way things are. They're just fine the way there are. I think if she gets married, my schoolwork's gonna get bad again. I really do. I'm afraid of that. Yeah. I'm not really worried about her gettin' married. I'm just worried 'bout my schoolwork." When no response came, he continued—looking his mother right in the eye. "Tell you what. You don't get married and I'll do my homework." Reading the silence as a demand for a better proposition, he added that he would keep his room clean and not give her a hard time. When she did not rush to accept his offer, he burst into tears. "Why not? Why do you have to get married? Okay," he said, trying to speak calmly through his heaving sobs, "here's my last deal. I'm giving you one last chance not to get married."

Now, I thought, was the time to remind Eddie of all that he'd been playing over the past few months. "Eddie, is it okay if I say something?" I didn't want to flip my only ace until I was sure that he was playing the hand.

"Sure, go ahead," he urged politely through his tears.

"Are you sure? Because I may be wrong. I am, lots of times, you know."

Again he urged me to speak my mind.

"Eddie, I think you don't want someone to steal your girl."

Both Eddie and Mrs. Welch laughed self-consciously, embarrassed by my acknowledgment of the romance that they, like most mothers and sons, shared. But neither balked at my words. Eddie explained that the marriage would make his parents' long-past divorce more real, and destroy his illusion that his mother and father would someday get back together. His mother tearfully listened and shared ways in which she felt the same.

As the day of the marriage approached, Eddie grew sadder in therapy. He drew that picture of Mandy, with a dog bone in her mouth, and longingly talked of her, his father, and his grandfather. He described times when not having a father was especially difficult—like holidays, at father–son games, "every night," and especially when he and his mother were not getting along. "Ya need to feel like there's at least one somebody that likes you, somewhere."

"You think about him every minute of the day?"

Eddie nodded, then asked, "This sounds weird, but can I be thinking about him even when I'm not thinking 'bout him?"

"Does it feel like you are?" I asked.

"Yeah," he replied, sounding curiously amazed at his self-discovery.

"Then you probably are."

Eddie proudly served as ring bearer for the wedding, and enjoyed the family's move to a rented house not far from his grandmother's. He looked like a different child, helping around the house, having fun playing basketball, and hanging around James. He and his mother became even better friends. School steadily improved, as did his friendships. The children who'd teased him were now his friends, and the teachers who'd once scolded now praised him.

Postscript: I'm tempted to end the story here, but the flukes of life would not allow that. Soon after the marriage, Eddie's family moved to a different town, where he gradually fared less and less well. When I contacted his mother about the book—about two years after the therapy had stopped—she was about to call me to resume Eddie's treatment. Eddie had confessed to his mother that I'd meant a lot to him and had been a help, but feared that I'd be disappointed in him. In fact, he believed that I would change my mind and not want his case in the book when I heard what had been happening.

When we began to meet again, Eddie rather quickly identified the sources of his attentional relapse and regained the progress he'd temporarily lost. He sorely missed his friends, the supportive school staff, and myself; and he stressed that he missed us not just as people in our own right, but also as witnesses to the progress he'd made, the obstacles he'd overcome. Eddie also talked about his great disappointment in there being no Santa Claus, tooth fairy, or Easter bunny. Some mild probing rapidly led to his disclosure that his father recently had called and wanted to reestablish contact. As of this writing Eddie still was working to understand how he felt about the call, what he should do about it, and whether he should ask his father the question he had wondered—and which had distracted his attention—for so long: Did he love him?

Children who have trouble concentrating are a varied group. They need individualized treatments involving various types of therapies—play, behavioral, and family; they also need educational plans and, sometimes, drugs. Though research eventually may identify those children for whom medicines are most suited, it will never thoroughly tease apart biological and psychological influences.

X

Growing Pains

She plumes her feathers, and lets go her wings.

—John Milton,
A maske presented at Ludlow's castle

Parents want their children to grow autonomous and confident enough to cope with life; at the same time, they wish them to forever remain young and dependent upon them. Their children are just as confused. They plead for independence and responsibility, yet continually sabotage their parents' sincerest efforts to provide them. Nine-year-old Cassie was no exception, nor was she pleased by my suggestion that her mother leave the room.

"No! No, don't go!"

Her forcefulness took me by surprise. Up to this moment she'd been thoroughly soft-spoken and cordial. I'd put Mrs. Adams into an awful position. I was recommending that she leave; Cassie was pleading that she stay. "What should I do?" her shrugging shoulders asked. The perplexed mother and her intimidating daughter looked to me for an answer.

Why did I push for their separation in this very first meeting? What was my rush to implement change in a relationship that had evolved over nine years? I reflected upon similar cases and my habitual choice to go more slowly. I knew what was at risk. If Cassie felt mistreated, she probably would not return. Her failed therapy would fall, almost squarely, on my shoulders. There seemed to be every reason to proceed with extreme caution. Yet looking at their present anguish, I knew there was an immediate need for relief, today—not the trivial relief that allowing their connectedness to go unchallenged might give, but the substantial relief of having their anxieties lightened. I could not, however, ease those anxieties without knowing what they were.

Before I could reply, Cassie's daunting glare had faded. "I don't feel well, Mommy. I think I'm gonna throw up. I want to go home. Let's go home, Mommy." I already knew about Cassie's frequent stomachaches, which were the main reason for her referral; however, her symptom was surfacing in the therapy earlier than I'd expected.

"My stomach hurts, Mommy. It hurts bad." She crossed and wrapped her arms around her sides, then pulled her knees up against her belly. "I want to go home. It hurts. It really hurts." When her mother did not respond, Cassie pressed harder: "It hurts bad, Mommy! Let's go home. Now, Mommy. Let's go right now!"

By putting the idea of her mother's leaving into her head, I'd sufficiently stirred Cassie to show me the lengths she would go to prevent it. Deliberately taking time, I calmly asked Mrs. Adams what she did in similar situations at home. Cassie sighed loudly at my question, unmistakably exasperated by its implied neglect of her demands to go home. "You've gone one step too far, mister," her frown cautioned. "Now you've really done it!"

Mrs. Adams attributed Cassie's frequent attacks foremost to separations from her and not getting what she wanted. During them she cried uncontrollably and protested that she, as a dying child, needed urgent medical care. In response her mother would inquire solicitously about the pain and attempt to physically console her, sometimes rocking the third-grade girl in her arms. The more Cassie's stomach hurt, the more babyish she became; the more babyish she became, the more her stomach hurt. Occasionally she was rushed to the hospital, but more typically she recouped spontaneously, especially if given her way or distracted by a friend. Sometimes Mrs. Adams felt that Cassie conjured up her pains at will to accomplish what she wanted; at others, she feared her daughter suffered from a serious yet undiagnosed condition. She wondered whether the pain reflected emotional conflicts, and to that end she had arranged for this therapy. "That's why," she addressed her daughter, "we need to stay and figure this out."

But Cassie was not persuaded. She paled and her voice weakened. "I'm sick, Mommy, real sick. I need a doctor. I need to go to the hospital."

Without doubt she wanted and, I was growing more certain, expected to get her way. I was even surer that whatever its terms, her way was not what she needed most. If Cassie and her mother left now, coming back next time would be even harder. I looked into Cassie's watering eyes and quietly asked if her stomach hurt.

Unoffended by my obvious question, with dramatized effort she gave a small nod. She worried, she revealed months later, that a bigger one would have exacerbated the pain and have led others to think she was not as sick as she claimed— the latter an injustice she often felt.

"A lot?" I followed.

"Yes," she peeped.

Fully cognizant of the question's heavy-handed transparency, I asked whether her stomach had begun hurting when I suggested that her mother leave the room.

"No!" she angrily denied.

I'd struck a chord. Did she want me to know about and help with her true feelings? I pushed on to find out.

"So, it hurt before then?"

She resumed her sickly composure and nodded feebly.

"Oh, I see. My asking your mom to leave didn't cause your stomachache, it only made it worse."

"Yeah, but it didn't give it to me." This qualified agreement—in its admitting that some relation, however minimal, existed between her pain and my initial call for separation— represented a major concession. She sat up comfortably.

"Cassie, I'm going to ask that your mom leave for a few minutes now."

"No! No!" She doubled up reflexively and weeped.

"You'll be fine. I'll be right outside the door," her mother encouraged in a shaky, disbelieving voice.

Cassie grew more distressed. "Can we leave, Mommy? I want

to go home. I'm gonna throw up. My stomach hurts really bad."

"We can leave the door open. I'll just be a few steps away."

But Cassie would have none of it. "I'll die, Mommy. I'll die. Really, I will."

"You won't die, sweetheart. You'll be fine." Her mother reached over to pat Cassie's leg, but her gesture was rejected with a kick.

"I'm not okay. I'm sick. I'm dying. I'm gonna die, Mommy. I'm dying."

Had Cassie not looked so robust, I'd have considered sending her off to the emergency room myself. I knew that Cassie was in good health, but as I'd just heard, there was little reason to tell her. She'd readily discount any challenge to her proclamation of ill health.

"You're dying?" I asked softly and very seriously.

"Yes," she answered somberly. She found my sobriety neither condescending nor histrionic, but felt it well suited the gravity of her situation.

"What a scary thing, to be dying," I replied in the same tone. Her mother shivered at my words, then intently watched for her daughter's reaction.

As a beginning therapist, I'd have couched my comment in gentler terms—"What a scary thing *to feel like* you're dying," or *"It sounds as if you are worried* that you are dying." I soon learned, however, that those therapeutic qualifiers—*feels to be, sounds as if, looks like*—intended to convey some tentativeness and give room for disavowal of my remarks, often diluted patients' experiences and made them feel misunderstood. I would not suggest to a child with fatal cancer that "It's scary to feel like you're dying," for that would minimize the terror and reality of his actual dying. Instead I'd say, "It's scary *to be dying.*" Though Cassie was solidly alive, she believed herself to be dying. And that psychological truth mattered more than any medical facts.

"But I don't want to die," Cassie spoke earnestly, needing to convince me.

"Of course you don't."

Cassie's weeping slowed but deepened. Her tears, which had been partially crocodilian and for others' benefit, were now wholly her own.

Mrs. Adams noted with surprise that I hadn't told Cassie that she was fine. At first she was shocked by how frankly I spoke, uneasy that I hadn't said something more hopeful, more comforting to her daughter. "I always tell her that everything will be okay, that she won't die. But I"—she paused to compose herself—"but I can't promise her that, can I? No one can." She recognized that Cassie knew as well as the grown-ups that being mortal is perilous and uncertain. "I try to put her mind at ease, but I never seem to. She knows I can't promise her she won't die, doesn't she?"

I nodded. False reassurance reassures little and, at that, only fleetingly.

"Sometimes she asks if *I'll* die, and who will take care of her and make her sandwiches the way she likes them."

"What do you tell her?" I asked.

"That I'm fine and she doesn't have to worry about me dying. I know, I know, you don't have to tell me." Mrs. Adams extended her tissued hand from her eyes as if to fend me off; however, she was pushing away her own words and awareness. "I know what you're thinking. I can't promise her that, either." She fell silent and watched her hands twist a wet tissue apart.

"What is it?" I asked.

"Cassie's grandmother, my mother, died when I was sixteen." Her lower lip quivered. "That must worry Cassie."

"That must worry Cassie?" I asked. Cassie did not jump in to resolve our speculation, understanding—so I believed—what was happening and what my comment was up to.

"I guess it bothers me, too. I don't want to die young, either." She laughed self-consciously. "For that matter, I don't want to die old. I guess I just don't want to die. Maybe it worries me even more than it worries Cassie. I don't know. It probably does."

When I suggested that death worried them both, they smiled, somewhat embarrassed by their display of emotion. They were more relaxed, but were certainly not freed of their fears.

"Shall we try now?"

They both looked at me in dismay that I hadn't forgotten or given up. "Oh," Mrs. Adams recalled, "you mean I really have to leave?"

It was important that I persist. They'd already learned that I was not afraid of their anxious fantasies. They also had to see that I was not afraid of their being apart physically. A real separation, even if only for a few minutes, would symbolically set the tone for the entire therapy.

"We've made it through the worst," I congratulated myself, seeing that Cassie did not fuss when her mother stood up and walked out. My confidence renewed, I questioned her about school, but she did not answer. I tried less threatening topics—her favorite television shows and snacks. Still nothing. I offered her toys and games, all of which she declined by silently sitting still. I was beginning to get the picture.

"You want nothing to do with me, do you?"

She smirked loudly.

"Nothing at all."

Cassie purposely looked at me and rolled her eyes; she then turned away, toward the door.

"You're very upset with me, aren't you?"

She wanted to ignore me forever, but could not stand another second of her angry tension. Her body tilted forward, while her face led the attack. "I hate you. You're a mean, mean man. You're the meanest doctor I ever met."

"Because I asked your mother to leave?"

"And just for that"—Cassie stood up and placed her hands on her hips—"and just for that"—with principled determination she deeply inhaled, then scowled—"I'm never gonna play with you ever!"

"Never ever?"

"You heard right! I'm never gonna play with you or your dumb puppets." Those were the toys that, I later learned, most intrigued her.

"That's a very long time."

"That's just what you deserve. You don't deserve anyone to play with, forever and ever!"

I placed my detective dog puppet on my right hand and looked into his face. "Yeah," I made him say to me, "that's just what you deserve. You took away her mommy. You don't deserve anything better." The dog glanced over to Cassie, who strained not to smile, and then back to me. "And you think she's gonna play with you? You must be kidding."

Without any direct suggestion by me, Cassie picked up a

cow puppet for herself. "Yeah, that's right," she seconded my dog's proposal. "You tell him." Her puppet further told mine that she was worried because her parents planned to go away for a weekend without her. Within ten minutes of her having established an embargo against me and therapy, Cassie was playing and talking. If I had not taken her initial threat seriously, if I had not believed that she truly believed those words, she would not have made peace so quickly or left her first meeting as comfortably.

Cassie's stomachaches were not at all unusual. Many children feel pains—in their stomachs, heads, and virtually all other body parts—without being sick. These aches can make physiological sense and mimic those of real disease, or can be bizarre and anatomically illogical. Like the fickle shimmying and pings that bedevil our cars but disappear when the car is taken into the shop, these symptoms often vanish the very moment the child lies upon the examining table.

These children frequently visit doctors, especially after hours, and yet those frightening, expensive, and time-consuming emergency-room evaluations seldom benefit them. The physician, under great pressure to treat acutely ill patients, may not sense the emotional meaning of the child's pain. And even should she suspect it, the environment is typically not conducive to nor is there a sufficient relationship with the child and family for her to intervene adequately. Moreover, families, who prefer that things be left status quo until the next late-night visit occurs, may adjudge this to be just as well.

Physicians, who are pressured by worried parents, fearful of malpractice suits, or skeptical of psychological explanations, further may refer the child to specialists or conduct more tests, even when quite sure that nothing is wrong. This may unnecessarily subject child patients to inconvenient, uncomfortable, costly, and risky diagnostic procedures. But these extensive work-ups can fail to put a child's mind at ease; in fact, they may endow the symptom with greater legitimacy and heighten the child's fears. "If it's really nothing, why do I have to keep seeing more doctors for more tests?" asked a boy plagued by migraines.

In spite of clean bills of health, pains notoriously persist. Children may remain convinced that something malignant goes on inside their bodies, something that even the big machines cannot detect. Prolonged physical assessments also can encourage susceptible parents to adopt their children's symptoms as causes célèbre to distract them from their own empty or otherwise unhappy lives. The search for illness can immobilize families, who may decide to put off important decisions or the seeking of non-medical help until the physical source of the symptom is uncovered. (And often it never is.) By recommending therapy early on, Cassie's doctor had saved her from some of these psychological side effects. And fortunately, her mother had been receptive and committed to the idea.

There was an abundance of data in Cassie's history to support a psychological hypothesis for her symptoms. According to standardized test scores and teachers' reports she was quite bright, yet her third-grade schoolwork was only fair and her concentration was erratic. Going to school, especially at the beginning of the year and on Mondays, had always been difficult and sometimes required her being forcibly carried onto the bus by Mrs. Adams. Cassie frequently missed school because of morning stomachaches, headaches, and general malaise—though she generally felt fine by midday.

Her early childhood history was unremarkable except for two major separations. At age two, when her mother was preoccupied with her younger sister's birth and subsequent month-long hospitalization, Cassie was cared for primarily by a grandmother. About a year later, Cassie herself was hospitalized for severe respiratory croup, following which she seemed to favor her father. She presently lived with her mother and two sisters, one younger and one older. Her parents had separated two years earlier because of constant physical and verbal fighting, some of which she'd witnessed. But now they were attempting to reconcile, so she saw her father almost daily.

When Cassie and her mother returned for their second visit, they were arguing—about what I didn't know. Cassie's big, cheery hello seemed to be an intentional dig at her mother as much as a genuine indication of good feeling for me. She eagerly left her belongings and mother in the small waiting area adjacent to my office. We spent most of the session huddled in the small alcove, which was the part of the office farthest from the doorway. A small, fuzzy beige calf with gray and brown spots, long eyelashes, and tiny pink felt udders spoke at length and in a hush about treats, toys, games, and friends.

"Why are you whispering?" I asked.

"Sh-hhhhh!" she silenced me. She quickly removed her first finger from her lips to indicate silently that I should give her a minute before saying anything more. Taking a pencil and paper from the desk, she wrote, "Mother might hear."

"What will happen if she hears?" I wrote back.

"I don't know, but she might kill us. We need to hide our self" was the reply. Cassie was much angrier than she recognized or could bear. She imagined her mother to be as murderously furious at her as she was at her mother.

"You're worried that your mother will hear us in the lobby?"

"Yes!!!" she wrote back with gigantic exclamation points. At the hour's end, I asked Cassie to stand outside the office while I spoke, so that she could judge the acoustics for herself. Though she could not hear anything, the experiment did not put her anxieties to rest. What she feared her mother knowing was not primarily what she said but what she thought. And no door or walls, however thick and insulated, could provide that kind of protection.

For many weeks Cassie came to sessions agreeably. She played out complex scenes in which a baby girl cow climbed a large oak tree until she could go no higher and was too frightened to shimmy down. "Help me! Help me!" Her mother, a larger fleecy yellow cow puppet, ran about screaming, "Help me, someone! Please help my baby!" Cassie emphasized that the mother cow was much too panicked to retrieve her child. Only a kindly bull fire*man* walking by was able to rescue Baby Cow. To show her appreciation, Baby Cow rewarded him with hugs, ice cream, and a good brushing. Did this play embody her essential situation—a child who could neither be all grown up nor a baby, who resented feeling so dependent on her mother, who often judged her mother to be more anxious than she, and last, who more easily enjoyed her father's attentions and help?

Back on the ground, Baby Cow bragged about her adventure.

"But weren't you scared hanging from that branch?" I reminded.

"You must be mistaken," she corrected my puppet. "You
heard my mother. She was scared, not me." Baby Cow's (and
Cassie's) preferred awareness of her mother's worry primarily
served to avoid her own anxiety over being caught up in trees
(and growing up).

Cassie came in the next week complaining of a bad headache; she was immensely frustrated that the school nurse had
given her an aspirin instead of the customary dismissal to go
home sick. With my encouragement she confessed anger that
I'd requested school staff to keep her in class unless she was
very ill. "If you hadn't opened your mouth, I could've gone
home," she rebuked. She then played a little mouse that could
not decide whether to escape from or stay in a maze full of
both hazards and tasty cheese. Cassie, too, was indecisive, only
her mazes were home, school, and therapy with me.

I soon became a surrogate—with all the complexity that
implies—for the baby cow's heroic fireman, who in turn stood
for the original object of her affections, her father. For most
of the following month Cassie meticulously cleaned my office,
cheerily whistling as she worked. She disposed of pieces of
hardened clay and paper scraps left by other children, she
shelved books, and she stacked papers. Even message slips
were arranged into a fan to make them easily readable. I felt
like a father whose daughter, pretending to be her mother,
his wife, makes him breakfast and brings his pipe and slip-
pers. I had grown used to children messing up my office and
ordering me about, so her wish to please me was initially
flattering; but soon her doting grew uncomfortable. There
was a foreboding sense that her eagerness to do for me was
not singularly a sign of affection, and involved some need to
control our relationship by being neat and nice. As this became clearer to both of us, her interest in taking care of me
waned.

Several months into our work together, suffering fewer
stomachaches and spending more days at school, Cassie arrived in a huff. Mrs. Adams gently hinted that she'd had a
very bad day and had thrown a whopping tantrum. Cassie did
not resist my invitation to enter the office, but once in, she
aggressively and firmly buried herself in a chair. She wrote,

"No!" to my suggestion that we play with the puppets, and likewise refused the clay and tiddly-winks, two of her favorites.

"What is it?" I wrote.

"Nothing!" she wrote back. "This day is horrid. Even my favorite cookie is horrid. Everything is bad today!" She did not elaborate on what made everything so bad.

We sat in quiet tension until, with only a few minutes remaining, I inquired why she'd rejected doing the very things that she loved. She angrily scribbled a note, threw it on my desk, and stomped to the door, where she lingered for my reaction.

I slowly unfolded the paper and read, "Because I DON'T WANT TO, that's why!"

I looked up at the pouting face that dared me to say something, that dared me to make her day. I could have said something encouraging or chirpy—such as "Cheer up" or "Tomorrow will be better"—but I'd have been rubbing salt into a wound, as do the highway patrolmen who tell speeders to have a nice day after writing out their tickets. I could have reflected her stated position—"You sure let me know that you just didn't want to"—but such parroting would have added nothing to what we both knew. "Till next week, Cassie," I said with a straight face, for this was not the time for smiles.

She began to speak but decided not to, opting to slam my door shut. As I sat down to record my notes of the hour, including mention of the distraught state in which she'd left, I heard the sound of a girl and her mother walking down the hall, happily chatting and laughing.

My allowing Cassie to neglect me, to be hostile in absentia, had safely sanctioned her being mad at me. I had not retaliated by getting mad or withdrawing or intrusively demanding that she explain her behavior. She was on the prowl for a combatant, for a dog to kick. If I had fought with her, she'd have escaped herself and blamed me for everything—her tantrum, her bad day, and her feeling rejected. Left to war against herself, she openly discovered that it was angry Cassie who "didn't want to be with me" and not me who didn't want to be with her. We had planted the seeds of understanding as to how her passively expressed anger spited herself, and kept her from getting and feeling the very attentions that she craved from others.

The succeeding week she asked that I read her a story, from a book she'd brought, that defined friends as people who "return each other's letters." "I might have ignored your spoken questions last week" was her underlying message, "but I returned your letters. Even while angry at you, I wrote you back and remained your friend." Our mutual trust had been strengthened.

From our earliest moments together there was little doubt that both mother and daughter were equal investors in Cassie's stomachaches and her developmental quandary. Yet not until the fourth month did I know the specific terms of their partnership. A favored aunt on her mother's side had brought her to therapy. Mr. and Mrs. Adams, progressing well in their attempt to reunite, had gone to Atlantic City for the weekend—the first trip they ever had taken without their daughter. It was the prospect of that same vacation that had terrorized Cassie in her initial hour with me. She did not appear overly distressed as she told me that her parents had said good-bye that morning, but it was much too early to assess her reaction. She'd just been dismissed from school and had eaten an ice cream cone on her way to see me. The reality of being left behind had not settled in, so I assumed.

Cassie calmly gestured for me to enter the small alcove at the far end of the office, where she then corralled me, using my captain's desk chair as a security gate. "You," she authorized in a low, solemn voice, "are hereby sentenced to three days in jail." She further instructed me to rest my chin upon the seat so that I peered through the slender spindles of the chair back—a behind-the-bars look that very much pleased her. "You will sleep alone in the dark and eat crummy food," she tormented, adding in a whisper that I should act very upset.

"But I want my mommy and daddy," I cried. "I want to be with them."

"Ha, ha!" she laughed with mock cruelty. She told me that my parents hated me and had left me in jail so they could have a fun time (something, she strongly implied, they could not do with me around). Having served me bread and water, while describing the outrageously wonderful pizzas and desserts that my parents were savoring at the best restaurants without me, she tossed me a pencil and paper. "Write them a letter!" she commanded.

Not wanting to disobey my strict warden, I wrote my parents a letter. "Dear Mom and Dad, I am lonely in jail and want to be with you."

After Cassie read what I'd written, she wrote me back a letter to me from my parents. "Shut up, son. We hate you very much. Love, your parents." If that had not been hurtful enough, my merciless guard then made me read the letter aloud so that she could humiliate me. "Ha, ha, ha!" she gloated. "They're glad to be without you! Ha, ha! You'll never see them again."

"That's what I'm afraid of. I'm so mad at them." I raised my voice. "I feel like making *them* be all alone. Then, *they'd* know what it feels like." I tried to put into words what I sensed my jailer felt beneath her mean exterior and was trying to make me feel instead.

"You're sick now," she suddenly dictated. "Play sick."

"I'm sick?"

"You have an awful stomachache. Call your parents and tell them you're very sick and need them home." She handed me the plastic yellow telephone, then answered my play ringing on the desk phone (the hotel's).

"Mommy," I whined, "I'm sick. I've got a stomachache. It hurts, Mommy. It really hurts." I tried to use the same words that I'd heard Cassie herself speak months ago.

"We'll be right home," she pleasantly said as my parents.

"Oh, boy," I rejoiced, but before I hung up, the phone rang again.

"I have something to say," Cassie, as my mother, said very angrily. "We've changed our minds. We're not coming home. You're growing up and will be okay. If your stomach hurts, tell your therapist."

"But—but, Mommy. My stomach really hurts. I'll die. I really will. Won't you come home to take care of me and my stomach?" I begged.

"You can die for all we care," she ranted. "We're not ruining our vacation for your stupid stomach!" Swept up in the play, Cassie grabbed my receiver to assume my role—the imprisoned child—and talk with my imaginary parents. "You're making me mad," she yelled, "and that's giving me a stomachache!" She ran to pick up the other phone and again became the mother. "Good, I'd rather *you give your stomach a headache than give me one.*"

A complicated story was unraveling. Cassie fell ill, not consciously but unconsciously in order to obtain more of the attention she sought and to safely vent the rage she felt over her mother's not always being available to give it. Concretely speaking, she beat up her stomach rather than her mother, and Mrs. Adams, understandably, could live with that. She did not want her daughter to feel sick, but neither did she want to be the target of her fury. Nor did she like to be aware of the comparably intense anger she herself could feel toward Cassie and her other children. By becoming fragile and pained rather than angry and defiant, Cassie received her mother's attentive care in lieu of wrath. This complex arrangement prevented both mother and daughter, who loved each other very much, from becoming too directly hostile with each other.

After Cassie released me from "jail," she initiated an open discussion of her concern that something might happen to her parents when they were away. Upon my relating this to her past reluctance to attend school, she admitted worrying that her parents might fight or that one of them might die or leave in her absence. She felt compelled to stay home to make sure that all was okay.

Over the early winter, Cassie progressed steadily. She seldom experienced any body pains and had nearly perfect attendance. Her concentration, grades, and satisfaction in school had improved markedly. During this period she made drawings and clay sculptures of cross-bred animals—such as elephants with long trunks and kangaroo pouches, and cows with sharp, assaultive horns and tender, vulnerable underbellies—play which helped her to negotiate feelings about her sexual identity. Like most children Cassie occasionally wondered what life would be like as the other sex, and fantasized about mothering babies of her own.

Cassie initially could not express frustration about her sisters without lecturing herself on the need to love and respect them. This self-directed moralizing, rather than curbing her natural envy and resentment, served more as a testimony to the awful guilt she felt for harboring unloving feelings and thoughts. Gradually she openly complained about sharing her bedroom, her toys, and other possessions with her sisters, especially the youngest, whom Cassie disparaged as "the baby."

She also did not like sharing people. Her wish to own others exclusively vividly came into therapy after she'd felt slighted by a friend's closeness with another girl. "I like mouse so much better than you, Ox," she repeatedly told my character. "He's my best friend. You're nothing to me!" She teased and rejected Ox until nudged to see that it was Ox's predicament with which she identified and which she hated to feel. "No one wants to be the one left out, do they?" she asked.

"No one that I've met," I answered honestly.

As her more generic quest for sole ownership of people resolved, her wish to control her father's attentions became more acute. For weeks we played detectives, "good pals," who together ran a private eye agency. Her blossoming romantic fantasies eventually found a more amorous outlet in the case of a thief who had stolen a diamond wedding ring because she wanted "someone all for herself." This play led to Cassie's explaining that sometimes she wanted her father for herself, and that seemed only fair because her sisters seemed to monopolize her mother.

Cassie felt great shame over her strong wish to exhibit herself and her skills—as revealed, for example, in her calling a swordfish a "weirdo" simply because he liked to impress aquarium-goers with his fancy swimming. She pursued this issue more deeply in her creation of a gymnastics school for puppets. At first Beauty and Zippy, its founding members known respectively for their good looks and speed, rationalized that they exercised solely for health reasons, but gradually they openly admitted in television interviews that they loved to show off their jumps and somersaults in front of large crowds.

When Cassie heard that therapy was going to be brought to a close, a decision based on her good progress, she felt very confused—pleased that she'd have more free time to play, sad that we'd no longer play together. For several weeks we played a hide-and-seek game in which puppets unable to find each other instead found discarded clothing—clues that the others had left without having notified their friends.

Cassie's feeling that she'd lost her early childhood and her mother playfully peaked in her final detective adventure, the most elaborate of our series. Having read a make-believe newspaper headline about a boy who lost his blanket, Cassie volunteered her sleuthing skills to help find it. "Let's see. Where should we begin?" she asked. "We need suspects! Bring me suspects, I say." She gestured for me to prop Mrs. Cow in my desk chair.

"And you must be the boy's mother," Cassie said, squinting as if to unnerve her adversary. "What do you have to say for yourself?" Placing her hand inside the puppet, she answered her own question for Mrs. Cow: "He's too old for a blankie. He needs to grow up." Cassie, again as the inspector, pensively rubbed her chin. "Hmmmmm. Too old, you say? I see. Very interesting." Through her professional demeanor I could see she did not like what she had heard. She called for the next witness, the bull.

"And you," Cassie accusingly pointed at the puffy brown-ringed nose, "must be the boy's father. What is your excuse?" Taking the puppet, she spoke in a very fatherly, grown-up voice for Mr. Cow. "I agree with my wife. He's much too old to be carrying a blankie. Much too old." She made the bull shake his head disapprovingly. "Yes, much too old, indeed." She then told both cow parents to wait in the lobby (my chair), while she printed the following front page story using black marker and typing paper.

THE CLINIC NEWS

Little boy had a blanket wawa. It is missing. Where is it? Please call Detective Adams 385-6767

Cassie leaned back in the chair, pretending that a ruler in her mouth was a smoking pipe—a regular chip off the old Sherlock Holmes, she fancied herself, in yet another variation of a father–daughter bond. "Mmmmm, where can that fuzzy wawa be? Where could it be?" She slowly swiveled her chair and surveyed the room suspiciously. "Where could that wawa be?" Suddenly she jumped up and yelled, "Bring the boy here, now. I've figured it out. And call the paper to give them the big news."

"What should I tell them?" I asked, sensing the thrill of her discovery.

"Tell them that Detective Adams found the blanket, wawa. But that big questions remain, like who took it and why don't the boy's mom and dad want to let him keep sleeping with his blanket and why don't they let him carry it around anymore." She silently motioned for me to bring in baby cow as the boy. As she requested, I took his front paw and escorted him to meet her as detective.

Cassie knelt down so that she faced the baby cow that stood in the chair. "Now, don't be scared, little boy. I won't hurt you. I just want to ask you some questions. And," she spoke in a stern but caring manner, "I want the truth. Now, take your time and tell me the whole story."

Feigning nervous hesitation, she spoke for him. "I, Michael Winks, hid my blanket so that I can find it when I want to. I know I need to grow up, and I am growing, but sometimes I need to be a baby, too." She then called in his parents, and after delivering a gentle slap on their hands, she sentenced them to a family ice cream party, her treat. Though we spoke briefly about Cassie's recent frustration over her parents' attempts to curb her thumb-sucking, there was little to be said or explained. Her play had best spoken for itself.

In what I consider to be one of the most touching and insightful episodes in *Sesame Street*'s illustrious history, Ernie longs to jam with a big jazz band, but just can not bear to put down his trusty bathtime buddy, Rubber Duckie, even for a minute so that his hands can be free to play the saxophone. With understanding for his good friend's heart-wrenching predicament, Hoot, the wise old jazz owl, reassures Ernie that he does not have to send his duckie away on a plane, train, or rocket; he just has, in the words of the song, to "Put Down the Duckie" long enough to play that song. Comforted, Ernie finally does put him down and plays a mean solo, after which he quickly snatches his friend back into his arms. "Ooohhhh, Duckie," he coos, while hugging and kissing the little yellow plastic bird. "I missed you so much. I'm so glad to see you."

Ernie and Cassie both knew that growing up meant giving up. Crawling and walking brings great adventure, but takes an infant away from mommy. Feeding herself is fun and satisfying for a little girl, but not as gratifying as suckling the breast or lovingly being spooned applesauce. Generally in healthy development the child's curiosity and quest for competence exceeds the pull to stay safely where she is or to retreat to where she was. And so she begrudgingly gives up her diapers and reckless excretions because she likes feeling clean and in charge of her bowels. Or she endures the pain of leaving her mother because the exciting activities of preschool and the company of other children make it worthwhile. We all do this growing with colossal reluctance—kicking and screaming all the while, each in our own way*— as did Cassie with her stomachaches and school phobia.

On our final day, Cassie brought in prizes she'd won at a school fair that week. After joyfully telling me about them, she went to work drawing a make-believe edition of the *Boston Globe.*

"You usually print the clinic news, but today it's a big city newspaper," I pointed out.

"Oh, we want the whole world to read this!" she exuberantly explained.

BOSTON GLOBE

Beauty and Zippy, in their LAST big show, delighted the crowds with jumps and dancing! Cassie did a fine job of training and deserves credit for this wonderful show!

Cassie was now ready to accept the admiration for which she yearned, and to feel the pride of growing up and a therapy well done.

Growing up is a bittersweet experience. Children need to have both sides of the progression understood and accepted. If they are pushed out, they go forward on unsure footing, ever liable to fall back. If held back, their future looms bleaker, scarier, and less likely to be entered. Every child, however young, has a past that she idealizes and for which she longs. Parents need to respect the child's love and mourning for that past, be it person, place, thing, or idea.

---

*This description of growing up was given to me by Murray Cohen, Ph.D.

XI

For Shame

"Conscience—the thing that aches when everything [else] is feeling good."

—Unknown*

Sex fascinated Joshua. Whenever his parents went out, he flew to the basement to pore devotedly over old copies of his father's *Playboy* magazines. And when they were home, he instead riffled through the family library, even the literary classics, to hunt down sexy passages. His pleasure was not complete, however, for he dreaded that someone might come downstairs unannounced and discover him. To guard against that nightmare, he kept a copy of *Pilgrim's Progress* on the floor beside him, carefully propped opened so that he could quickly assume the identity of an avid, wholesome reader. "I wonder if it looks strange that I'm always reading that book," he sheepishly worried. "I really should read it one of these days in case they ever ask me what it's about."

His interest in sex did not wane when he was outside of the home. Trips to the mall were opportunities to peek at new and different risqué materials, which he hid inside of more

*In Prochnow, H. (ed.) *Speaker's Handbook of Epigrams and Witticisms.* New York: Harper & Brothers, 1955.

innocent-looking books, such as one on Mexican cooking. I silently chuckled, imagining his nude centerfolds shielded by a recipe for hot tamales. Even in disguise he could not escape his lustful bent; his culinary cover was as hot and spicy as the underlying treasures. "And when people walk by," he complained, "I feel kinda like I'm burning up inside. I'm not sure, but I think I turn bright red. They must know I'm getting those funny feelings when they see me on fire." He worried, with good reason, that his embarrassed flush gave himself away. After all, what in a food recipe is embarrassing? His blush, his own scarlet letter, advertised and condemned his crime well before any other judge could do so.

Images of my own adolescent sexual curiosity, predominantly pursued in an attic rather than a cellar, flashed by. I recalled running to the dictionary—something I did not do for vocabulary homework—to look up words like *nunnery, teat, pudendum,* and *coital*. I might not have known a word's exact meaning, but I uncannily sensed whether it held erotic potential. Most anything French, which for some reason I equated with sex, had excited me. I intimately related to what my new patient described.

Joshua really loved sex, or at least he loved thinking about and looking for it. Of course he did. He was healthy and eleven and his parents had raised him with loving care—the very same reasons Joshua feared sex. He feared it would ruin his character, stunt his growth, drive him to commit illegal carnal acts, cause him to lose his parents' love and admiration, and ultimately result in a total loss of control and insanity. "But," as he appraised, "nothing too serious to worry about."

From his first hour with me, I knew I was in for a treat. Here was a very bright, articulate, and witty boy who dearly wanted help with his great inner distress. "Ya gotta help me with this," he pleaded. "Ya gotta keep me outa that basement. I can't help myself." After a moment's pause he continued. "Hey, I know what I'll do. I'll just tell you that I'll never go down to that basement again. I'll just promise you. That way, before I go down, I'll remember that the next time I come here I'll have to admit the truth to you. Yeah, that's it. *You can be my conscience."* Joshua again left me room to comment, but I had nothing to say. "Don't you have any advice that can keep me from going down there?" he asked nervously.

"Good luck," I responded without jest. I knew well that there was nothing more to offer yet.

"You mean I'm stuck being sex-crazed?"

I waited easily, for this was not a sex-crazed boy. Sex-crazed boys talk about sex and do not, as did Joshua, experience and talk about the anxiety and guilt of it all. No, his was not the talk of a wild child at risk of even mild sexual misbehavior, but the talk of a responsible and moral boy who hated himself for what was happening to his mind and body. Although he had plenty of good conscience—more than enough to be a good boy and good man—he felt hard-pressed. In a pubertal imbalance of power, the little cartoonish devil on his right shoulder had grown into a more formidable opponent for the angel on his left.

"You don't think I can just forget about it?"

I shook my head from side to side. Unquestionably he could not.

"I had a sneaking suspicion I was stuck with it," he replied with apparently no surprise. I mused to myself how well that two-worded phrase, "sneaking suspicion," captured the broader conflict he'd just laid out for me, the sneaking curiosity and the suspicious guilt it evoked. Like everyone else's, Joshua's unconscious seldom, if ever, took a break. Before leaving, he stopped at the doorway to make sure he hadn't promised me to stay out of the basement, and sighed with relief when I confirmed that he had not. He incidentally added that he liked my office, because it—being decorated in "one of his favorite colors, drab"—relaxed him.

I reflected upon Joshua's plea for my help in curbing his impulses and wondered how society at large might view my passive acceptance of his curiosity and desire as normal, healthy, and within his own authority. Poor Freud, I thought, had been so misunderstood. Caught up in his inestimably pioneering discovery of the powerful influence that fantasy itself wielded on the psyche and the body, he unfortunately overly deemphasized his original (and in itself overly generalized) belief that all neuroses stem from childhood sexual abuse. Embracing neither promiscuity nor perversion, he was entirely an advocate of responsible sexual behavior. But he

did not view external control as the answer. He believed that
civilization's only hope was self-control: who, realistically, is
available to oversee every blind alley, parked car, dormitory
room, and suburban home? No, Freud believed that a person
can manage his or her own sexual impulses only by fully recognizing, understanding, and coming to terms with them.
Consider the prevailing medical and societal attitude to which
Freud's gentler suggestions appealed and by which they were
violently assailed, as in this treatise on masturbation written
by a London physician of the time:

> In general the best attitude to adopt to the practice is
> that it is a deplorable breach of manners, that it is
> disgusting like nose picking. It is right that we should
> endeavor to provoke in the child a sensitive aesthetic
> sense which is offended by the act. . . . [If] change of
> scene and new and suitable company [fail to] divert the
> child from exclusive concentration on the ever-present
> temptation, apparatus for restraint [may be needed]. . . .
> If the thighs are rubbed together at night . . . adopt
> bracelets of webbing worn above the knees and carrying
> between them a light metal bar. . . . If it is practised by
> manipulation the hands must be confined. At the worst,
> confinement in poroplastic armor, as for spinal caries or
> severe poliomyelitis, may be necessary. But whatever
> device . . . if possible the child should in no way connect
> the apparatus with its real object, the prevention of the
> [masturbatory] act. . . . It is worth while taking endless
> trouble to convince a little child that his legs are so
> crooked or his back so one-sided that the apparatus has
> to be worn. . . . All [of the child's] interest and attention
> must be centered upon some imaginary complaint while
> the real enemy sinks out of sight.*

I wondered how many children had been raised by these
methods, and with what horrid consequences? I also questioned whether these methods had not been some other form
of sexual abuse, or at least an excuse for inflicting excessive
and inhumane discipline in the name of morality. One had

*In Cameron, H.C. *The Nervous Child*. London: Oxford University Press,
1924, pp. 97–99.

to wonder further about the sexual health of someone who had so severely feared masturbation as to resort to such punishment. This brief excursion in history rejuvenated my conviction that my purpose was not to tame Joshua, but, paraphrasing and masculinizing one analyst's words, to enable him to become master of his own sexual thoughts and life.*

The circumstances of Joshua's referral were unusual. He was an all-A student well liked by his teachers. At home he was a good son to his stably married and well-educated parents, and a good brother to his seven-year-old sister. Despite some social discomfort, he had good friends. The strong work ethic, honesty, and fairness to others that he so admired in his father were established firmly in his own character. The facts of his life—combined with his readily observable warmth, deep interest in and caring for people and the world, and rich sense of humor—suggested that he was a rather well-adjusted boy. His parents brought him on another psychologist's recommendation, primarily because he seemed tense and unable fully to enjoy his many accomplishments. It did not take long for me to see that their perceptions were accurate.

Joshua was anxious, almost as anxious as I imagined I was at age eleven. Unfortunately, for an anxious person, beginning therapy becomes just one more thing about which to be anxious. What if I "probed his mind and found him to be crazy"? What if he said things that upset his parents or hurt my feelings? He was very pleased that the waiting room radio made just enough noise so that his mother could not hear our conversation. "That's perfect. She doesn't know what I'm saying, but she can tell that I'm talking." Joshua explained that by talking, he meant working. After all, he was here for therapy, not to have a good time. I did not bother to tell him that our time together was for whatever he chose to do, for I would have been wasting words. If he really believed the time to be his own, he'd not have needed my help.

From the very start Joshua feared he would break something in the office. When his hand or back brushed against a

*In Sharpe, E.F. *Collected Papers of Psycho-analysis.* 1950. Reprint. New York: Bruner-Mazel, 1978, p. 4.

wall, he would jump back as if jolted by an electric fence. He chastised the Boston Museum of Art for their exhibition of a tall blue vase, portrayed in a print that hung on my wall. "Don't they even care about it? Anyone could just kick it over by mistake." And upon my accidentally bumping the desk and prematurely toppling a domino tower we had built, Joshua dived to the floor. "I thought it was all over," he confessed with relief after checking that the desk's protective glass was not broken. Anything but a destructive person, he feared being one.

Conflicts around competition preoccupied the early months of Joshua's therapy, as did our games—which he invited me to play—of cutthroat dominoes, the rules of which mandated that we play rough, tough, and "take no prisoners." As much as he hated to lose, he was fearful that his victory would make me mad, dislike him, or think that he was greedy; in his own words, he also wondered who'd "want to get therapy from a loser, anyway?" and thus found winning no bargain, either. Sometimes he successfully averted winning by playing badly. When he could not, he vigorously excused my loss as a forgivable result of his better luck, my leniency, or the distracting demands of being a therapist. Joshua related all of these feelings to the cribbage and word games that he loved to share with his father.

To illustrate better how he felt, Joshua built a "competitometer." Lower readings indicated that he was bored or playing an unworthy opponent; higher ones brought "WORRY" and "PANIC" that he might ultimately lose and become a "FAILURE." Only the middle ranks of the scale, "INTEREST" and "CHALLENGE," were tolerable to him. They represented the optimum condition in which two equally matched competitors raced neck and neck, ideally to a dead-heat finish. Joshua could neither win nor lose without losing.

This tentative balance between closeness and competition also pervaded his classroom life; he wanted to be popular and a good friend, yet also enjoyed being one of the smarter pupils. His aspirations—wanting both to be outstandingly special and to belong—often clashed. He liked being called on and praised for his work, yet sometimes other kids seemed to like him more when he was not so successful. Rewards based on academic achievement felt rather precarious to him. "What happens if I lose my intellect?" he pondered. Joshua wanted to be liked for who he was, not because of good things and in spite of bad things—though he also wanted the good things noted and celebrated. He viewed this revelation as further proof of his greedy wish to have everything, to have "his cake and eat it, too."

Joshua began his twelfth session by telling me that "nothing horrible had happened that week," and so he had no idea what to do or talk about.

"Is therapy only for horrible things?" I asked.

He unequivocally replied that it was, and compared being in therapy with riding in a taxicab. "How can I talk about happy things and brag about myself when the meter is running and my parents are paying the bill?"

The hairs on my neck stiffened at his metaphor. I hadn't been so stung since another teenage boy, whose mother chose to pay weekly in cash, posted a handmade sign outside my office door—"PROTECT YOUR VALUABLES! PICKPOCKET IN VICINITY." I disparagingly thought about a local famed therapist who, rumor had it, charged by the minute, and was chilled at the thought that my own analyst possibly could ever do that to me; however, I soon caught on to myself. I was trying not to feel anything like a therapist who charged by the minute, who did this for the money. But I did charge for my time and therapy. Although I had chosen this work for many additional reasons, being a therapist was my livelihood; it paid the mortgage and bought groceries. To leapfrog over Joshua's concerns—to tell him to say just what he liked and not worry about the cost, or that money concerns were too dirty or trivial for therapy, or was a matter just between me and his parents—would have been wrong, unfair, and selfishly intended to lick my own wounds. The treatment contract that we shared was based upon payment of money, and that issue, vital to every course of therapy, could not be denied.

"Your parents don't want you spending your expensive time in here bragging or talking about happiness?"

"Well, not really. They told me to talk about whatever I want. It's just a sense that I get."

"You mean, *you* don't think you should be enjoying yourself here?"

His face wrinkled up all over. "Gee, I guess it's sort of up to me, isn't it?" Joshua then talked about birthdays, other children's birthdays, belittling friends and his sister, Elise, for enjoying them, while slowly recalling how much he missed his own. Insistent that he was not dropping hints, he timidly admitted that he'd like a party. "Don't have to get me any-thing special," he volunteered. "And don't worry about the snack. I'll eat anything."

"Anything?"

"Yeah, anything. Just about anything will be okay. Actually, anything will be great!"

"So a cookie would be okay?"

"Sure, anything. A cookie'd be fine, but, uh, would it be okay if I made a suggestion, just a suggestion?"

"Sure."

"Cupcakes are okay, too."

"Cupcakes?"

"Yeah, any kind of cupcake would be good."

"Any kind?"

"Any kind *you* like. Likc, you know those chocolate ones with the chocolate frosting and white squiggles on top? I think they may have white filling, too." With similar congeniality he gave a blanket okay to any beverage while spontaneously endorsing apple juice in well-refrigerated twelve-ounce cans. It was a little frightening to imagine what the menu planning might have been like had Joshua thought that he cared what we had for a snack.

The day before his next session, I bought a cupcake and juice, but I forgot to bring them to his hour—perhaps be-cause I was running late; more likely, because I don't usually offer snacks and had misgivings about doing so. I'd witnessed too many children too busy eating to lament their unfulfilled birthday fantasies and realities. Nevertheless, I'd agreed to cater this event.

As soon as he entered the room, I recognized my oversight. While Joshua looked for signs of his party, I deliberated and decided not to say anything yet. A premature explanation would have denied his deserved reaction. How angry can a child be at a grown-up who is profusely apologizing? No, I had goofed and my punishment was to wait it out with him. I'd eventually acknowledge my failing, once he'd had ample opportunity to feel and respond to it. Joshua said nothing about the missing snack, but proceeded to berate teachers who forget to bring in corrected papers and parents who break promises. At my wondering aloud whether he'd known any therapists who were forgetful, he said that he didn't, but that he could understand some lesser kids being mad at me— but for what he did not say.

"What might those children want to do?" I asked, simply accepting the stated anger rather than again pushing him to name its source.

"Oh, gosh." He tried to slow the fantasy that my question stirred. Having scanned the room, he postulated a mousetrap kind of scheme triggered by a fastball thrown at the wall over my desk that ultimately would shatter the windows and de- molish the furniture. But he abruptly stopped his gleeful de- scription of the escalating damage, fearful that it could result in "someone's personal injury." When I queried who that someone might be, he replied that I possibly could lose con- trol of my rage and kill the child who'd destroyed my office. In his usual good form he assured me of his firm belief that I would never commit murder intentionally, but only if I could not help myself.

When finding his favorite snack waiting at his next session, Joshua gobbled it up. Cupcake and juice went everywhere, over him and the office. They may have tasted good going down, but not for long. "Now I've shown you my true colors," he said. "I knew it wasn't worth it. No party ever is." As a self- imposed repentance for the greed and selfishness that Joshua feared his exuberant enjoyment of the snack had shown, he spent the remainder of our celebration cleaning up every crumb, so that his family and other children would not be made to feel envious over a party they had missed.

I wished there had been magic words to make the good feelings more palatable to him: "But it's your day, Joshua. Enjoy!" But he did not need my consolation. My job was to help him understand what interfered with his pleasure, and to help soften the stern internal court that relentlessly sum- moned every one of his thoughts and deeds for a hearing.

"Is it hard to enjoy good things?" I asked.

"All the time," he sadly confirmed.

Joshua's feelings concerning his mother's help with school- work were no simpler. " 'It's wonderful, but . . .' she always says. She always has a but." His mother, whose verbal skills and concern for his schooling made her the perfect literary adviser, habitually reviewed his writing with an editor's red pencil.

"Gee, she just grabs your work and marks it all up?" As one who writes, I empathically could feel my blood pressure rise at the vision of his mother's unsolicited critiquing.

"Not exactly, I kinda ask her to," he responded in a hand-over-mouth, I'm-not-sure-I-really-want-you-to-hear-this, delivery. It turned out that he more than kinda asked. He sometimes demanded, sometimes late on the last night before his project was due.

"Well, if you don't like her criticism, why do you keep asking her for it?"

"Why can't she just say she loves it, that it's the greatest thing ever written?"

"Oh, you don't really want her help?"

Again he mumbled, "Not exactly. She's really good at writing and makes my papers better."

Ah, the plot thickened even as it clarified. "You want her help, but you don't like it."

"Exactly," he stated in no uncertain terms. He wanted both unconditional admiration and constructive criticism, even if they were absolutely incompatible.

Joshua considered himself to be the guardian of his parents' perfectionist hopes, and estimated that his failure, should it ever occur, surely would be too much reality and disappointment for his mother and father to endure—a perception tested during his school's annual spelling bee. Joshua had done well the previous year, and confidently anticipated even greater success this time around. He spoke little about the first level of competition at his school, but dwelled on regional competitions and the eventual finals scheduled for the White House. "What about the poor kids who'll lose, who won't go as far as me?" he sympathized. Losing in a relatively early round on a relatively simple word saved him from much more of that worry. He was so fearful that his winning the contest would make him the target of others' envious wrath, he misspelled a word that he knew well. Joshua, while complaining plenty about his mother's overemphasis on the bee and on grades in general, initially denied any upset; upon my inquiry, however, I discovered that he was also quite disappointed in himself over losing. I had assumed that he was, indeed, for he'd all but booked his hotel reservations for Washington, D.C.

For several therapy hours Joshua examined who it was that really cared too much about his schoolwork, he or his parents. He decided that all three of them were confused, wanting him to enjoy learning, earn exceptional grades, and not worry about them. But he recognized that it was hard to care very much about something, then not care if it doesn't turn out well. He subsequently began wondering whether his mother and father had caught grief about school from their parents, and he concluded that no one escapes the good and bad influences of one's mother and father—a wisdom that many adults never attain.

As usually happens in psychotherapy, Joshua's feelings for me changed—growing deeper, more complicated, less exclusively agreeable, more tangible. His expressed wish that his mother could be calmer and "as good at looking bored" as I was proved to be an indirect complaint, for many times he wanted me to be more emotionally available and responsive, like her. As do many patients, he originally valued my neutrality and reservation of judgment, but over time he felt that I didn't even care enough to criticize him.

I was to disappoint him further, when Joshua rushed into his hour and was joyfully setting up a soldier toy hide-and-go-seek game that he'd created over the weekend. For over thirty minutes he worked earnestly, talking little and then only to confess the guilt he felt over playing (and not discussing his problems). Although he replied "nothing" to my query as to what prevented him from doing both, he dejectedly picked up the green men and returned them to the toy chest.

"What happened?" I asked, in a fog as to why he'd given up the play that had seemed so important to him.

"What do you mean, what happened?"

"You were so excited about your idea, but you gave it up and now look very unhappy."

"Oh, I'm not sure if I was bored or just too excited."

"Too excited?"

"Yeah. I really should talk. You were right. Boy, I don't know what got into me. See, this is what I've been trying to tell you. I get too carried away with games and fun. I was just having too much of a good time, too much fun." Though a guilt-over-pleasure theme was clear, it was not until he told stories of his homemade cards and presents seeming to go unappreciated that I fully understood.

"You brought me a new game today—a game you'd made up on your own, just for us."

Joshua tried not to cry. He nodded. "It's okay. Talking's more important. That's what we're here for."

I explained that, in fact, his playing was just as important, but that I could see why he thought it wasn't, especially the way I'd behaved. I wondered myself why I indirectly (through my question) had suggested that he talk while he play rather than simply having noted his conflict about playing. As soon as I saw his mother in the waiting room, I recognized what had prompted my blunder. I worried that his mother, hearing that we were not talking, would be displeased with me as her son's therapist. Unresolved feelings from my childhood— fearing that I'd be seen as shirking my duties—had blurred my view of Joshua's feelings and had led to my unconscious, disruptive comment and failure to accept his gift graciously.

Over the next two months Joshua grew more and more upset. He harshly rebuked himself for having those "funny feelings again." A television show about parental sexual abuse had saddened and infuriated him. "Sex is just no good!" he preached. Noting the ghastly things it could do, he decided that he'd be better off "just to stay home and never grow up and get sexy." And being alone, formerly a welcomed chance for his extracurricular reading, increasingly bothered him. He worried that his parents might become so fed up that they would leave him or enroll him in a faraway private school, the latter, he assumed, seeming more probable, because his parents would choose the more responsible alternative.

I marveled at the power of his fantasy. With a much younger or less healthy child, I might have challenged his perception and pointed out how dearly I knew he was loved at home. But that was not called for. His perceptions of others were somewhat distorted, based on the psychic upheaval early ad-olescence and psychoanalytic therapy were inducing. Al-though he sensitively felt his parents' conflicted feelings, what he felt more vividly was his own self-hatred and horrid fear

that becoming a sexually mature person would result in something terrible.

If anything, Joshua's feelings about himself and all that he
loved were ambivalent and complex. So when he broke the
news that the family dog had died, I did not offer any prompt
condolences. Nor did I sympathize with how sad he must feel,
for I did not know what he felt. I just listened. Joshua eulo-
gized Ferdinand as "kinda funny, stupid, wild, sluggish," and
more a vicious tyrant than a protective watchdog. He told
how, according to family lore, the puppy's lunging at his crib
twelve years ago had inspired his first spoken words: "Down,
boy." "I just wished I'd given Ferd a good enough pat to make
his tail wag before I left for school. I patted him there after
he died, but it was like rubber," Joshua rued. "It used to be
the softest part of him."

"You didn't get to say good-bye."

Joshua teared, but instead of directly responding to my
words, he described his parents' grief. "What really worried
me," he admitted, "was that the shock could kill my mother,
that my mother could die. That's what worried me." Losing
his dog had stirred up worries about losing people, especially
his mother. If I had expressed too much sympathy for Ferd,
which would have been easy given that I recently had lost my
own dog, Joshua might have felt uncomfortable telling me his
genuine feelings, that he was more concerned about someone
who lived than the animal that had died.

Joshua was growing up. While becoming more aware of his
wish to be a little boy, his interest and capacity as a junior
high student continued to develop. He campaigned for class
president, successfully refused drugs and cigarettes, and
joined the track team. But he wasn't rushing to throw out his
"kidness," either. He devised wonderfully nasty (as yet not
implemented) pranks for his sister, and ate an entire tray of
frozen orange juice sticks that his mother had made especially
for him. Joshua took great and comparable pride from all of
these contrasting achievements.

He was looking much less anxious, too, and living with considerably more zest than he had when we first met. He par-
ticipated in regular school activities—sports, theater, student
government, and musical productions—as well as special programs, such as interscholastic college bowls and student ex-

changes; he also felt more confident, more popular, more willing to compete and more satisfied with his life. His slightly fallen grades did not trouble him, and he defied his parents a bit—in a respectful and kindly manner, of course. He'd even not so accidentally cracked my footstool in two. "Here." With the faintest smile he calmly handed me the unequal halves. "I think it's broken. I hope you can fix it." Given this impressive progress, Joshua, his parents, and I all agreed that it was time to stop treatment and that three months would be ample for a therapeutically proper good-bye.

The question of whether to work or play, which dogged Joshua at every turn of his therapy and life, heightened once the termination date had been set. He played earlier in each session, harder, longer, and with greater enjoyment. Although his playing still evoked discomforting pride, he now could express it in words rather than by avoiding the toys that brought him so much pleasure. Anticipating their absence, he more acutely noticed the room and playthings—their colors, textures, functions and even smells. He recounted with frustrated regret the time he had wasted not playing, and now realized that he had been the only one holding him back from that fun.

Like most children, Joshua wondered about the terms of our ending; however, unlike most, he was willing to talk about it. "Why continue to meet weekly, then just stop?" he asked. "Why not wind down? I could come every other week for a few months, then every month for a few years, and then once a year for the rest of my life." He surmised on his own that my more definitive strategy would intensify the impact of our good-bye. "I guess it's good to end abruptly to prepare for when someone leaves or dies fast. But," Joshua posed optimistically, "I guess winding down slowly would better get me ready for when someone leaves or dies in a wind-down kind of way." He also thought that we should meet for longer and longer sessions to make up for the time we'd be losing, the times we'd never see each other in the future.

Therapy was getting harder for both of us. As we approached our final hour, I wished more than ever to give Joshua snacks, to share information about myself, and to console him actively with kind words and hugs. But it was not in his best interests to get more and more of me just before losing me completely. He needed to grieve for me in order to be able to live life fully while enduring the inevitable, continual deprivations and separations of human relationships. And in order to grieve for me, he had to lose me. He could not feel alone as long as I talked and "did" for him—and so I waited longer to respond to questions, to offer assistance and to comfort pains. Paradoxically, I had to give Joshua the space to feel alone so that he would have that experience to examine while he still had me and therapy. To spend our final time together avoiding the reality of the coming loneliness would leave him out in the cold, alone with his minimally resolved feelings of aloneness.

Joshua did not like being alone any more than I enjoyed leaving him that way. He suddenly saw danger everywhere: dramatically describing the great risk of his becoming a drug addict, the murdered witness in a drug-dealing trial, the victim of gang violence, and an academic dropout—unless, of course, a deadly childhood disease didn't take him first. His underlying message was twofold. Overtly he felt frightened and vulnerable at the prospect of ending therapy; covertly he was trying to keep me. Having calculated that his therapy was ending because he'd made such gains, maybe, he hoped, it would be continued should his life become a shambles. And Joshua was testing that premise within the safe confines of therapy, unlike less fortunate adolescents left to search for attention, caring, and personal definition on the streets.

Joshua, as do most children and adults, viewed life according to zero-sum economics, under the assumption that resources—gold, oil, and love—exist in limited quantities. Caring seemed to him as much a commodity as pork bellies and jelly beans; someone's taking more meant that someone else had to take less. As was to be expected, Joshua's younger sister was his chief competitor in the "care market" they shared. Her class took better field trips, and she was given better toys, nicer clothes, and more attention by almost everyone—or so he assessed. Her special Sunday morning time with their father particularly irked Joshua. He judged that relatives, even a favorite aunt, preferred Elise, mostly because she was "cute, little, and *a girl.*" When he noticed that his school's cafeteria charged more than Elise's did for the same items, he resentfully decided that his lunch money was directly subsidizing the "bargain-basement prices" she enjoyed.

Up to this time he had made few references to my having a family, but his sentiments for his sister were now being transferred to my own child, whom he'd seen being wheeled in his stroller. Joshua rationalized that I could not buy him better birthday snacks because I needed the money to take care of and buy toys for my own children. An unfamiliar car in my driveway evoked his fantasy that "contented mothers were drinking tea in the living room while their babies slept peacefully beside them." His jealousy of and anger at my young son were palpable, yet he vehemently and spontaneously insisted that he did not feel those ways. Watching crows fly by the window, he warned me that vultures are known to kidnap small children. He asked, repeatedly and out of the blue, "Why would I ever want to hurt your baby?" when no one, least of all me, had suggested that he did. Joshua knew that in a couple of short months he would be losing what my child would not—me. What a bind he was in—both loving me and wanting my child, a child he knew I loved, out of his way.

Not until one of our last sessions did the basic mystery come to light. Joshua, who'd maintained his high grades despite liking school less, grumbled about teachers who assign too much homework. He reminisced about nursery school, where instead of being required to do homework, he received approval merely for wearing clothing of a certain color or spelling his name with toothpicks.

"Those were the days?"

"Yeah," he dreamily affirmed, "I think you stop making nostalgia at about five."

"You stop making memories?"

"No, you keep making memories," he corrected with assurance, "but it's no longer very good nostalgia."

"Gee," I pursued, overriding the temptation to let the discussion end with his pithy comment, "did anything happen when you were about five that ruined memories?"

"No, nothing much." Joshua was subdued. "No, nothing much happened at all. The only thing that happened was Elise was born." He looked at the wall as if in a trance. "She's lucky."

"Because?"

"She's still kind of a baby. Yeah, she's kind of the family baby."

"Those *really were* the days."

"Yeah," he sadly agreed, "they sure were."

The following week, while I was updating the magazines in the waiting room Joshua arrived, looking as downtrodden as I'd ever seen him, followed by a bubbly little girl and Mrs. Andrews, who carried a large straw basket covered by a red cloth napkin. Joshua politely introduced me to his sister, then walked into the office. His mother cheerfully told me she'd brought cookies, lemonade, coloring books, and a cribbage board. "Don't you worry about us," she said. "We'll just have ourselves a little picnic out here."

Joshua sat down and tried to express what he was feeling, but he could not. Frustrated with himself, he took out the army men. "Maybe these will help," he mumbled. Halfheartedly he arranged the infantrymen into sheltered fighting positions so that I could see only the tips of their little rifles sticking out from under his seat cushion and behind the chair legs. Having second thoughts about his initially designating himself as his force's general—"That's kind of selfish to want to be the leader, don't you think?"—he promptly decommissioned himself. Every now and then we could hear his mother and sister having sufficient fun to transcend the soundproofing. Trying to distract himself from these disturbing intruders, Joshua rather obsessively wiggled a soldier into a small hole underneath the desktop. As he heard each sound of joy from the reception area, he winced and pushed harder on the figure.

Suddenly he panicked. "He's stuck. Oh, God. He's stuck. Now I've done it. I'm sorry, Dr. Bromfield. Don't worry, I'll buy you a new desk." Joshua ran to his chair. "I'm sorry, really I am."

Having given him a few minutes to collect himself, I asked if he wanted me to help him get the man out; sometimes sharing in the repair can help a child overcome his guilt. But he declined, stating that he'd done enough damage for one day. I unbent a paper clip and easily retrieved the piece.

"Whew!" Joshua looked as if the weight of the solar system

had been taken off his shoulders, but that he still carried the earth and a few other planets.

"What is it, Joshua?" I asked quietly.

"I miss it."

Though I knew what he missed, I asked to be sure: "What do you miss?"

"Life before Elise. Sometimes—no, this is a terrible, terrible thing." I waited many moments. "Sometimes I've imagined life without her or wished that she was never born." He paused for several moments more. "Sometimes—now, don't take this the wrong way, because I'd never really do anything—but sometimes, sometimes I think *I* deserve to be dead. Not that I'd ever commit, you know"—his voice and eyebrows raised together—"suicide." He was close to tears. "I don't know why I feel so bad. Why am I hating myself?"

"Are you sure you don't know?" I obviously suspected that he did.

"No. Do you?"

"I have a hunch. Do you want to hear it?"

He nodded that he did.

"What would it have taken to have a life without Elise or for her never to have been born?"

His eyes teared up. "You think I'm a murderer?"

"Of course I don't, and you're not." He was truly horrified that I could have such a bad thought about him. We sat in deadly stillness.

"Is it possible—no, this is terrible."

I tilted my head to encourage him to go on.

"Is it possible that when Elise was still in my mother, I wished she would've—" His voice gurgled over the final word, though I knew what it was.

I nodded gravely.

"That doesn't make me a terrible person, does it?"

"It doesn't make you one, but *you feel very much like one.*" Though Joshua was far from letting himself off scot-free, he had confessed his fantasized crime and appeared much relieved for having done so.

By the session's end he smiled and talked about his upcoming school play. "By the way," he asked as he stood up to leave, "I wonder why all this came up today." Before I could respond, one of Elise's delighted squeals pierced the wall. Knowing that we shared the same thought, it was our turn to laugh.

Joshua's love for his father infiltrated and predominated what remained of his good-bye. "How can I be so upset about losing you," he asked seriously, his attachment to me making him feel like a traitor, "when I have a father of my own whom I like and love?" He feared that his desire, of which he had grown aware, for his mother to favor him over both Elise and his dad would result in his father's retaliatory refusal to love him anymore. Needless to say, that fear primarily said more about his own sense of guilt than about his father. To his great relief, he was learning that much of what made adolescence and sexually maturing so frightening was actually old stuff: worry that his wishes to be his mother's favorite (and father's, too) would lead to his losing both and being all alone.

Although in his final hour Joshua reviewed all of the benefits he attributed to therapy, he identified two gains as the most satisfying. He could break things, like my stool, without hating himself; and he could catch peeks at magazines or romance novels without dreading that he'd be caught. "Oh, gosh," he sighed, "tears are coming. I think the lump in my throat has reached my eyes. I didn't want this to be like one of those movie endings when I'm crying hysterically, telling you how I always loved this and then drive away as we wave to each other and I cry all the way home."

I observed that it sounded more like an ending from real life.

While he buttoned up his jacket to leave, he whimsically wondered whether we might continue his therapy by mail. He soon nixed that idea as impractical because emotions tend to change more quickly than letters can be delivered.

Adolescence makes enormous demands. Teenagers confront their maturing bodies and a constant barrage of hormonal, academic, and social pressures. In no other phase of life are the opportunities for growth and confusion, humiliation and despair, so pervasive. No less burdened, parents walk the tightropes that their children string for them: hold but don't baby; admire but don't embarrass; guide but don't control; release but don't abandon. The list of dichotomous impossibilities goes on. The only certainty upon which battle-scarred parents can rely is that this struggle, which may seem endless and to no good end, is needed to complete the work of childhood. It allows children to leave, become themselves, and find others to love and love back; and it allows parents to allow their children to do so.

Ending

XII

No Secret Recipe

"It is no child's play."

—Geoffrey Chaucer, *The Merchant's Tale*

Are there specific personal qualities that make somebody especially suited or unfit to be a child therapist? Are his present life circumstances and motivations for being a therapist relevant to his work? Is it preferable that his childhood was either wonderful or traumatic? Should he be a parent? Should he be in therapy himself? To paraphrase an old nursery rhyme, what are child therapists made of?

One can assume that a child therapist must hold some basic warmth and good feeling for children. Many able child therapists—having (as I did) volunteered at special schools, been camp counselors, or coached youth sports—know prior to entering the field that they enjoy being and working with children. However, I am somewhat wary of those who speak too much of their love of children, especially when that love is contrasted with a lesser devotion to adults. "Why," I ask, "do you so prefer children to grown-ups?" Responses that they are simply nicer or more fun concern me; those suggesting that children haven't yet lost their innocence, been spoiled, turned rotten, or become men or women really concern me. Children often wish to please those whom they love or fear, and may appear angelic as they sleep, but they are no more saintly than their parents are possessed by the devil. How can someone who prefers to treat children because of their alleged child-like purity, help them to mature if he fears they will only become more like the grown-ups he dislikes or he feels have gone bad?

A therapist who brags of having only good thoughts about children is usually just unaware or unaccepting of the possibility that he could do otherwise. Unable to admit his inevitable anger with child patients to himself, he may reveal it in other ways—such as unconsciously demanding loving and nice behavior in return for his own. He may find that his patients, in contrast to those of other therapists, seldom give him a hard time, and often flatter or bring gifts. The refusal to see his occasional, only human aggression toward child patients—who out of their own psychological condition may insult, devalue, threaten, reject, and not get better—can ironically lead to an even more hostile act: the therapist's rejection of the child's true feelings. In my supervisory experience, I have found that those who proclaim their special affection for children are no more effective as therapists than those who do not, or those who simply treat all people, regardless of age, with care and respect.

How playful does a child therapist need to be? He must play sufficiently well to engage children and show that he genuinely appreciates the play and toys that excite them. Since play is a principal mode for children's communication, he must be able to think and speak that language, to query and comment in its terms, especially in the idiosyncratic dialect spoken by each child's play. And not to be minimized, he must himself find play interesting or he will soon grow weary of his patients and profession.

Being too good a player can be a liability, too. A therapist who plays too vigorously or too well may overpower the child. A child whose parents did not play responsively with her may need a therapist who does; yet she does not require an extraordinarily robust playmate as much as she needs someone who can use play primarily to confirm and enhance her self-understanding. By too easily assuming direction of the play, even if at the child's invitation, a therapist runs the risk of expressing his personal needs to the neglect of the patient's. Excessively active playfulness in a therapist may indicate a tendency to find others' play less stimulating or a wish to avoid uncomfortable lapses in play—lapses, analogous to the talking patient's silences, in which the child's longings and resentments often hide, and which must be endured, acknowledged, and explored.

How smart does a child therapist have to be? He needs to be quick enough to know what's happening, yet he does not have to be smarter than or even as smart as his patients (though he'd better be able to recognize and cope when parents and children challenge the adequacy of his intellect or academic credentials). Several years ago, early in their daughter's therapy, a husband and wife asked why I didn't have more diplomas, citing another therapist whose entire wall was covered. Only after I'd acknowledged to myself my slighted feelings and indulged in a fantasy of wallpapering the walls with certificates of study could I hear and address their underlying anxiety as to whether I was good enough to help their child, and their arrogant way of expressing that worry— a manner that they eventually confessed had lost them many friends and alienated their child's teachers. More recently, a second family probed to know my IQ, wondering if I was brainy enough to deal with their genius son. What soon surfaced, without my having to reveal anything about myself, was their thoroughly unfounded fear that they themselves were too dumb to parent such a gifted child. The ineptitude they suspected in me perfectly mirrored the ineptitude they unfoundedly saw in themselves. The successful outcome of that therapy was their coming to see IQ scores as numbers of limited meaning, telling relatively little about their son, his needs, and their capacity to meet them.

A child therapist does not have to be a math whiz, but he needs to know language well enough not only to hear what children say, but to respond in ways within the child's emotional and cognitive grasp. Think about this comment made by a therapist to a five-year-old boy following a disruption in his play: "The big father horse first ran and jumped with the little horse, but he suddenly went off to play with the mother horse. You then made the little horse run away and hide in the barn. I wonder if the big horse's going to spend time with another horse made the little horse mad. Is that why he ran to hide in the barn? And is that the reason that you stopped

playing and won't talk to me now? Are you feeling too mad
to play? Is that what's going on right now with you?"

That mouthful, which would in all likelihood exceed what
the boy could follow or retain, may say less than the more
economical "The little horse isn't the only one that's gone off
to feel bad" (implying that by withdrawing, so had the patient), or the even plainer "He wants his dad to play with
him" (as did the boy, and which is why they both ran off
angry). The shorter, sweeter wordings are better geared to the
child's language level and more sharply spotlight the emotional meaning of his play. Moreover, the more succinctly the
therapist speaks, the less time he spends planning what he
will say next, and the more time he can dedicate to understanding the child's leaps of fantasy.

The child therapist must appreciate the gradations of language and how to regulate them. "It sounds as if you might
be experiencing a loss"—more tentative and emotionally
weaker than "You're feeling sad about your grandmother's
death"—might fit an older child who is intolerant of the
slightest feeling; whereas the more potent "You miss her terribly" could feel more empathic to a child more aware of her
immense grief.

Familiarity with both the king's and the cook's English, the
language spoken at school and on the street, is invaluable.
Therapists do not need to converse habitually in slang or with
profanity in order to connect with patients, but they must be
comfortable with earthy speech and to know when to exploit
its powers. Sometimes only strong words can capture strong
feelings. Moreover, a therapist who is offended by the names
of body parts and bodily functions will be of no help to the
child who struggles to understand and accept in himself the
real things—the glands, precious fluids, and carnal acts—to
which those terms refer.

A child therapist does not require sheer intellect as much
as he needs to think flexibly, to see the concrete and the
abstract simultaneously. If two colored pencils fighting over
a sharpener made me think of nothing but two pencils fighting over a sharpener, I would have missed the deeper competitive and sexual theme of one eight-year-old boy's play: two
long things vying for one hole. Randy was murderously jealous that his beloved sister, who'd raised him as a surrogate

for their alcoholic mother, was engaged to be married. And if I saw only the symbolic, I would have been blind to the immediate reality that stirred the inner conflict—the fact that my pencils had broken points. I thereby would not have no-ticed that my allowing other children to use and wear down my pencils had made me (in Randy's eyes) a two-timer, the culprit incognito with whom he could vent and resolve his rage over his sister's love for another. A child therapist con-tinually must keep watch to see, hear, and feel how the simple and complex, the superficial and deep, the gross and sublime, push and pull at each other.

Overgrown intellects, having outlasted at least a decade of formal education, may be prone to miss the emotional con-tent of play; they may prefer thinking to feeling. They can more readily and contentedly see a theoretical oedipal trian-gle than one particular little girl crying outside her parents' locked bedroom door. They would rather speculate on the subliminal derivatives of her obstructed libido than feel her sad, angry loneliness. Theories about the psyche,* including the associated technical terminology, are generated in the mind. Just as hunger has little meaning in the absence of a gnawing stomach or a soul in need of love and attention, hypothetical mental constructs wield power only as far as they apply to what people think, feel, and do.

Some clinicians view therapy as a puzzle to be solved quickly and by themselves. They take pride in seeing what others can-not, while they are reluctant to see what everyone else sees. Such therapists may be very bright and conceptually sophis-ticated, but are too impatient to let the child and the therapy naturally unfold. Once they believe, oft times mistakenly, that they know what's going on in the patient, they lose interest. Their lack of pleasure in watching a child do his own psychic crossword, their wanting to take it over, impedes the therapy process. A therapist who takes more joy in his own than the

---

*A related topic, itself worthy of an entire book, is the relation between a therapist's orientation and what he sees. Not surprisingly, clinicians tend to see what they believe is there to be seen: behaviorists are prone to see learned behaviors, cognitive-behaviorists faulty and negative belief sys-tems, family therapists dysfunctional systems, psychoanalysts internal con-flict, etc., though certainly not all clinicians of a particular perspective agree on what they see, either.

child's insights sabotages a fundamental aspect of therapy: what the child discovers on her own is more personally mean-ingful than what the therapist figures out for her. How much simpler life would be if we grew best by being told what we ourselves cannot see, or what another, usually older or wiser than us, already has experienced or learned from his mistakes and pain!

As the discussion of intelligence implied, a child therapist needs to be attuned and receptive to feelings. That should go without saying, for thoughts *and* emotions are what rule us. But, in the trendy vernacular, how feely is ideal? A child ther-apist who relies upon logical deduction to make probabilistic guesses about emotions will frequently miss what actually is felt. He needs to be comfortable enough to observe, with eyes, ears, and heart, what children feel. He needs to have the stom-ach for psychic pain (as well as for love and other feelings) in the same way that the physician must have one for blood and guts (though all patients would benefit if both doctors could tolerate both kinds of suffering). And he needs to have some awareness of his own feelings. As Samuel Johnson's proverb reads: "Those who do not feel pain seldom think that it is felt [by others]." How the therapist deals with his own distress has much to do with how he receives and treats that felt by his patients.

Consider how, as a trainee, I sympathized with the horrid plight of children from broken, abusive, and neglectful homes. I felt deeply for their hurts, yet disavowed any direct famil-iarity with their circumstances or sorrow. I believed that I personally had nothing about which to feel upset—at least, nothing resembling their traumas. Since I provided the chil-dren with some relief and insight, what was the danger in my wish to see myself as nothing at all like them?

Since I preferred to view myself as being very human, see-ing patients as so different from me dehumanized them some-what. I tended to pathologize patients, to see what they did in therapy as signs of physical or mental disease rather than unique expressions of universally human experiences, ones I also shared. Only as I grew more aware of how I felt could I sense what they felt. For example, when I recognized how terribly lonely and misunderstood I often felt, I began to un-derstand psychotic speech not as a random neurologic symptom, but as a meaningful response to ways in which I'd made patients feel alone and misunderstood. One does not have to be orphaned to fear abandonment or abused to feel mistreated. Unless I can tolerate those feelings within and toward myself, I ultimately and unconsciously will ask the child not to get them all over me. And when I push away feelings, I also push away the child who feels them.

Effective therapy requires effective interventions—saying or not saying something, doing or not doing something—at the right time. This requires an empathic gauging of how the child is feeling moment by moment. Is she growing too anxious or too sad, or does she need to feel a bit lonelier or more uncomfortable? I do not want to overwhelm a child, nor do I wish her to lose an opportunity for growth. In order for me to know how both I and my patients feel, I must be able to tolerate and sit still with feelings. If I cannot stand loneliness, I might be prone to interrupt silences or force myself into the play, whether or not these actions suit the child's wishes or needs. Discomfort with sexual feelings may lead me to dress dolls that a child has unclothed or suggest a board game when he begins to play out a rape. If I am not at home with aggression, I will be liable to stifle or punish hostile play, or redirect anger meant for me toward others who are not in the room—such as teachers, siblings, or parents.

What jeopardy is posed by the child therapist who is excessively emotional? The inordinately impassioned overly identify with their patients, perhaps children with whom they share some special commonality, or in whom they see or would like to see themselves. They go far beyond comprehending or empathizing with a child; they experience the child's sentiments or predicament as their own. This can distort their perception of what is happening and their efforts to find the best way to aid the child. A therapist who feels a child's abuse as his own may become too frightened or outraged to help that patient see how he has led himself into a dangerous situation or could have avoided such harm; or worse, he may be so swept away by the victim's perspective and pain that he cannot refrain from providing comfort— perhaps soothing words or affectionate caresses—which can be antitherapeutic, if not abusive in itself. A therapist whose emotions are not clearly demarcated from others' may confuse the patient who struggles to clarify her own identity. It is the therapist's responsibility to keep one foot on the floor, physically and psychologically.

Can a therapist be too keen on feelings? We are all familiar with caricatures of those who seem to get a little too much of a kick out of others' upset, who crave the sound and fury of others' emotions. They consider it their job to foment psychic riot by throwing gasoline on inner fires. This style occasionally is effective with constricted patients who grew up with unresponsive, unaffectionate parents, but more often it can overwhelm them or keep a flame lit under patients who already are agitated. While therapists need to pay constant attention to patients' emotions, we must beware not to use them to entertain ourselves or distract from our own depression or emptiness.

When I applied to graduate school in clinical psychology, the chair of a fellowship committee wondered aloud why anyone would want to spend their days listening to other people's problems. He then asked what I thought about the premise that people became psychologists in order to deal with their own problems. I wanted to question his own motives for becoming an academic bureaucrat, but anticipated that easily would be seen as defensive and proof of his proposition. Instead I politely agreed without giving any details about my personal issues; fortunately, he let me be. At that time I did not understand the wisdom that underlay the dean's question: that *why* I became a therapist had everything to do with *how* I would be a therapist. He recognized that my reasons would do much more than simply determine what profession I pursued; they also would directly and profoundly influence the way I treated patients. Only later did I gradually discover this essential truth for myself.

I initially believed that my prime motivation for becoming a psychologist was to help, if not completely rescue, children. Although I realized that I could never physically replace a missing or abusive parent, I held exaggerated expectations of what therapy could accomplish. I aspired to make everything good again—to be psychologically the lost father, to undo abuse and restore a child to her original mint condition, whatever that was. This optimistic spirit sustained me in my work with extremely damaged children in hopelessly bleak situations. Besides, I reasoned, what could be wrong with wanting to help?

As a result of this feeling, I occasionally did too much for child patients. I focused more on feeding them directly during the therapy hour to the exclusion of teaching them how to fend for themselves, how to grow and harvest their own emotional nourishment while not with me (the Peace Corps model). In one painful-to-remember case, I inadvertently fostered a neglected little girl's fantasy that I would eventually adopt her. Too cowardly to challenge that unrealistic belief, I unknowingly promoted it and subsequently disappointed her. Rather than help her to overcome her situation, I left her as vulnerable as ever to the traumatic whimsy of her environment. Sometimes I steered children's play toward happy endings, wanting them to leave the hour happier and more relaxed than when they came. This was cruel to those who reentered a reality that was not at all happy, and who needed play therapy to express their utter lack of hope and cheer. I slowly learned that, try as I might, I could not amply compensate for a lost or bad parent, nor could I rewrite a child's history. This required that I come to terms with the mortality of my own childhood. Admitting that I could not help a child to escape or relive his one and only childhood past meant acknowledging an equal finality to my own. My delay in mourning days gone by, good and bad, had obstructed the goal of helping my patients do the same.

A zeal to give comfort can backfire in other ways. The therapist's idea of help may differ from the child's or the parents', which quickly raises the complex question of whose therapy it is. For instance, a child with intrusively empathic parents may sometimes need to feel misunderstood in order to forge his own identity; one never having been given space to be by himself may need to be left alone, in the therapist's presence, to mourn and grow beyond past losses. That may not jibe with a therapist's need to give a hand more actively. The therapist who cannot sit patiently with a child's (and probably his own) problems may need to prevent even a doll from jumping off a play bridge, or prematurely resuscitate persons whom the child has deliberately brought to harm in play.

Parents may disagree with the therapist about what is in the patient's best interest. And sometimes the child himself does not want the kind of help offered. A therapist who rigidly needs to help, and who unconsciously demands appreciation and therapeutic progress in return for that help, may be unable to permit or tolerate patients thwarting his best intentions. Consequently, he may fail to grasp the psychological meaning of the child's reluctance to accept help. He may become angry, frustrated, or unable to meet the child where he is, becoming less able to provide the very help he feels so driven to give.

Over years of introspection I gradually came to see that much of my motivation for doing child therapy was an urge to mend and restore my childhood. As I listened closely to my patients' dreams and longings, I also gave an ear to my own; sometimes I simply gave children the consistent attention, understanding, and admiration for which I sorely yearned. I relished watching children play at being naughty, saying and doing what I had not been able to say and do as a child. While helping children to accept and forgive themselves for thoughts and deeds they hated, I vicariously assuaged guilt over mine. Creating an atmosphere that allowed children to master their destinies playfully compensated for what I could not control in my own childhood—the feedings, the hugs, the bedtimes, the good-byes, the deaths. I insured that my child patients could govern in play what in actuality ruled their lives outside the office. In sum, I hoped to assist children in knowing themselves better and sooner than I had, to give them the play therapy—with its pleasures and benefits—that I regretted not having had as a boy. As is perhaps obvious to the reader, underlying this wish was my illusory fantasy that had my childhood been different, had I been in play therapy, I would not have had to grow up and face life's pervasive uncertainties—the unavoidable losses and mortality that ever threaten all of us, and that terrorize most of us.

How, in general, does a therapist's childhood influence his work? Do patients profit more when it has been enchanted or when it was less than perfect? Before answering that question, I immediately must point out its inherent fallacy. No one's childhood is charmed—except as memorialized in photographs, third-person retellings, or the most repressive of memories. No one emerges from childhood unscathed—some more, some less. Every child knows more loneliness, rejection, fear, worry, ridicule, humiliation, and hunger than he cares to recall. There are, however, those who had it worse, much worse. Some children's mothers die during their birth; many children have never known their fathers. For a multitude of reasons, probably at least half of the country's children grow up without their biological mother and father in the same home. Too many children are molested or beaten; far more are abused psychologically. Given this dismal qualification, let me restate my query. Does either a less than perfect or a much less than perfect childhood better prepare someone to be a child therapist?

Someone who has had a dependably loving, safe, and nurturant upbringing has been given a significant head start in developing his capacity to trust, use sober judgment, be capable of mature and intimate relationships, think clearly, contain impulses, tolerate his feelings, and derive satisfaction from his discoveries and work—all of which can enhance a child therapist's functioning. But there is no guarantee that he can or will pass on to others the good, intangible things that he received. Nor is it law that a bad childhood precludes a career as a therapist. There are many extraordinarily resourceful therapists, having grown through and been strengthened by grossly imperfect childhoods, who can better endure the enormous pain of their patients and give them the skillful caring they themselves never knew.

Some assert that only the rehabilitated can rehabilitate others. This modern twist to the ancestral adage "The well fed does not understand the lean," holds that the sobered best help alcoholics, recovered drug addicts best help users, and past victims of abuse best help those who continue to be hurt. Some of this opinion derives from clinical experience with and testimony of adult patients who credit their survival, for example, to the peer support of Alcoholics Anonymous or a group for battered women. How this applies to child therapy is not simple.

Certainly there appears to be a ready basis for understanding or camaraderie between those who've traveled the same experiential road. Children may quickly come to feel close to a grown-up who disclosed having been similarly mistreated, though this bond often loses its leverage as the therapy progresses and as the child eventually faces herself. A therapist's firsthand experience can catalyze or hinder. His knowing repeatedly how his father's fist in the face felt may enable him to know why his equally beaten child patient finds crying and accusing his father so difficult; on the other hand, the vivid closeness of the experience may stop him from seeing the subtle, all-important ways in which his life and his patient's have differed. One sexually abused therapist may feel greater than ordinary concern and empathy for an incest victim, while another finds that she holds resentment and disgust for the child who fared no better than she. No equation can predict how common ground between therapist and patient will affect treatment. (This discussion especially applies to the many, if not the majority of therapists who were drawn to the profession because of having grown up to become adult children of their alcoholic, abusing, depressed, neurotic, critical ... [fill in the blank] parents, the previous generation's adult children of their own similarly imperfect parents).

It is of no surprise that the present as well as the past affects a child therapist's work. No differently than the patients they treat, therapists are affected by what happens in their lives. The effect may be general—as when illness or fatigue interferes—so that the therapist's patience, attention, or judgment are compromised with all of her patients. Or the effect may occur or be intensified specifically with certain patients, in certain situations, or around certain issues that more acutely tap the therapist's current wounds or dilemma. During the week my daughter's birth was imminent, I had difficulty watching one child play out a baby being born dead. This was too close to my own worries over the birth. As a result, I was not very empathic with my patient's wish that my child never come, and could not fully help her to understand those feelings. Two weeks later, after my child's healthy delivery, I could respond more synchronously to the play and the jealous theme.

The therapist's life situation may be prolonged, as with a long-time failing marriage or a battle with chronic disease; or temporary, perhaps affecting the weeks following the death of a loved one or the day after an argument with a spouse. He can be preoccupied with financial burdens, a new car purchase, or an upcoming medical examination. He may be irate over his daughter's choice of boyfriend or forlorn over an aged parent's sudden deterioration. The therapist is not immune from life, and the therapy is not immune from the therapist's reactions to that life.

But life changes do not necessarily encumber the therapist; they can also enlighten him. Having children made me considerably more attuned to parents, especially single parents. I directly experienced the utter fatigue and frustration I'd previously known only secondhand from the descriptions of parents. Spending one or two hours per week with a child (in therapy) is both much different from and easier than parenting her day in, day out. I now understood how onerous the slightest demand or suggestion that I make as therapist might feel to a parent who already works twenty-five hours a day, and how terribly helpless and just plain lousy it feels to believe that you are ruining rather than raising your children. I am sure, however, that having children makes some therapists more dogmatic, less understanding of other parents, and rather preoccupied with their own overwhelming schedules. Conversely, I know many childless therapists who are admirably skilled, sensitive, and dedicated in their work with parents. Almost every sort of life circumstance—whether good or bad—brings opportunity for a therapist to grow or recede, to see with more or with less clarity.

Harry Stack Sullivan,* arguably the most influential of American psychiatrists, warned therapists against the natural susceptibility to use patients to satisfy their own needs for security and safety. A therapist who does not feel loved may seek admiration from his patients, while another whose relationships with his own children or grandchildren are strained may encourage his child patients to be on happy, unconflicted terms with him. Another may seek to escape awareness of what frightens him by focusing on similar fears in the chil-

*Elaborated in *The Interpersonal Theory of Psychiatry*, New York: Norton, 1953.

dren whom he treats. Most alarming and occurring with stag-geringly high incidence, a therapist lacking healthy outlets for emotional and sexual intimacy in his nonprofessional life may indulge his desires with vulnerable patients. Although ther-apy is a mutual relationship and patients inevitably contrib-ute to the therapist's growth, it is not their responsibility to soothe his anxiety, distract him from personal troubles, or give meaning to his life. Their role is not to make him be or feel useful, or compensate for ways in which his life outside of therapy is lacking, disturbed, or stressed. Even the most well meaning of therapists must take care not to exploit his patients or the process in order to preserve his own comfort, esteem, and sanity.

This may give the erroneous impression that the therapist should keep himself out of the therapy; nothing could be further from the truth. That would leave the patient with an empty shell of a man rather than a warm-blooded, caring person. The notion that a therapist is objective is a myth, as is the popular trend to equate the therapist's silence with neutrality. Although it is usually a good tactic for the thera-pist to leave most of the time for the patient's talk or play, this is occasionally carried to an extreme. A therapist's rigid unwillingness to talk (even when he has something useful to offer) or interact (to say hello, express condolence over a death, take seriously a patient's concerns over fees and schedule) represents neither a therapeutic ideal nor a dispas-sion toward the patient. It more likely is a defensive push against the thoughts and feelings that being with the patient evokes, perhaps a sign of the clinician's discomfort, not his impartiality.

We all, including therapists, are limited by who we are. At any point in time, none of us can think, say, do, feel, bear, or understand any more than we are able to. Every therapist's experience with and understanding of his patients is perva-sively and perpetually confounded by who he is. He cannot change that, but he can strive to keep his own character in mind when he draws inferences about what he sees and hears in the consulting room. To this purpose, the child therapist must continually assess what he thinks and feels during each hour. The fantasies and sentiments that come to him during sessions, though often incisively informative about the therapy process, are by no means perfectly reliable barometers of what is going on inside the patient.

I take much objection with the therapist who unquestioningly shares his own associations or daydreams with patients, who believes that everything running through his mind holds precious significance for the patient playing or talking across from him. Such a therapist may automatically attribute his sensations—his anger, boredom, or excitement—to patients, disregarding facts about his own past, present, and inner world. It is more critical that the therapist regularly share his thoughts and feelings with himself, that he ponder them to better know how he is listening to or playing with the child. *A child therapist cannot be too aware of his patients' and his own feelings,* especially as they are distinguished from and relate to each other. The greater his capacity to know them, the less likely he will use patients to protect, gratify, tranquilize, or arouse himself.

How does a therapist watch out for blind spots, keep herself on the clinical straight and narrow? One way is to seek supervision from a more experienced clinician or regularly share her work with a colleague, thereby coming to see what she could not or preferred not to see on her own. However, the surest and deepest way for a child therapist to gain understanding of herself and her work is through the self-exploration of a personal therapy. Coming to awareness of and grips with her own conflicts reduces the likelihood that they will be detrimentally played out with patients. Moreover, there is no better way to learn about our patients than to know ourselves what it feels like to be a therapy patient—to be the one who feels pathetically stupid, defective, bad, hopeless, and humiliated. After a therapist herself feels the intense anxiety of therapy or knows moments in which she truly cannot remember or feel something that is obvious, she becomes more empathic with her patients. Although I've had much instructive supervision, I've learned most about being a therapist from my own analysis. And probably of all that I've learned, my most influential discovery has been that I primarily *needed and wanted* my own therapy—not, as I first believed, to become a more insightful or empathic therapist (though that has happened to a certain extent), but to confront and quell the painful conflicts that originated in me long before I had ever met my first therapy patient.

(It is surprising, amusing, and mostly worrisome how many therapists, even those dismayed by or critical of their patients' reluctance to persist in treatment, have never felt that they had the need, time, or money for therapy of their own. Of course, going without therapy does not mean that one will be a bad therapist, only that he will not understand himself and his work as fully as he might. Even the brightest and most well-adjusted clinician is prone to psychological nearsightedness, if not blindness, in the service of self-deception.)

But then again, treatment does not perform miracles on either patients or therapists. Talking therapy seldom reforms hardened criminals, makes good persons of the corrupt, or gives heart to the heartless. Gaining awareness of a conflict may enable some therapists to conduct themselves more effectively and satisfyingly; but that insight may bring little change to others. It may not be enough for a therapist to know that he has an exaggerated sadistic streak, unethical financial ambition, or an incontrovertible sexual perversion. If he continues to act upon them with patients, he remains guilty as charged. Because someone is aware that he has a penchant for robbing banks does not pardon the deed.

This brings up what in my opinion is the child therapist's most essential quality—good character. In what field is personal integrity more crucial? A therapist takes vulnerable patients off into a private room, where he becomes privy to the most basic aspects of their lives and selves. If that therapist lacks self-control and is without a clinical conscience, the child and the therapy are sunk. No differently than a parent with children, a therapist cannot conduct shady business practices or tell white lies about his lateness and forgotten appointments and expect patients to live honestly with him. Great intellect or psychological talent do not make up for a therapist's moral delinquency, for irresponsible or abusive behavior.

Though I strive to accept my patients as they are, I am neither nonjudgmental nor valueless. I cringe inside when a child describes his brutal treatment of the family dog, or spends his therapy hour devising better ways to humiliate a deaf child at school, ways that I know will be implemented the next day. I listen patiently not because I condone those things or don't care enough to stop them, but because that's the only way—however slow—that I know of coming to see why a child is so hateful or uncaring. I do not yell or punish; I do share my concern over the way in which a child mistreats others, and try as quickly as the therapeutic situation allows to show the child how his abuse of others connects to that he received from others. One of my strongest commitments to child therapy stems from my belief that therapy helps children grow closer to and more accepting of themselves. A child who can like himself, or at least not violently hate himself, will better treat not just himself but others and his environment.

By working backward from the memories of adults on his analytic couch, Freud elaborated on the linkage between an individual's early and later experiences. His idea that what happened to us as children affected how we live as adults, however, was not revolutionary. Centuries before him, novelists—based on astute observations of human nature—richly described how early life events could lead to an adult's resilient triumph or tragic self-destruction. They saw life in its truest, most complicated form and realized that no simple rules exist to predict what becomes of someone. They knew that character requires some adversity in order to grow sturdy, and that a perfectly privileged, indulged childhood does not so much prepare as it sets up a child for a mighty downfall. Nor was it a mystery that a singularly malignant childhood mostly produces a hardened, emotionally underdeveloped adult, and that some kindness and human stability are needed to keep a child's humanity vital and accessible.

Given this long historical awareness, I'm quite frankly surprised at how frequently child therapy gets no respect, and is estimated to be of less value than work with adults. Even in academic clinical settings, child therapy is occasionally thought of as glorified baby-sitting or women's work, terms that—accurately reflective of societal prejudices—simultaneously manage to disparage children, women, and men (who happen to be child therapists). What accounts for these mis-perceptions of child therapy?

The historical, and somewhat deserved, grandeur of psy-choanalysis has fostered a popular tendency to view the backward reconstruction of an adult patient's childhood as nobler than the more contemporary understanding of the childhood with which a child currently grapples. By some in-tellectual bias or nostalgia, the past, like a fine wine, is prone to be judged as more valuable with aging; though, as the cases in this book demonstrate, even children have a past from which they have arrived, to which they continue to be at-tached, and that requires illumination and demystification. Pragmatically, one surely can argue that addressing a child's problem promptly, thereby allowing development to get back on track, is as worthwhile therapeutically as treating the con-sequences of that emotional arrest in an adult thirty years down the road.

Some believe that children are too immature to be com-mitted allies in a therapeutic endeavor. Such proponents contest that children simply come to play and be attended to—as if we adults do not. In my experience, however, chil-dren, while not using sophisticated catchwords to describe their treatment, can have substantial experiential understand-ing of and appreciation for how therapy works. They can sense just as assuredly as any adult when therapy relieves a stomachache, reduces a fear, or enhances self-esteem. And why should the work of treatment—looking at oneself, ac-knowledging faults, revealing pains, feeling humiliated—be easier for the child than it is for the adult reliving such child-hood experiences? Children's capacity and wish to better un-derstand themselves, to feel less alone and helpless in a big, dangerous world, are grossly underestimated. There are many adults—even those who regularly come and pay for treat-ment—who do not cooperate with the seamier, more hurtful aspects of therapy. I have found that patients' variance in how they comprehend, accept, or avoid the toil of therapy is in no way explained by age.

Generalities better describe all patients than they distin-guish between the young and the old. Most patients seem to like hearing nice things (though that might cause later shame and guilt) to hearing less than nice things. Most seem to dislike frustration and loss. They all react when I mess up, am late, or listen poorly. They all want to be loved and admired unconditionally (though none of us are). They all want to be safe, even if doing something dangerous. Most (though psychologically many cannot) would rather use the money spent on therapy to buy other things, often toys such as video games, baseball gloves, ski vacations, fancier cars, and house additions. Most wonder how I treat other patients, and envy those whom they perceive to have more of what they want and who (so it looks to them) do not need therapy.

The goals of treatment are not so different, either. Both children and adults want symptomatic relief—to have fewer headaches or feel less anxious—and both are quite impressed when they achieve it. Both want to function better, to feel less helplessly at others' whims. Though a child's development typically is more ongoing and fluid, therapy can allow even an adult's psychological and cognitive growth to go on. Just as therapy might free up a boy's concentration, it can help a grown-up to learn and remember better. When therapy goes well, it can enhance both decision-making—in the boardroom as well as on the soccer field—and the capacity to give and take love, both for the child with parents and the parent with children. Both young and old patients are equally capable of improving their self-image and softening their consciences.

The principles and techniques of adult and child therapy also are quite comparable. I watch and listen carefully to both children and adults. Bad observations or unempathic interpretations lead to detachment or interruptions in both play and talk. Though it's often easier to see with children, who may feel less bound to decorum, grown-ups do not pull away or change the topic any less frequently. The work is the same—slow, plodding, and hard. I need to follow the patient's rhythm regardless of age, and my decisions to hasten or slow that pace are made using the same therapeutic judgment and scale.

Empathizing does not change according to the age of the patient. Although developmental considerations (about physical growth, intellectual maturity, etc.) sensitize the therapist in thinking about all age groups, trying to understand what

an individual child feels is exactly the same as trying to understand what a grown-up feels. I treated a seventy-two-year-
old woman, for example, who was most distressed over her
perception that her mother had always favored her sister,
while many much younger patients have been swamped by
fears of death, an issue some have designated to the developmental province of an older generation.

Often children are treated as if they are simple, incomplete
people, who grow complicated only with age. Parents and
therapists who anguish over their own birthdays may be surprised when a child is not thoroughly joyful over hers. Children's experiences need to be explored as fully, and without
assumptions, as do grown-ups'. Childish-sounding complaints
are not to be taken at face value. I explore boredom, tired-
ness, or a wish to skip a class skating party with as much
reserved tenacity as I would an adult's apathy, ennui, or decision to skip the company picnic.

Conducting both child and adult psychotherapy has been
instructive; developmentally, they inform each other. A five-
year-old boy's castration anxiety enlightened my understanding of a forty-four-year-old executive's fear of success. Treating
a little girl who had been mistreated by her mother enhanced
my therapy with a married woman who, also having been
abused as a child, avoided parenthood for fear that she would
mother no better than she had been mothered and that her
children would grow to hate her. Working with adults shows
how the ways of childhood evolve to become the more enduring warp and woof of personality, and continually re-
minds me of the psychological dilemmas with which the
parents of my child patients contend. No less, my perennial
exposure to children's life as it is today helps me to see my
adult patients' childhoods more concretely and vividly, as they
lived them.

Ideal therapists exist only in our imaginations. In actuality,
all therapists, whether treating the young or old, are continually bombarded on two fronts: from the patients and themselves. At the very least (and they can do no more), they should
(as do their patients) strive to better see, feel, and know how
their own inner tensions and self-ignorance distort their perceptions and hinder their therapeutic work. After all, what

makes child and adult therapists alike, and what makes child and adult therapy alike, is exactly what makes children and adults, therapists and their patients, alike: we are all human beings who began as children.

XIII

Oops!

"The perels of hem that offendyn and erryn."

—Edward Arber,
The Revelation to the Monk of Evesham

"The most troublesome cheese doodle to fall from the skies"—
so might begin a diary of my misadventures as a child therapist. I looked up to see from where it fell. And there, well
above the adjacent stone garage, between what would be the
third and fourth stories of the huge maple tree that rose behind the clinic, a boy sat comfortably. The branches formed
such a natural seat that he did not have to hold on: one free
hand held the can of snack food, while the other dropped its
contents below. In the few minutes during which I'd spoken
with another one of the six boys in his therapy group, Kip—
its most daring and agile member—had climbed well up into
the tree.

"Wow, look how high he is!" one child announced. "How
ya gonna get him down?"

"I'm glad I'm not him," said another, nodding in my direction. "He's gonna have to call the fire department to bring
the ladder truck!"

Maybe, I thought—working hard to put my real fear that
he might fall and get killed, out of my head—all he needs is
some recognition for being special. "You really want us all to

see what a good climber you are. Boy, and have we!" I said.
He continued to drop doodles.

"I don't think that helped," one child chirped.

"I don't think so, either." I smiled toward him, unable to
miss the humor and satisfaction that he—a child habitually
wallowing in his own hot water and others' disfavor—found
in my hour of terror, in what looked to him to be my royal
screw-up.

The orange puffs continued to fall. One glanced off my
head. "Gotcha that time," Kip cheerfully called. His predicament did not worry him; in fact, he did not even consider his
situation to be a predicament.

Obviously, however, it was my predicament. What could I
do? I did not want to order him down. That's not my style,
and besides, I was treating Kip in part to remedy the effects
of his harshly authoritarian father, a man whose excessive
control had led his son to be such a rebel in the first place.
More to the point, screaming for him to come down would
probably have just made him climb higher, until only a helicopter could save him—and incidentally make me look that
much more foolish and impotent. The hubbub of the gath-
ering spectators distracted me from the momentary and dis-
maying awareness that even in this turmoil, I continued to
care about what others thought of me. Refocused on my task,
I considered a bribe, a promise to reward a hasty descent with
a privilege or a treat. But that also was not in my therapeutic
repertoire, and likely would encourage further and more ex-
orbitant extortion by Kip and his fellow group members.

"What are you doing in that tree, anyway?" I called upward
with outer calm and inner desperation, hopeful that my un-
pretentious question would cause him to reflect on his reason
for scaling the tree—and magically eliminate his need to be
there.

"Throwing cheese bombs at you" came the predictable reply.

"Are you angry, Kip?"

"No," he responded pleasantly, and in all honesty, he did
not look angry. "Are you?"

"You're wondering if I'm angry." More useless psychology
talk. This was not getting any better.

"You are starting to look a little pissed, ya know, Dr. Bromfield," Kip's best friend observed. "Are you worried you're gonna get in trouble?" Two others debated whether I'd be sued, and for how much.

They read my fears accurately. I was indeed worried and angry. Should he slip, I decided, I would throw my body under his. Perhaps I could break his fall, and in the bleakest scenario, we would go together (sparing me the awful consequences—the phone call to his mother, the clinical investigation, the likely lawsuit, and worst of all, the unforgivable guilt over my carelessness).

But as the hour passed, the novelty faded. Chuckling onlookers went their way. The group's co-leader, a very experienced child group therapist who took such events much more in stride, urged me to stop psychobabbling and join the basketball game that the other members had resumed. "Have faith," I urged myself. "If his friends aren't worried, there's probably no reason to. Ignore him and maybe he'll return to earth." Wisdom from Freud's *Standard Edition?* More likely the *Ladies' Home Journal!*

Kip did come down by the hour's end. Safely. "Ran out of doodles," he explained matter-of-factly, "and besides, I gotta meet some kids at the arcade."

For the first time I understood parents' common and strangely paradoxical tendency to threaten to kill the child who ever again crosses the street without looking, who ever again frightens them so. It's bad enough that we cannot send our children into the world wearing construction helmets, chastity belts, or germproof bubbles; why do we have to be reminded of that? As does the jaywalking child to his parents, Kip forced me to see my limited capacity to keep him safe. In so doing, he made me feel small and helpless—ways that I, like most grown-ups, hate to feel.

I can smile now, having gained some clinical maturity and distance, but it wasn't quite as easy when I was an insecure beginner. As a novice, merely sitting with a patient was a challenge. During those formative years I experienced my fair share of awkward moments, as when a boy locked me out of my office. Crouched in the hallway against the thick gray steel door, I tried—in a loud whisper, so as not to be heard by my professor in the adjoining room—to persuade my hostage-in-reverse to surrender. (Adam eventually grew bored and let me in.)

Though some mishaps just seemed to happen, I usually brought them on myself. For example, once naively believing that a good child therapist should be able to win over the most oppositional and unreceptive child, I gladly accepted one parent's responsibility for bringing her reluctant child from the lobby to my office. It took one trial of dragging that screaming child by the hand to expose the foolhardiness of my assumption. Of course, her mother thoroughly enjoyed witnessing the purported child expert flounder. "Don't feel bad," she gleefully consoled. "Sarah's a handful for anybody." She was right, too—about both her daughter and my need to keep in mind that a therapist, however well trained and skilled, is just another person, an anybody.

If hauling children to my office was stressful, having them flee once there was mortifying. One child, following her very angry play, ran into the waiting room proclaiming that I'd been mean; a second, who'd told me sexy jokes, accused me of dirty talk. Truly flabbergasted and fearful that their parents would believe I'd done something wrong, I followed those children out, not entirely unlike an older sibling who rushes to tell his side of the story lest he be unfairly blamed. (In actuality, I found that parents knew pretty well what their children were up to, and quickly urged them to return to their therapy.)

My sensitivity to what parents thought of me and my work frequently came up. I initially felt criticized when they complained—a common fact of the child therapist's life—about their child's bad grades, misbehaviors, and general lack of therapeutic progress. Many times I felt tremendous pressure to conform to popular opinion calling for me to forsake the patient principles of therapy and push the child more actively—via confrontation, punishment, or drugs—to do what others wanted him to do. But over the years, through the benefits of my analysis and others' supervision of my work, I grew less wary of the parents who prowled my superego and waiting room, and far less frequently feared their disapproval or judgment of my guilt by association with their children. (As a result, I saw more clearly how parents' hyper-criticism

of their children and me often reflected their own stern consciences and critical parents.)

If, as some say, life's most indelible lessons are learned
through humiliation, perhaps my most instructive experience
occurred in the special education classroom to which I served
as consultant several years ago. Having been amply warned
by the teacher and school psychologist that the students were
exquisitely impulsive and required a high degree of structure
and supervision, I should have been fazed, but I wasn't. I'd
twice met with the class and all had gone smoothly. Only after
the principal's summoning of Julie, the classroom's reliable,
firm, and skilled teacher, had left me alone with the group
did I realize it had been her presence, not mine, that had
created and maintained the illusion that I exerted control.

Literally seconds after Julie's departure, the children began
to show signs of strain. Civil requests became unruly demands
for more attention, water, and more trips to the bathroom.
One child left his seat to visit another; three children milled
about the sink. All twelve were soon ricocheting off the walls.
They first hurled curses, then things—pencils, paper, food.
Nothing I said slowed them down, primarily because they
didn't hear me over the noise they so busily made. I looked
at the clock. In less than five minutes, all hell had broken
loose. I was lost. I thought of running for help, but that would
have left the children alone. I considered pressing the inter-
com buzzer and screaming for help, but I was too overwhelmed and proud to avail myself of assistance. Two
children, a boy and a girl, had begun undressing under a
desk. I was at the mercy of fate.

Just as we were about to go over the edge, I heard the door.
"At last," I sighed, "Julie is back." But when I turned, I instead
saw a crowd of faces watching through the large door window. Those teachers—looking a little concerned, somewhat
amazed, and a lot entertained—later admitted that seeing my
obvious bewilderment and ineptitude had gratified them immensely. This pleasure revealed less their sadism and more
their frustration over the lack of respect and admiration of
which they, as educators, were so frequently and undeserv-
edly deprived. They generously sympathized with me over the
children's reckless behavior, knowing—even if I didn't—that
I was the one who had been out of control, and knowing—

even if society didn't—what a demanding and important job they held.

When Julie came back, I immediately cited a need to make a patient's appointment—a face-saving, however valid, excuse to escape—and hurried out to my car. I wanted to forget my awful day at school. As I drove off, my heart went out to the children who, I surmised, frequently felt this way. For several minutes I empathized with their having to go back and face teachers, before recognizing my apprehension that I, too, would have to return. To my grateful surprise, when I did— and as often occurs in the lives of children—my horrible day with the class was followed by our best meeting yet. Moreover, the children still looked to me for help, and the teachers still sought my consultation. Although this ordeal taught me—the hard way—that underestimating patients' needs and overestimating my powers to manage them was dangerously overreaching, its greater and underlying moral was that being fallible and accepting help did not make me less of a therapist or a person.

The spontaneity that can make children so appealing can also make them hazardous to one's social health. In the waiting room children have invited me to taste a half-eaten ice cream cone (I didn't), chew some already chewed gum (didn't), directly bring my nose to a rancid two-week-old tuna sandwich (didn't, though no one in the lobby could avoid smelling it), sing a full-length disco song so that the child could demonstrate her dancing (did, but only after we'd gone into the office), clap while the child recited a brief rhyme for his parents in my presence (did, right there), rub my hand across a military crewcut (didn't), and show how much money I had in my wallet (didn't). Every child therapist could generate an impressive list of her own. Although these public appeals can make a therapist feel put on the spot, they represent merely the tip of an iceberg. When considering these requests, I strive to understand whether I am complying or refusing for sound clinical reasons or out of personal discomfort (not that they need be mutually exclusive).

Though I routinely let children verbally insult or describe ways in which they'd like to debase me, I do not permit them to harm me physically. When playing a game of indoor copy-me basketball or Simon says, I may be asked to perform wildly antic slam dunks, make silly faces, or waddle like a duck—all of which I am generally willing to do. A pretend school scene may require that I play an outcast on the playground or stand in the corner like a dunce. Children, the ultimate victims of powerlessness, notoriously want to control everything in therapy—the play, the toys, and the therapist. "Draw this!" "Say this!" "Go here!" "Keep silent!" Child therapists who cannot tolerate being bossed and used in such ways experience considerable anguish and obstruct their patients' play.

I do not, however, allow a child to berate me endlessly if therapeutic benefit does not seem to follow. A therapy that involves nothing more than the patient's hostile devaluation of me functionally can completely become a psychic toilet bowl to which the child comes to leave his weekly dump. Though this may bring some relief, it does not enable the child to integrate those parts of himself that he'd prefer simply to excrete and be rid of. That child needs to understand that he vigorously disparages me in order not to feel so disparaged and worthless himself. A therapist who is truly masochistic or unwilling to protect himself—when called for—can overstimulate a child's sadism, promote disrespect for the therapy and himself, and ultimately, make the child feel very unsafe. There is a major difference between letting myself be abusively manipulated in fantasy and actually being mistreated. I cannot imagine a single clinical indication that warrants my allowing a child to hurt me.

Each therapist must determine for himself what he can tolerate comfortably. If I believe that I must put up with everything the patient dishes out, I inevitably will feel resentment and my patients somehow will pay. It is reasonable for a therapist to exercise some measure of free will. At times I have suggested that a therapist-puppet stand in to take play pies in the face meant for me, declined to play Nerfball soccer because my back was sore, and often not brought to the office games or toys that I strongly disliked, though they might have some therapeutic value. Demanding that child patients treat me cordially and respectfully by conventional standards— being polite, not being fresh, using nice language—however, is not acceptable; nor is it defensible to avoid acknowledging my preferences and limitations—what I will not or cannot do—by adjudging the children's requests as wrong, sick, silly, or bad. As long as being a child carries the risk of humiliation, so will the work of being a child therapist.

If it is human to err, I categorically belong to the world of mortals. But the intent here is not as much to chronicle my mistakes—though that might be amusing—as to discuss how they affect therapy and, once committed, what can be done about them. A child therapist is destined to make many mistakes, but he is not doomed to mismanage them, to heap insults upon the original injuries. At the very least he can control the damage; at best, he can lend some understanding to his patient and perhaps gain some for himself.

What, to begin with, is a mistake* in therapy? It may be a social faux pas that hurts more deeply than the fanciful French label might suggest. While one patient did not so much as blink when I called him by the wrong name—as compared to another's dropped jaw and pronounced flinch—weeks later he confessed that my wayward greeting had roused his deeply running, previously unspoken fear that I preferred others, such as the person to whom he supposed my misnaming had referred. A miscalculated bill overstating what is owed me, or failure to show a child patient or his parents a common courtesy—such as not saying hello on the elevator, or not asking how some well-discussed baseball tryout or elective surgery turned out—can temporarily disrupt a previously steady relationship.

Errors can also occur around the basic conditions of therapy, such as the scheduling of sessions. One fragile teenage girl, the first patient for whom I ever was late (by about fifteen minutes), profusely forgave me for "being only human," then canceled the next three hours for a doctor's visit, a cold, and a final exam—overtly good reasons. Only after resuming did we both discover that she hadn't missed therapy as much as she had skipped it, out of hurt. If I had truly cared about her, so she understandably figured, I would have been there

---

*Here I elaborate the sorts of errors that pervade even the soundest course of therapy. I do not address what can be considered therapeutic crimes: ethical and legal violations, sexual abuse, insurance fraud, lying to patients, etc. These more serious, inexcusable, and sometimes irreparable infractions are qualitatively different from the blunders about which I write, and warrant a much lengthier and thorough discussion.

on time. Had I initially and more forthrightly acknowledged what I'd done, or rather what I'd failed to do, and resisted the temptation to so easily accept my patient's pardon as the end of the story, I'd have made her sacrifice of a month of treatment less necessary and less likely.

I must be wary when attributing my misbehaviors to external conditions beyond my control, such as unexpectedly heavy traffic or last-minute duties at the hospital. These excuses, which can look deceptively aboveboard, often discourage patients from complaining, especially those who do not easily assert their needs. Besides, in many instances I know ahead of time that there's road construction or that I will be covering emergencies, and accordingly can leave extra traveling time, reschedule patients, or warn them of my possible delay. To use a patient's or parent's habitual lack of punctuality to rationalize my own—to decide "she won't mind" or that "it's no big thing because she's always late herself"—is particularly crooked and woeful. The likely significant meaning of her untimeliness becomes moot and impossible to address if I respond with confounding inconsistency of my own.

Now when I am late, I generally acknowledge it frankly with neither excessive defense nor apology. "I'm late, aren't I?" I'll say, or "How late am I?" Though children and parents commonly deny caring, they virtually always know precisely how many minutes they've been waiting for me. If my schedule allows, I make up the time at the hour's end; if not, I add it to the next hour or prorate the charge for the present one (depending on how late I am and what suits the patient). Alternatively, some children have requested that I give them a written IOU that they can cash in when they want or need more of me and therapy. Others have asked for interest payments—an extra minute or two—on their lost time, for good punitive measure, and I have obliged, mostly as reward for the openness of their feelings toward the insult I've dealt them.

Short of unethical malpractice, forgetting a patient's hour is about the most painful misdeed that a therapist can inflict upon his patient. Such a blunder can derail the most engaged patient and evoke uncharacteristic wishes to skip sessions or quit therapy altogether. I've been amazed, in my experience and that of the trainees whom I supervise, how frequently

patients who have been stood up by their therapists soon return the favor, neither coming to nor calling to cancel their
next hour.

At the least, patients deserve to use my foul-ups to their
own psychotherapeutic advantage, though this is not always
easy for me to permit. Having, as a trainee, discovered that
I'd forgotten a patient's appointment earlier that evening, I
frantically telephoned her: "I'm so sorry. It doesn't reflect
how I think about you. Do you think you can forgive this and
go on with treatment? I've just been preoccupied. . . ." I truly
believed I was being sympathetic, conveying heartfelt regret
over my oversight—and, in part, I was. I recognized less that
I was defending myself against her anger and disappointment, certain to come my way, by flogging myself before she
did. In one of her last sessions many months down the road,
that young woman disclosed that seeing my great upset over
the missed hour had deterred her from sharing her own. How
much fury could she have shown to a therapist who was on
his hands and knees begging for mercy?

If I say something dim-witted ("Different strokes for different folks"), insensitive ("Well, maybe that's why people at work
don't like you"), or simply off base (such as hardheadedly
suggesting that a child's angry play is a reaction to my upcoming vacation, when he did not yet know that I was going away),
it is my clinical duty to bear its full consequences. Although
an explanation for the basis of my assertion or trying to restate more tactfully what I'd originally meant may eventually
be warranted, I must for the time being play wait and see.
Saying, "But I didn't mean for you to feel hurt," may comfort
me but leave the patient chilled. The child may feel she is
being told that she had neither the right nor justification to
react as she has. She may profit more from my observing
aloud that my comment has hurt her or has not been very
helpful, or was dull, tactless, or off the mark. As is true for
parents, my best intentions to speak kindly and constructively
do not soften the sting of words that children hear as unresponsive, critical, or mean-spirited.

Even in times of personal innocence, I purposely may put
up with a patient's accusation that I am guilty. Rather than
immediately lay the blame where it belongs—"But I didn't
forget the name of your teacher; you've been calling her by a

different name lately"—I may temporarily own it—"You can't believe that I didn't remember her name." Once the child has felt understood and explored his sense of being unheard and unremembered, he then may talk about his need to indict others for the difficulties in his life. Although there are situations—with, for example, patients lacking conscience—in which I resist taking responsibility that is not mine, I cannot imagine any good clinical reason for my defensively arguing that my view of reality is truer than the patient's.

If, for example, a chronically angry patient has repeatedly rejected my comparably long-lived insistence that he is angry, maybe I have missed the more pressing aspect of his immediate experience. Perhaps his most immediate reality, what he feels most at that very moment, is not anger, however strong, but his need *not to feel or show* that anger. My stubborn hammering at him, "But you *are* angry," may succeed in forcing a confession, but to what end? Confirming a patient's reality, such as that boy's reluctance to share anger, is generally the most direct and shortest route to helping him be able to look at others and himself more openly.

And in that most basic of questions—whose reality is it?—lies the catastrophic potential of therapist errors. Some of the most troubled people have grown up in homes where they were forced to believe, at least outwardly, and under the threat of abusive punishment or exclusion from the family upon which they depended, that what they experienced was not and had never been. By parental mandate they were not to hear the demeaning, smell the alcohol, feel the incest, or see the hypocrisy. For a therapist to deny his own actual words or deeds, however trivial or benign, or to dismiss them as patients' distortions, is crazy-making of an equally abominable and reprehensible order. Though many are wont to proclaim all that transpires in therapy as grist for the therapeutic mill, some therapist slips and sins are better off designated and treated as the useless chaff or toxic black fungus they are.*

---

*In this regard, it is interesting that patients who file complaints to ethics committees and licensing boards often are most enraged and vindictive over not the primary transgression, but the therapist's subsequent refusal to sincerely admit wrongdoing and express regret.

* * *

Every therapist—even one who is conscientious, ethical, and in no way abusive—often speaks and acts in embarrassing, unhelpful, and hurtful ways. Though supervision, therapy, and experience generally enable him to make fewer and less grave mistakes, he unavoidably will continue to err throughout his practicing life. His aspiration should not be to know precisely how to handle each mistake but to accept and recognize his clinical and human imperfections, and allow for the patient's fair and justified right to do the same.

XIV

Going Forth

"This is a terrible hour, but it is often the darkest point which precedes the rise of day."

—Charlotte Bronte, *Shirley*

If caring about patients, like loving our children, is risky, then working with Kenna was downright dangerous. Her history of abuse and neglect was tragic beyond belief—and prognostically dismal. Her mother's boyfriend had molested her in every conceivable way almost daily since at least her second year. Although her mother vowed she knew nothing about it, that it happened in her absence while Flex babysat, a social service investigation cast serious doubts on her claim of innocence. For many years she'd been hooked on heroin and prescription narcotics, a habit she supported by prostituting. In their one-bedroom apartment, Kenna frequently heard and watched her mother having violent, deviant sex with assorted boyfriends, girlfriends, customers, and addicts. Her biological father could have been any of many anonymous men. One only can imagine the life that Kenna led or, stated more accurately, to which she was subjected.

Her salvation came when she was four, by an unexpected twist of fate. A neighbor, furious that her husband had accepted sex from Kenna's mother as payment for drugs, phoned in an accusation of child abuse that fortunately—in

218

spite of the caller's dishonorable motive—was pursued and substantiated. Found thoroughly doped up, Kenna's mother readily admitted being too strung out to care for her daughter and asked to be relieved of the burden. It was done. The state human resources agency took custody and placed Kenna with a young couple as their first foster child. Despite rugged times with both the girl and the legal bureaucracy, times that would have tried a saint, the couple—who were unable to have their own child—adopted her. Soon afterward they brought her across the country to New England, where they hoped to give her a fresh start in life, and where our mutual story began.

We first met a few weeks after Kenna's sixth birthday. She looked her age but seemed older, her rough and sordid childhood somehow palpable. Her twitching eyes and fingernails chewed to the bone suggested tremendous inner tension. When she introduced herself by slyly revealing her underwear, Mrs. Trosi—who, like her husband, was reserved in looks and personality—acknowledged her daughter's excitement about meeting me, while gently pulling the hem of her dress back down.

"We've tried buying only pants and overalls, but she takes them off no matter where she is," her husband lamented. "I guess the issue runs a lot deeper than what clothes she wears."

I rapidly learned that things had not been going well. In the therapeutic kindergarten class she'd recently joined—a program designed specifically for seriously distressed children—Kenna seldom paid attention, frequently caused commotion, and continually sought physical contact with others. She could comfortably accept hugs and pats from the teachers, but she was not nearly as easygoing with children. In better, and usually tired, moments she could play a game as long as her leg or arm rested against a peer's. More typically, her classmates rejected Kenna's pushy attempts to lie on or prop herself against them, which led to her fighting and wrestling—retaliation that simultaneously expressed her frustration while obtaining some of the bodily relatedness, however combative, she craved. During the school day she carried herself in a sexy way, and was ever prone to lose control of her impulses: she undressed; invited children to the bathroom; masturbated herself and tried to do the same to others; and on two occasions she peed on other children's art projects that had earned the teachers' praise. Limits on these behaviors made her feel overwhelmingly criticized and deprived, and usually evoked her wild cursing, biting, spitting, and destroying anything that she could lay her hands on.

While recounting this background, Mr. Trosi interrupted himself to ask whether they should even be discussing these matters in front of their daughter. He feared that certain topics might upset her (though she neither appeared to be bothered by what was said nor had corrected, as we suggested she do, anything with which she disagreed). But before I could respond, he confronted his own worry: "Who's kidding who? She knows better than me what's been done to her." "And what she's done, too," his wife added. Surely, there was some question whether Kenna consistently recognized her own actions, but I saw no need to refine their fundamentally perceptive observation.

Children know when they have been raped, unloved, demeaned, deserted, or unfed. They know whether loved ones have died or babies have been born. And they often do know when they themselves have abused, neglected, or let down others. After all, they are the ones who live the very childhoods we may experience only secondhand. They may not like hearing the words that tell of those truths, and may blame their messengers, but it is precisely the underlying, traumatic realities that cause their pain, and that others' well-meaning denial or tactful euphemisms can never undo.

"We don't allow her to do wild things at home," Mrs. Trosi continued. "But we don't know how to prevent her from doing them when we aren't around." She described Kenna as behaving much better with them ("It must be the undivided attention she gets"), though exquisitely vulnerable to feeling criticized and unloved. Unlike her behavior in school, she did not avoid the hurt she felt at home by attacking; instead she stopped talking, playing, and eating until one of them could draw her out. Of all her problems, her parents were most concerned over and frightened by the night terrors from which she woke with bloodcurdling shrieks, often soaked with sweat and urine.

Although I knew practically nothing about these people, I sensed that Kenna had found herself a good home. Yet I could not suppress my wonder, and some suspicion, as to why any couple would voluntarily adopt a child so obviously troubled and seemingly damned by her early history. The beginnings of an answer came quickly.

"We never could have imagined handling this situation," Mr. Trosi further explained with a smile. "But once we'd lived a few months with her—"

"And what months they were," his wife good-naturedly interjected.

"Yeah!" Kenna put down her clay and with a child's pleasure backed into her mother's solid hug.

Mrs. Trosi nuzzled her cheek against her daughter's. "But it was worth it, wasn't it?" They both beamed.

Though I was witnessing love and smiles, all I could see was the dark underbelly—the sadness and rage that such a thing could happen to a child, or to any person. Nightmarish images of her abuse flashed by. How, the question gnawed, could her parents ever make sense out of what happened? What did they think about when they tucked her in at night or sent her off to school in the morning? So much of what parents fear for their children already had befallen Kenna. I envisioned them praying nightly for a miraculous exorcism of the neglect and trauma that had been done to her body and spirit. Maybe she should see a hypnotist, I thought. Maybe someone could convince her that the abuse had never happened, that it was all a very bad dream.

I recalled a young patient with whom I'd done volunteer work at a state psychiatric hospital almost twenty years earlier. After he'd been raped by a stranger on his way home from school, his parents believed he was too dirty to be their son or to live in their home anymore. He was institutionalized because he had nowhere else to go. At the time I could only condemn those parents, but now, sitting in the presence of a family that had embraced someone else's brutalized child, I wanted to understand them better. How much pain and self-hatred had they known? What horrible childhoods of their own had made them so unable to cope with their son's misfortune? And how could they have lived with themselves, without him? I imagined two lonely old people—having dedicated their lives to not facing what had happened, to not remembering the son they once had and maybe once loved—unexpectedly discovering a baby picture that somehow had escaped their self-protective destruction many years before. My eyes welled, my senses cleared. I suddenly understood why Mr. and Mrs. Trosi had adopted their foster child: they had grown to love Kenna and just never could have given her up.

The hour almost was up. I looked toward Kenna snuggled in her mother's arms, then over to the several blue-trunked, green-bushed trees that she'd sculpted. They looked big and strong.

"She thinks about trees a lot. She notices them everywhere, even in books and on television. Is that a problem?" Mrs. Trosi asked. Kenna's brow wrinkled in anxious anticipation of my verdict.

"And trees are everywhere, aren't they?" I rhetorically asked Mrs. Trosi on her daughter's behalf. I wished to convey acceptance of Kenna's obsessive interest, the meaning of which I did not yet know.

Kenna smiled warmly at me, then made a single red apple, which she carefully attached to the tallest of the trees. Her gift thanked me for my comment and understanding, and suggested that big trees, whatever or whoever they were, probably had not been wholly bad to her. I also was reminded that to a small child, even someone of modest height, such as myself, can appear to be a mighty sequoia.

"Would you like to help with the things your mother and father have been talking about?" I asked.

"Would you like to come talk to him?" her mother translated.

Kenna nodded enthusiastically. Given the urgency of the situation and her expressed willingness to come, we decided upon a trial of twice-weekly play therapy. (As my practice was almost an hour away, her parents decided they would continue receiving parent guidance from a therapist nearer their home, with whom they requested that I periodically communicate.)

The following Tuesday, no more than ten minutes into my initial individual session with Kenna, the therapeutic stew already was boiling. Before beginning, I'd demonstrated that the office door could not be locked, so that she always would be free to find her mother (whom, I was told, would be bringing her to sessions). Given the abhorrent traumas that Kenna had known when left with Flex, we agreed that Mrs. Trosi would not leave the adjacent waiting room during sessions. Kenna said, "Good," then proceeded to run a security check of her own. She immediately examined the windows to make sure that no robbers could enter to hurt us or steal the toys, and explored every nook and cranny "just in case," though she did not specify the dangers for which she hunted and prepared.

Unabashedly she asked that I join her at my desk, where she built a domino fence around two other dominoes. Rapidly rubbing them together, as if kindling a camp fire, she squealed that they were "gonna do nasty"—a term that came up again and again in her treatment—"until they lose their spots." Her legs wiggled in rhythm with her hands until she could no longer stand it. "I have to pee," she yelled, running from the room. Returning from the bathroom, she refused to come back to play. "I think he's too upset to work anymore today," she rather confidently told her mother. Mrs. Trosi wisely did not force her daughter back into the office, but explained that they would wait until their scheduled time to leave. She wanted her daughter to get used to this new place and not to run off in a panic. It worked. After reading with her mother for the remaining twenty or so minutes, Kenna left considerably relaxed, and even peeked in my doorway to bid me a hearty "See ya Thursday," the other day of the week on which we'd be meeting.

Kenna began her second hour more subdued, sitting calmly and drawing at the desk. She instructed me to draw geometric designs exactly like hers, and testily chastised me for lines that wandered even slightly. Intending to convey empathy for her wish to be mirrored, I said, "You want me to do just like you," but this only agitated her further. She drew a stick girl, while demanding that I resume my copying of her. Then, grabbing my picture and holding a crayon like a knife, she slashed a heavy mark from the bottom of my figure's trunk, downward and between its legs. In a flash these paper people were furiously going at it, face to face, doing two-dimensional nasty. She blushed, giggled, and again ran off to the bathroom. She came back to clean up, though not before proclaiming to her mother that I'd been "coloring dirty stuff." By offering too much understanding too soon, my comment ironically had backfired. I had unleashed her intense and traumatically oversexualized longings for and apprehension of closeness, which ran from her core so near to the surface. Kenna's reaction warned me to proceed even more slowly and with greater caution.

Kenna tested me ever more severely in her third hour. Noticing a small horsefly on the inside of a windowpane, she panicked. "It's a honey hornet!" she cried, running for serious shelter under my desk and behind my legs. "Look out! He stings!" I restrained my instinct to reflect or explore her fear of the bug. Although this danger likely embodied various inner anxieties and memories, treating it merely as a psychic symbol would have cataclysmically undermined her growing trust in me. She truly feared that bug on its own terms, however actually small and harmless, just as I would have feared a giant rodent. Facing a menace my own size, would I have been able to sit serenely and explore my associations to the rat, or would I have run from his sight? The answer was obvious. More sensitized to Kenna's plight, I temporarily shed my therapist's sweater to don a valiant knight's armor, and shooed the fly out the window. Assured of her safety, and heartened that I had not trivialized her fear, she spoke, describing with relish how "soft and ticklish" the insect's furry tongue could feel, while stressing that the surrounding sharp teeth could severely bite at any moment and without any warning—seductively sweet, unpredictably malevolent. Who— Flex? her mother? herself? me?—was the original honey hornet? Her ento- and etymologically fascinating choice of bug— some hybrid of a food-producing honey bee (female), aggressive hornet (male), and the references to honey (nurturant, endearing), and horny (sexual)—suggested that the answer was not a simple one.

Over the succeeding few weeks Kenna's play became more coherent, employing the consistent theme of hide-and-go-seek. From her permanent station under the desk, she eagerly directed my bull puppet, whom she called Milkie, to look for her in all the wrong places. "Make him cry for me!" she said. And so my Milkie, befuddled and moaning her name, stumbled about the office, searching the chairs, drawers, toy chest—everywhere but the place where his presumed loved one hid. When Kenna sensed the time running out, she finally would authorize me to find her. "Milkie! Milkie! Milkie!" she rejoiced, snatching the puppet from my hand. She spent the last few minutes of each hour happily curled up in her hiding place, clutching Milkie to her chest.

Although it was unclear who or what Milkie represented to Kenna, their ultimate reunion was unquestionably comforting. I wondered why she repeatedly delayed its occurrence until the final minutes of each hour. Did she feel too guilt-ridden or fearful to be discovered sooner? Was her play primarily intended to show me what life was like for a child who had spent countless hours alone, or in the company of a stoned or otherwise preoccupied mother, waiting for someone to come and take care of her? Was she heightening the story's pleasurable and relieving climax by allowing the tension to mount; or mastering and revenging her own helpless hunt for those who'd abandoned her by controlling the futility and fulfillment of Milkie's quest for her? Moreover, she had assigned me not the female cow but the male bull puppet, whom she referred to as masculine, and who was linked to something milky. I assumed that each of these hypothesized dynamics played some role in her play, and that the repetitive happy ending—Kenna cuddled under the desk—served mostly to comfort her as she braced herself for her imminent (until the following session) separation from me.

We'd been meeting for six weeks, and Kenna—having found a safe place in which to release some of her inner tensions—was looking slightly calmer. Her tantrums at school were a bit less explosive, and she was not quite as aggressive. On the other hand, she was telling everyone at school that I was not her therapist or doctor but her boyfriend. When asked, and even when not asked, what we did together, she did not describe our drawings or puppet play. Instead she merrily boasted how I "kissed, hugged, and did nasty on her," evidently behaviors, in Kenna's mind, that would have demonstrated my love for her.*

Her teachers, laughing but visibly unnerved as they recounted these stories to me, expressed much relief when I kiddingly shared my fantasies of their wanting to ask whether I "really did those things with her." Through the years I'd become somewhat inured to seeing shocked faces when I divulged believing in children's sexuality and that incestuous feelings can reside in the healthiest, most upstanding of parents. (Why else would mothers feel such shock when they first see their sons kiss a girl their own age, or fathers so enjoy Mr. Mom's cordially greeting his daughter's prom date with a revving chainsaw in hand?) Occasionally others, including clinicians, have faulted me because I've recognized that a young woman still loves the father who abused her, or have expressed an inkling of understanding for what has led an abuser to become what he is. To some, anyone who, upon hearing of an abuse, does not immediately cry, "Off with it!" himself becomes a perpetrator, and is unfairly seen as condoning misdeeds that he judges, no less than his critics, to be incontestably and calamitously wrongful.

Sexual abuse is a frightening business. Even the most enlightened parents, appreciative that children routinely fantasize about sex, cannot help but worry when they hear their children talking about it. We want our children to be candid with us, and yet, like parents who ask their adult children to keep their plans for romantic cohabitation to themselves, we would rather not see or be reminded of our young children's (and by direct association, our own) sexuality. And yet we all know that something has to be done to prevent these abuses from happening, something that requires awareness of the sex all around us and in ourselves.

Nevertheless, I could have managed without the added stress and controversy. I would have preferred Kenna to ad-

---

*Some would have suggested that Kenna be treated by a woman because her abuser was male. Without going into a broader discussion of that idea, I think it was arguable as to whether Kenna felt more betrayed by men or women, Flex or her mother. It's also arguable that Kenna would not have shown a female therapist this all-essential material. Most likely, she would have progressed well with any clinician who had been there for her, therapeutically regardless of gender.

vertise me as someone who played and talked with children about their feelings. But I did not mention to her what the teachers had told me. She had the right to say whatever she chose about her therapy and her therapist; she was in no way obliged to guard my reputation. As it happened, her wishes for me came more fully into the open at the very next meeting.

"My God! What happened to her?" I thought. Kenna's face and arms were covered with bloodied scratches. I hadn't heard of her mistreating animals, but I somehow suspected that she'd picked on the wrong cat. Kenna went right to work and said nothing about her bruises. Again and again she answered a play phone—telling the unidentified caller that I was too busy playing with her to take calls from other children—until her impatience over the self-engineered and relentless ringing grew too great. "This is my special time," she spoke loudly. "We work hard during this time and I'm not sharing it with you or nobody." Then, hollering, "What? You're crazy. He is not. He's mine. He's my boyfriend!" She threw the phone at the window and, blushing bright red, ran under the desk, where she remained for some time.

I let her know that I was interested in what she felt, but that I'd wait for her to tell me when and if she wished. Upon surfacing, she walked straight to me. "What would you like?" she asked sincerely, explaining that she was a waitress at a diner who would cook me a good breakfast so that I'd "never die." She hummed tensely while pretending to scramble eggs and brew coffee. When she noticed that our time had elapsed, she dropped the play skillet and fell to the floor herself. Clinging tightly to my legs, she tearfully pleaded for me not to make her leave. Once her crying subsided and she'd relaxed her hold on me, I said, "Kenna, you didn't like someone else saying that I was their boyfriend."

"No," she snarled. She then told how Lisa, a classmate who was also fatherless, had threatened—assumably out of envy—to call me to tattle that Kenna had been a bad girl at school. Kenna believed Lisa's prediction that, hearing such an unfavorable report, I would no longer like her. Just as she had tried her best to behave at school, before she'd thrown the first scratch of a vicious cat fight with Lisa, Kenna had tried her best to reassure herself in play that I was irrevocably hers.

But it hadn't been enough; she was petrified that I would reject her. In desperation, and in spite of the crushing humiliation, she served me a healthy meal, trying to take care of me in the hope that I would forgive and keep her. As difficult as it was to witness, I knew firmly that this was only a preview of things to come. Much worse things had tragically defined Kenna's earlier days.

Kenna's emotional wounds needed to be opened and cleaned, and prepared for fuller, long-term healing—an exquisitely tedious and painful process. Memories of the abuse overflowed. For days she played a little girl whose mother, off "doin' nasty in the bathroom," had left her vulnerable to "getting beat or made to do things she didn't want to do." "I ain't doin' that. No way I doin' that with nobody. I can't do that with nobody," Kenna suddenly—while drawing or playing a board game—screamed at the air, her eyes terrifiedly shot up into her sockets. "You can do it, but I ain't. You doin' it with someone else, not me. I gone somewhere else. I ain't here." I wondered whether these behaviors and the regressed language were memorials to how she'd originally coped with the overwhelming acts and feelings of the abuse. She had protected her soul—her feeling self—by dissociating it from the flesh being violated in such harmful and confusing ways. But now she wanted herself back.

There was no end to the venomous self-disregard in which Kenna held herself. "Do you know about the hungry caterpillar?" she asked, adding that her teacher had read the book to her class that morning. I knew the story well and could have responded with a resounding "Sure, I do," creating a warm, cozy moment of sharing, but I wanted to know what she thought about it, so I asked. "See," she gloomily began, "there's this bad caterpillar, and her mother tricked her into eating something bad, and she died and rotted and maggots ate her for supper." Her story was a far cry from the story I recalled about a friendly caterpillar happily eating his way through apples, pies, muffins, and pizza in order to grow. Yet Kenna clearly heard it differently, as a fable of a caterpillar whose greedy appetite was rightfully punished. The black-colored filter through which she had experienced that pleasant tale similarly contaminated her perception of an office print that depicted a mother sending a girl off to school with a well-stocked picnic basket. Kenna speculated that the mother had packed sandwiches laced with rat poison so that she would never again have to see her child's "stinking, ugly face," a face so repulsive that it made her vomit.

Having been neglected and abused early in her life, at a developmental period when she perceived herself to be the center of the universe, Kenna could not recognize that her mother and Flex had failed. She felt herself to blame for her own mistreatment. If, as she maintained, kids got the caring they deserved, then the neglect and abuse she received must have proven to her that she was enormously foul and worthless. I yearned to tell her that she wasn't bad, that she wasn't to blame, that it was their fault. But never having been trustworthily loved, and thereby not feeling lovable, Kenna would not have believed me. I instead expressed how terrible it must have been for her, not to be the root of all evil, but to *feel* that she was. By accepting rather than benevolently contesting how horrid she felt about herself, I began to make her feel understood, accepted, and loved.

Over the next two months, Kenna's behavior at school became less overtly sexual. She was able to accept friendly hugs, and play games requiring physical contact without becoming wild or aroused. I was not surprised by the guardedly optimistic report, for she increasingly had been channeling her sexual feelings into the treatment. For many intense weeks she had brought bananas and lollipops to sessions, eyeing me longingly as she provocatively licked and ate them. When her mother asked whether she should prohibit Kenna from bringing those foods, I could not think of any good reason to. Sex, and whatever it represented, was on Kenna's mind, whether we liked it or not.

Her demands escalated: "Touch my belly." "Rub my butt!" She begged me to "dance sexy" with her, and when I refused, she threatened to break my things and never come back. This actively reached its peak, coincidentally enough, on Valentine's Day, after she'd handed me a large, blank homemade heart. "Do me. Do me!" she commanded, shoving her right forefinger in and out of a circle that her left hand made. "Do me!" she yelled. "Do it now!" When she went to pull my hand—apparently to do something "nasty"—I set a firm limit.

"You can't do that with me," I calmly explained, "but you can use a doll or puppet to be me, and do whatever you'd like."

Her eyes teary with rejection, she began fondling a female doll's crotch and bottom. Her rubbing grew frenzied. She sucked and licked the plastic body all over, until suddenly she whipped it past my head—glaring at me, absolutely enraged.

"I didn't give you what you wanted, did I?"

"No-oooooooooooooooo!" she howled for the better part of a minute, then broke down to a muffled cry.

"Can you tell me what you wanted?" I asked, strongly sensing what that was.

"Touch me," she whined. "Do it to me!"

"I think there's something more that you want, something you want even more than nasty," I softly offered.

She peered at me in nervous expectation, her face tightened like a vice.

"I think you want me to give you a card, just like the one you gave to me."

Kenna bowed her head. I felt a saddening recognition of the underlying reason that such a young girl could solicit sex from me, a grown man, so much more easily than she could request a little piece of paper. Kenna was able to ask me to "do her sexy," because she—however frustratedly—could endure my refusal of that. But my refusal of her wish to "be my valentine"—that she could not have handled. Before departing, she cut out a construction paper heart and dictated my inscription to her—"For my favorite girl."

Slowly and steadily the sexual bravado faded, leaving a lonely little girl who sorely wished to be loved. She brought me an acorn on Father's Day (a baby tree for me to take care of?) and asked if she could call me Daddy, "just in make-believe because I never had one," while promising that she would not forget that I "really wasn't her daddy" when it was time to leave. She wistfully described how as her father I would feed, bathe, and play with her. I'd be the "best daddy" even though I wouldn't "make her dance sexy."

"I'd take good care of you, and not even make you do things you don't want to."

"And I'd be the best girl in the whole world." Here was the

corollary of Kenna's law: a child who is taken good care of must be a good child.

"The best father with the best daughter?"

"Yeah," she sighed. "But you're not really my father, are you?"

I shook my head from side to side.

"But I can pretend. Can't I?" Her spirits lifted.

"Of course you can. Anytime you wish!"

For the first time ever, Kenna left the hour in a good mood and without saying good-bye. After all, as we'd just determined, she didn't have to say farewell and could pretend that we were still together whenever she liked.

In the months to follow, Kenna alternately drew closer, then repelled both me and her wishes to be my beloved baby. She brought books such as *Goodnight Moon,* which I read to her while she fantasized being an infant in a crib, safely and soundly in my watch, and herself played good mother to a baby doll. But whenever she seemed to recall that babies could be harmed or abandoned, she instantaneously embraced the aggressor's role and savagely abused the babies she'd recently rocked and fed. Twice she ran to the waiting room to rip pictures of babies out of parenting magazines. "Kill the babies! Kill them all!" she chanted to herself until she was exhausted, eventually crying and confessing that she felt "cold and hungry."

"You'd rather scare and hurt little babies than be hurt and scared yourself."

"I hate Kenna! I hate Kenna! I hate Kenna!" she ranted, whacking her fists against the sides of her head. "I just wish she was dead, all dead."

"That's how much you hate Kenna?"

"Yes," she affirmed through her sobbing.

Though she continued to deal with her abuse and abandonment, Kenna's self-hatred diminished considerably. For weeks, rather than portraying herself as a wicked child, she played a frisky dog I'd adopted from the pound where she'd been left by her real dog parents. She crawled about the office on all fours, pretending playfully to chew up furniture, peeing and pooping on the rug, my shoes, and the bed. Kenna scribbled black lines on memo slips to make newspapers that she'd grab out of my hand with her mouth—presumably papers I was reading like a stereotypically busy father—in order to get me to play with her. Little clay dog bones became the treats she lived for. My job, she made clear, was to train and love her, because she wanted to live with me and was trying her best to be a good doggie. Kenna left each of these hours with a cheery "Bow-wow!" She originally asked—and was angry when I did not comply—that I respond to her canine farewell with affectionate pats on her back. After much negotiation we eventually agreed that in lieu of patting I would bark, "Arf, arf," in as deep and proud a daddy-dog voice as I could invoke.

Kenna emphasized that puppies, like babies, misbehaved in lovable and acceptable ways not as a result of malice but of their physical immaturity, of their not knowing any better, and for want of their masters' doting. This play was thrilling. She had begun to assert her wish for caring in a less sexual, hostile manner. The dog bones, though certainly phallic, were more benign and nurturant than the more baleful objects she earlier had brandished. Moreover, rather than eat the bones, and as insurance should she ever again be without a home and food, she buried them in the ground—a sad but adaptively resourceful thing to do.

Following this dog play phase, Kenna improved remarkably. She became relatively popular at school and had become fast friends with Lisa. Her concentration was enhanced, as was her academic learning and performance. Psychological testing revealed that she was superiorly bright, especially in language. She fought less and seldom tried to touch others inappropriately or expose herself. At home, she tolerated more frustration and required less constant reassurance that she was loved. Her night terrors had vanished. No one—Kenna, her parents, teachers, or myself—could have been more pleased with her progress.

In therapy she also showed marked change. She now—and had for months—spent her hours in restful, pleasurable activities. Using water colors she quietly painted wishful scenes of rainbowed and sun-drenched teddy picnics, describing in detail the wonderful and richly symbolic foods the mother and father bears brought: the endless apples, honey, and peanut butter sandwiches, the pizzas as big as the moon, the chocolate milk shakes as "tall as me." She played game after game of Candyland as it was meant to be played—delightedly cheering her jumps forward, far more delightedly cheering mine backward. Though she continued to seek my attention and caring—usually seated right next to me, at times leaning against my shoulder—she no longer made sexual advances. She fantasized that had I been her father, I could have made her mother better, and that we all could have lived happily ever after. This soothing reverie brought good feeling, not tears.

The smooth sailing could not last forever. In the sixth month of relative quietude, toward the end of our second year, Kenna, who ritually greeted me with a big hello, walked into the office without a word or a glance. After she'd sat for several minutes, she walked toward the dollhouse, never having before used it. My curiosity was piqued. I excitedly anticipated her doll play, and the window to her inner life that it was sure to open. But just as she was about to pick up a bear, or so I thought, *"Whack!"* With all of the brawn that a small girl could muster, she rammed her lowered shoulder into the roof and flipped the house into the wall. She fell to the floor on top of the plain wooden furniture that spilled about. Embarrassed and distraught, she frantically squeezed her head and body into the plywood lean-to created by the dollhouse tipped against the toy chest. Only her lower legs and feet, twisted as tightly as old-fashioned licorice, could be seen sticking out from the near end. What accounted for her attack on the house? I mentally dissected the present and previous hours, everything we'd said and done, but could not detect anything likely to have triggered her eruption. Something else was going on, to which I was not privy. Seeing that my sole question—"What is it, Kenna?"—brought no reply, I spent the remaining time silently watching the dollhouse rise and fall with her breathing. What could it be? I was utterly daunted.

The suspense was not belabored. In the waiting room, Mrs. Trosi anxiously told me that much had happened since our meeting two days earlier. My imagination ran wild. Had her father fallen ill? Had she? Kenna, I judged, could never survive losing another mother. Were they getting divorced, or had the adoption somehow been nullified? Then it suddenly dawned. Of course. How could I not have guessed? It had happened many times, so I'd heard, supposedly an old wives' tale, but weren't they the truest? Having adopted a child, Mrs. Trosi had gotten pregnant. That must be it! She was going to have a baby. Just to be sure, I determinedly held off my smile and congratulations. I imagined Kenna walking into the nursery to meet her new sibling when her mother spoke.

Mr. Trosi's father had suffered a mild stroke earlier in the week. Even as we met, her husband was flying to his parents' home in Austin. I further learned that, after a sleepless night of soul-searching, catalyzed by this sudden turn of events, Kenna's parents had decided to move to Texas permanently. Having tried with some modest success to make it entirely on his own, Mr. Trosi felt now was the right time to accept his father's long-standing, open-ended invitation to operate his thriving appliance store, and so would be assuming that responsibility immediately. They would move in only two weeks. Mrs. Trosi explained, her eyes moist, "We know it's terribly short notice. And we know that therapy has been important to Kenna. But we think it's even more important that we all be together."

I looked at Kenna. She stared blankly ahead toward the doorknob, lower lip trembling. She'd had no choice but to assault and reject the dollhouse, which symbolized all of the things that she had lost and would be losing—her original mother, her home in New England, and her therapy with me. I grew angry and wanted to take Kenna by the hand and run. "But we're just beginning. You can't take her away," I wanted to protest. "She needs therapy! She needs me." But Mrs. Trosi knew this; she knew what Kenna needed much more than I did.

"And it's not like we have to say good-bye forever, is it?" she continued. "Maybe we'll move back someday, or maybe Dr. Bromfield will move to Austin? Would you like that, Kenna?" Her daughter eyed me hopefully.

Like parents who tell their child that a deceased grandparent has gone on a long trip, Mrs. Trosi wished to protect Kenna from the painful truth. However, at what price? Given such a glimmer of hope, a child may wait and wait and wait— perhaps secretly, perhaps through a lifetime—for someone never to return, instead of grieving and getting on with her life. Although it is every child's prerogative to fantasize a beloved's resurrection or immortality, parents who hide the plain facts do their child a profound disservice and prolong the agony.

Kenna needed to know that we would be separating for-ever, that we would be—as is aptly and not so affectionately known—terminating. In that phase of therapy Kenna truly would confront the threat of abandonment and aloneness that had pervaded every preceding hour of her therapy and life, and around which she'd defensively organized her whole per-sonality and existence. She needed to feel this good-bye of good-byes fully, and know that there would be no next ther-apy hour, no returning from vacation, no seeing me in Sep-tember. Unless she could feel my death—which never seeing me again psychologically approximated—she would continue to hold on to me in a way that prevented her from attaching to the people who would be there for her in the future: her parents, teachers, and other therapists.

I looked at Kenna and her mother. "It sure would be nice to think that we weren't really saying good-bye. But we are. We really are."

In an ideal world Kenna would have had many months to terminate her therapy, and it would have been ended at her initiative, when she (in conjunction with the grown-ups' as-sessment) felt satisfied with her progress. But then, in an ideal world Kenna would not have been abused. For good or ill, we live in an extraordinarily less than ideal world, perfectly full of imperfect people, parents, and situations. Kenna and I would have to make do with the time that we had. We would have to end and say good-bye, however hastily.

Kenna came to the first of her last four hours carrying vol-ume T of a children's encyclopedia. For almost fifty minutes we sat side by side, silently looking at pictures of Texas. My mind continually wandered to a boy with whom I'd begun therapy a few weeks before. Though we sat next to each other, I felt distant, and sensed that she did, too. We were still in physical proximity, but had begun to drift apart emotionally; she investing in her new home and state, I in my new patient. Our mutual withdrawal was not hard to fathom. Go to any airport and watch the hurried "I'm not going to say good-bye" good-byes. It is human nature to withdraw from those we are losing.

Feeling somewhat ashamed and guilty that I was not attend-
ing to Kenna, I considered being more active, asking lots of
questions. But I recalled observing, without exception, how
even rushed terminations had followed a natural pace of their
own. My previous attempts to propel the closing work of other
patients had always failed miserably, unproductively throt-
tling rather than hastening the process. As our minutes ticked
by, patience remained my virtue of choice.

Prior to Kenna's second hour, I was somewhat unsettled by
my newly found optimism concerning her plans, my thinking
that she'd be better off starting over again. Perhaps she would
profit by transferring to a new therapist or even by taking a
holiday from treatment. And there was a little bit of "good
riddance" present also. Her progress had been steady; she was
due for a major setback. "It's all just as well," I consoled myself. "Let someone else deal with her when she hits the skids."
I was working very hard not to have to miss her.

Kenna arrived at her second hour more charged—physically
restless, scratching, repeatedly going to the bathroom—but
not at all talkative. For over forty minutes she painstakingly
traced an armadillo out of her book. I tried to talk to her,
to enter her world, but she shut me out. When she noticed that her time was up, she put down the marker and
flatly described how armadillos "like to die and get hit by
cars."

I wanted to scream that they got what they deserved because they liked to play in the streets and along interstate
highways. If they just stayed at home.... But I commented
instead in a normal tone of voice, "They must be very upset
inside."

I might as well have plunged a detonator. "Serves him
right!" She spat on her well-done drawing, then grabbed a
fistful of crayons and completely obliterated it. "You stinking,
ugly armadillo! You ugly animal!" She walked out shaking,
her mother's arm wrapped over her shoulder. I shuddered at
the thought that this might be the way she went from here,
for good.

Though both patients and therapists look with dread to the
last hour, it is often the penultimate, or next to last, session
that brings upheaval. And so it was with Kenna. She burst
into the room disheveled and furious. I was strangely reas-

sured. I could feel her feeling again, related to and caring about me; I could feel her back in the room with me.

After several minutes of steely, hostile silence, she dashed to the dollhouse and grabbed a father and mother bear. She excitedly ground their fronts together. "You and your wife do nasty," she angrily jeered before rushing them, still in hot embrace, to the seat of the chair next to mine, her chair. "You and me do nasty," she yelled. "We're doing nasty in the office." Though her talk and play bore all of the trappings—the words and acts—of sex, it did not feel sexy.

"You've taken my wife's place," I noted.

She grew frantic—writhing her body, lifting her dress, and wiggling her tongue out provocatively. I did not want her to lose control, to be overwhelmed, and yet I also did not want to cut off this potentially relieving and insightful reenactment prematurely. I envisioned shutting this play down, and her driving to Texas with all of this inside her, all by herself. I decided to take the risk and let it proceed. Admittedly, knowing that her mother was right on the other side of the wall provided me immense support to persist.

Kenna slowly walked a large circle around the office. She said, "I seen men wearing plaid dresses and sucking black sticks." I recalled that her family had vacationed in Nova Scotia the preceding summer; her father had told me about Kenna's friendship with a kilted bagpiper who'd given her a hug and a lucky rabbit's foot when they'd left. But she needed no reminders of that trip; she was traveling somewhere else now.

She started to spin, while circling faster. "They whirl and whirl, spin and spin." She twirled faster. "They do hot and nasty, hot and nasty daddies," she squealed. "Nasty, nasty daddies." She spun faster and faster. Her astonishingly rapid rotating gave a strange coming-and-going sound to her shouted words: "Nasty daddies, nasty daddies." Her dress was flung above her waist. "They twirl and twirl and twirl till their bad, nasty thoughts fly out of their heads! Get out of here!" she now *really* screamed. "Get out of here, you nasty thoughts, you nasty daddies. I hate you, you nasty, nasty daddy!" She pounded her head with her closed fist and fell against the chair, to the floor. For many minutes she lay there, panting for breath. Her eyes were wet.

"You miss him very much," I said as quietly as I could to still be heard. "So very much."

Kenna exploded with tears. Her body heaved with such strain that I feared she might not be able to withstand the pain. "He was my daddy. He was my best daddy." She sobbed uncontrollably. "It wasn't my fault what he did. It wasn't my fault I loved him." Her voice trailed off. "He was my daddy."

Although Flex had done horrible, destructive, and inexcusable things to her, he also had been the only caretaker in her early life. Every day he fed, diapered, bathed, and played with her. Despite his abusive indulgence (and as noxious as it may be to realize), he gave her more affection and caring than her mother had. Never having been welcomed to her mother's breast, to be fed or held, her suckling Flex and his milkie became an overpowering and confusing experience for her mind *and* body—both frighteningly abusive and pitiably soothing. Kenna's only early nurturance had been so perversely and hostilely contaminated by sexual abuse that receiving even wholesome nurturance in the present brought her enormous shame and self-hate. To be given to in any way and to enjoy caring was to be deserving of lethal poisoning or neglect. Like the beaten dog that devotedly loves its cruel master, Kenna loved Flex because she had not known any other way to love and be loved.

I slept poorly the night before our final hour, anxiously wondering what it would bring. Would she grow even wilder, beyond her own or my control? Would she leave my office in worse shape, unable to function as well as when she came? Maybe Mrs. Trosi was right to suggest that therapy end on a happy note, with optimistic plans of someday being together again. Maybe her daughter could not bear an absolute goodbye. Though I imagined her yelling, crying, sexually provoking, demanding hugs and kisses even more intensely than she had the week before, I could not keep myself from thinking about what I feared most of all, something that was much simpler, and for certain: at ten to four the following day, Kenna would leave me.

To my surprise, when she showed up, she did not appear the least bit upset. She bounced in and eagerly announced that she and her mother had planned a surprise for that last day. I was delighted at the thought that she and her mother had arranged for a farewell party, since, wary that doing so might preempt her own emotional agenda, I'd decided against my wish to bring chocolate cupcakes. What a grand and happy way to end! However, once again I was set straight. Their plan was not for a celebration but for Mrs. Trosi to blow her car horn sometime during the hour; that would be Kenna's signal to leave. Although this was a wonderful scheme—endowing Kenna with the power to desert me before I evicted her, the prospect of her early departure disappointed me. Kenna, however, interrupted my pained awareness by handing me a small package wrapped in a brightly colored picture of an armadillo she'd drawn. "Open it!" she happily urged. "Hurry up!"

I unwrapped a small blue frame that held a creased, faded black-and-white photograph, the sort taken by a coin-operated camera. It was a picture of a much younger, broadly smiling Kenna sitting on the lap of a very tired-looking woman. I eyed Kenna, then that woman. I could not miss the resemblance.

"You wanted me to meet her before you left."

Kenna nodded proudly, with the same smile in the photo. "I look just like her, don't I?"

"You sure do, just like her."

I began talking, intending to tell Kenna her how hard she'd worked with me, how much progress she'd made, how much I'd enjoyed working with her, and how much I'd miss her. Yet when she sensed the direction in which my words headed— to all of the deeply heartfelt things she herself would miss— she abruptly jumped out of her seat. "There's my mother. Bow-wow!" she yelled, running out the door, never to come back through it again.

"Arf, arf," I halfheartedly barked back, saddened that she'd left early, understanding why she hadn't waited for her mother to honk. But she didn't hear me.

She was gone.

Child therapists and parents share much. We both strive to have a sustaining, good, and protective impact upon the children for whom we care, and to give them what we ourselves lost or never had. And in spite of our most valiant efforts to do otherwise—and often for our own and our children's mutual good—we both exploit our caretaking experiences to repair our own marred childhoods. And last, at some time we both must let go of the little hands, the handlebars, the car keys, and finally, the grown-up children whom we can only trust and hope will keep themselves, and their children, well—now, and when we are gone.